WINNER

WINNER

MY RACING LIFE

A.P. McCoy

with Charlie Connelly

To Eve and Archie

© AP Enterprises Limited 2015

The right of Tony McCoy to be identified as the author
of this work has been asserted in accordance with
the Copyright, Designs and Patents Act 1988.

First published in Great Britain in 2015
by Orion Books
An imprint of the Orion Publishing Group Ltd
Carmelite House, 50 Victoria Embankment,
London, EC4Y 0DZ

An Hachette UK Company

9 10

A CIP catalogue record for this book
is available from the British Library.

ISBN 978-1-4091-6239-1 (HB)
ISBN 978-1-4091-6240-7 (TPB)

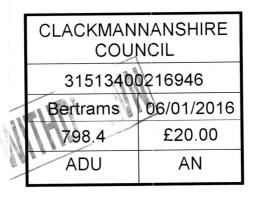

CONTENTS

List of Illustrations

Section 1

1. Deciding to retire was the toughest decision I've ever had to make. (Steven Cargill / racingfotos.com)
2. I rode my fastest hundredth on Arabic History. (Fiona Crawford)
3. I won my 150th winner of the 2014–15 season on Goodwood Mirage. (John Giles / PA Archive / PA Images)
4. Riding my 200th winner of the season on Mr Mole. (Edward Whitaker; racingpost.com / photos)
5. Back in the weighing room after revealing my retirement plans. (Bill Selwyn)
6. I came down when riding Goodwood Mirage in the Betfair Hurdle. (Bill Selwyn)
7. I won my first Irish Hennessy on Carlingford Lough. (Pat Healy / racingfotos.com)
8. The reception I was accorded by the Leopardstown crowd was amazing. (Alain Barr; racingpost.com / photos)

Section 3

List of Illustrations

ONE

Box Office, Sandown Park
25 April 2015

Two jumps from home the realisation hit me.

I'd been holding Box Office on the inside of a tightly bunched field and he was going well. After clearing the third last I eased across to the outside tucking in behind Richard Johnson, whom I could see was building to a strong finish on Brother Tedd and I wanted to go with him. Box Office was strongly in contention coming round the final bend for home and I was sensing a winner. As we approached the second last, however, both Brother Tedd and Grand Maestro began to pull away from the pack and, jumping in third place and coming up the hill towards the finish, it became clear that Box Office didn't have an answer on the day.

It was only then, when I had to reluctantly admit to myself the race was lost, that something other than the thunder of hooves and the rhythm of my own breathing muscled in on my thought process.

This is it, said a voice in my head, this really is the end.

I was now a matter of seconds away from the moment all the numbers stopped for ever. My career total of National Hunt winners would remain at 4,348 after this, my 17,546th ride. I'd never add to my twenty champion jockey titles; I'd never win another Grand National or Cheltenham Gold Cup. All the stats, the numbers that had governed my life for the last two decades, they were just a few hundred yards from being stilled for ever. My whole career, my whole adult life even, had been built on making those numbers click upwards as fast as I could but in a little over a couple of furlongs they would never move again.

I cleared the final fence of my racing career, saw the two leaders pull further away and became aware of a couple of horses in the corner of my vision. There was no way they were getting past. Box Office might not have had enough left in the tank to win that day but I was sure as hell that I'd ride the final furlongs of my career as hard as any I'd ever ridden before. I'd clocked up somewhere in the region of 40,000 miles of racing during my career, equivalent to going twice around the world, and now I gritted my teeth, reached for my stick and knuckled down for the last two furlongs of my racing life.

It probably won't surprise you to hear that deciding to retire was the toughest decision I've ever had to make. I imagine some sportsmen and women begin to notice things about their performance and sense the end coming: the reflexes aren't quite as sharp, the eye isn't as quick as it once was, injuries become more common and take longer to heal and the enthusiasm for the battle is dimmer than it used to be. They're aware of the questions and comments even if they remain unspoken. They see it in the eyes of the journalists and fans: how much longer can they go on? Are their best days behind them? Shouldn't they be thinking of calling it a day? As a professional sportsperson, whatever sport it might be, it can be very easy to keep going until you've passed your peak because it's hard to admit to yourself that decline has set in and you'll never be as good as you once were.

I experienced none of that, thank goodness. It would have been my worst nightmare: the whispers, the doubts, the pity – especially the pity – and it was something I was determined to avoid. Fortunately I was able to go out at the very top, and being able to say that makes me a very, very lucky man indeed.

Although it had come as a surprise to everyone, even those closest to me, I'd actually laid the foundations of my retirement several years before that emotional afternoon at Sandown. There were times in between when it had passed clean out of my head, there were times when I told myself I must be mad to even consider it, but I've always had a strong stubborn streak running through me. Sometimes it's a good thing, other times it's definitely not such a good thing, but that stubbornness was the reason I was able to retire when I did and in the manner I did: on my own terms.

The roots of that unforgettable Saturday afternoon reached back to 2010. I'd just become champion jockey for the fifteenth time and won the Grand National for the first time on Don't Push It. I was thirty-five years old and having an amazing year, one that would be crowned by receiving an OBE and being voted BBC Sports Personality of the Year. It may seem strange that such a successful year should have triggered thoughts of retirement, but it occurred to me that if I kept going the way

I was for another five years I'd have reached twenty jockeys' championships in 2015. It felt like a realistic goal: I was feeling good, riding as well as ever, twenty was a good, round number and I like good, round numbers. I would also be forty that year, another good, round number. I'd still be performing at the highest level and would be retiring on a considerable career high. It felt like the perfect scenario and was practical, sensible and attainable. I filed it away in the back of my mind and set about the business of riding as many winners as I could.

Time passed. I won more jockeys' championships to bring that landmark figure of twenty ever closer. I was still working hard, riding plenty of winners and still enjoying racing as much as I ever had, yet always there, lurking at the back of my mind, was this thought of retiring at twenty titles. The very factors I'd identified as governing the decision also succeeded in making the decision more difficult: how could I possibly walk away from the job I love when everything was going so *well*? Surely I was mad to even think about retiring? Surely I'd just be cutting off my nose to spite my face (which is, incidentally, one of the few injuries I've never suffered)?

All I could do was keep reminding myself that it wouldn't last. What I dreaded more than anything was reaching a point where I'd begin to hear people saying I wasn't as good as I once was, that I wasn't the jockey I used to be. I couldn't bear that, it would have left me absolutely distraught. That's why it was definitely the best thing for me to retire at the very top, on my own terms, while still being the best jockey I could be. I don't mind telling you there were times in my final season where it was absolutely tearing me up inside having to stick to that decision, but my innate stubbornness was always there, like a rock, anchoring my thinking and ultimately vindicating my judgement.

In April 2014 I secured my nineteenth jockeys' championship. I'd not discussed with anyone the possibility of retiring since I'd first thought about it, but at the Punchestown Festival that year I was at the home of my boss J.P. McManus and I broached the subject with him. I told him I was thinking of retiring at the end of the following season because I wanted to go if I was still at the top and lucky enough to be champion jockey for the twentieth time. I've always looked up to JP and valued his advice, and although my revelation must have come as a surprise to him, he was characteristically calm, rational and honest, as he has been throughout our time together. What he said was simple but exactly what I needed to hear: not to make any rash decisions and to ensure I did whatever made me happy. It had to be my decision and nobody else's, he said, and I had to do what I thought was right.

I made a particularly good start to the 2014–15 racing season. I always liked to work extra hard in the opening weeks of the campaign, racing at two meetings in a day if I could, haring around the country clocking up the mileage in an effort to ride as many winners as I could as early in the season as I could. Obviously I wanted to win all year round, but racking up a big pile of winners at the start of the season helped to put anyone else's aspirations of being champion jockey clean out of their heads. I tried to sicken the other lads as soon as possible; in effect trying to ensure there was no competition for the champion jockey title.

I was very lucky in that my agent, Dave Roberts, was brilliant at accommodating the kind of schedule I needed and almost psychic in the way he booked the rides that were right for me. Throughout my career I've been very fortunate in the people I've had on my side, and Dave Roberts has been a constant virtually from the time I first arrived in England as a teenager. Dave booked every ride of every jockeys' championship for me and in all the years we worked together I never once asked him why I was riding a particular horse, nor did I ask him why I *wasn't* riding a horse. As far as I was concerned it was Dave's job to get me on the best horses to make me successful and keep me winning and that's exactly what he did. I trusted Dave to come up with the rides, he trusted me to keep making the most of them.

I also benefited from another's misfortune: Jason Maguire, who had been second to me in the jockeys' championship a couple of years earlier, was injured in a bad fall at Stratford on the Monday before the Cheltenham Festival – the poor guy had to be resuscitated on the track and had half his liver cut out. Jason was Donald McCain's stable jockey, and his enforced absence and that of his regular back-up rider Timmy Murphy with a wrist injury meant that I was able to ride a number of winners for Donald in the early part of the campaign. Thanks to Dave's astuteness I had also begun riding for John Ferguson, one of the up-and-coming trainers over jumps. John is perhaps best known for being Sheikh Mohammed's bloodstock adviser but he's a very successful man in his own right and I rode a good twenty winners for him in the early part of the campaign. All these factors combined in my favour and almost before I knew it I'd reached fifty winners for the season faster than ever before, with a double at Worcester on 10 June.

I always set myself goals in life and am always wanting to challenge myself, to push myself further and harder, so when I rode my fastest fiftieth I thought, well, that's a pretty good start. I looked at the calendar, sketched out the season ahead in my mind and it occurred to me that if I could maintain even something close to the number of winners I was riding then I had a really good chance of achieving an unprecedented 300 winners in a season. That would be some achievement in any circumstances, but if this was to be my final season as a professional jockey it would be the ultimate send-off and the best way to show people I was going on my terms.

A big step towards that goal would be to ride my fastest hundredth, which I managed on Arabic History, one of John Ferguson's horses, at Newton Abbot on 21 August. I remember that meeting particularly well because after I'd won I did the 'ice bucket challenge' that was sweeping the country at the time and for which I'd been nominated by Ruby Walsh. It was a warm summer evening at the end of a hot, busy day so it turned out I barely flinched as the buckets of ice-cold water hit me. I quite enjoyed it to be honest, I found it refreshing, which I'm pretty sure wasn't Ruby's intention.

As I headed home that night it struck me that I was in a bit of a strange situation. Here I was, forty years old and riding my fastest hundredth winner ever, doing better than I had in any previous season. I already had a hundred in the bag and there were more than enough rides left in the season to make 300 winners a very real possibility. While an achievement like that would be a perfect landmark on which to retire, it also made me wonder if I was mad to even think of calling time on my career when I was clearly riding as well as ever, if not better.

My wife Chanelle was waiting for me when I got home and I told her I'd just ridden the fastest hundredth of my career.

'Anthony, that's great!' she said.

'Yeah, it is,' I replied, 'I think I might be getting the hang of this riding thing at last.'

She laughed, and I hesitated for a moment, uncertain whether to say what was on my mind.

'You know something, Chanelle?' I said. 'I think I'm actually getting better. I think I'm improving.'

She turned her head to look sideways at me as if to say, 'you're losing the run of yourself, McCoy'. But it was true. I was forty years old, had been riding professionally for two decades yet I was convinced I was becoming a better jockey. I thought back to the conversation I'd had with JP four months earlier when he'd advised me to do whatever was right for me. Deep down I knew retiring was the correct thing to do and had been my long-term plan for four years, but having made such a fantastic start to the season I wondered just what I might still achieve. I lay awake that night, thinking about how 300 winners in a season was definitely attainable. It had never been done before, over jumps or on the flat, and if I carried on the form I was in then it was a landmark well within reach. What a way that would be to retire, the ultimate high. The more I pondered on it the more determined I became: I'd work my socks off and reach 300 winners. It was a tall order and would take a lot of racing, but at the very least it would show that in my twentieth season I was still the best I could be.

There were smaller increments to achieve first. My next goal was to ride my fastest 150th, and when I arrived at Worcester on 9 October I was well on target. But that was about to change.

Late in the day I was riding Keep Presenting in a maiden hurdle in aid – ironically as it turned out – of the Injured Jockeys Fund. At the first hurdle the horse seemed to frighten himself somehow: he didn't refuse as such, but suddenly jammed on the brakes without any warning or apparent reason, jerking to the left as he took off. He hit the hurdle at a strange angle and down we went. I hit the deck and the horse landed sideways on top of me. Fortunately he was OK and jumped up pretty swiftly, but I'd had all the breath knocked out of me and knew straightaway I'd done myself some damage. As well as finding it hard to breathe I was in pretty serious pain from my ribs and my shoulder. Any jockey likes to get up as quickly as possible after a fall, psychologically you want to do it and it also lets everyone know you're OK, but I was very sore in the ribs and shoulder, could hardly move and could do nothing more than lie there groaning. As it happened, in the act of falling we'd brought down Noel Fehily on St Johns Point. Noel was fine and was standing up dusting himself down when he heard me moaning and came over to see how I was.

'Are you OK, champ?' he asked.

I tried to raise myself to look at him but couldn't move.

'No,' I gasped, still struggling to catch my breath, 'get the doctor, Noel.'

I didn't realise at the time but I must have got a kick in the mouth on the way down because there was blood coming out of it as I spoke; it can't have been a pretty sight.

'Get the doctor,' I repeated, 'get the doctor, Noel.'

The medical convoy must have had a restricted view of the incident: it seems they'd only noticed one horse fall and once they'd seen Noel jump to his feet they carried on following the race: they simply hadn't seen me go down. From my prone posi-tion I watched Noel jumping up and down and waving his arms, screaming at them as they drove on unawares into the distance. He walked back over to me.

'Noel,' I gasped, 'where the fuck's the doctor?'

'They drove past,' he said.

'What the fuck do you mean they drove past, Noel?'

I must have been getting my breath back by this stage as I was getting up a good head of steam swearing at poor Noel.

'Fuck me, Noel,' I said, 'I wouldn't want you saving my fuck-ing life, would I?'

When the race came round on its next circuit the medical staff finally noticed me on the ground and the doctor came run-ning over. It happened to be Doc Pritchard, my own GP who's done an amazing job of patching me up and getting me back on horses over the years.

'Right,' he said as he bustled up, 'what's wrong?'

'I can't breathe, doc,' I wheezed, in pretty serious pain, 'I've punctured my lung enough times to know what it feels like. This is definitely a punctured lung for starters.'

'OK,' he said, 'lie still and we'll get the stretcher for you.'

'I'm not getting on the stretcher,' I said. I was already thinking about my 300 winners and was determined to get up and walk away from this, work through the pain and carry on racing.

'Don't worry,' the doctor said. 'I'll help lift you up onto it.'

'No,' I snapped, still spitting out blood, 'no stretcher, it's mor-phine I need, just give me some morphine.'

I held up my arm, he pulled up the sleeve of my colours and gave me a shot of morphine. I think I was also given oxygen; either way, I began to see a little better through the fog of pain.

'Now,' he said, 'I need you to get on the stretcher and get in the ambulance.'

'I'm not getting in the ambulance.'

'AP, you need to go to the hospital.'

'I'm not going to any fucking hospital.'

Lying there on the cold ground by that first hurdle at Worcester, deep down I knew I was in big trouble. But there was absolutely no way I was going to admit that to anyone, especially myself. All that was going through my mind was the number of winners I was riding, and staying on course to reach that magical 300, so there was absolutely no way I was going to concede to any kind of medical advice no matter how sound and sensible it was. All I could think about was keeping going through the pain and riding more winners. Even the simple act of getting into the ambulance would have been conceding defeat. This was going to be a victory of mind over matter and I could handle any amount of pain and still ride. Nothing was going to stop me.

Poor Doc Pritchard. I wasn't going to do anything he wanted me to do. Eventually I got the medical team to help me up and I agreed to go to the ambulance as long as I walked there myself. But if anyone thought this meant I was going to the hospital they were sadly mistaken.

'Take me back to the weighing room,' I said as I climbed in to the back of the vehicle. The doctor went paler than I was.

'AP, you have to go to the hospital,' he said.

I looked him right in the eye and was as firm as I could possibly be.

'Doc, I'm not going to hospital. I'm going to the weighing room.'

Sure enough I got my way and lumbered into the weighing

room carrying a drip, got someone to make me a cup of tea with ten sugars, showered, got changed and was about to go home when the doc came back to tell me that my breathing difficulties meant my oxygen levels weren't high enough and he was genuinely worried. He told me I simply had to go to the hospital.

I thought for a moment.

'OK, well, if I'm going you're coming with me.'

I was jabbing a forefinger at his chest as if I was pretty much blaming the guy for my injuries. Doc Pritchard has known me for years, he's done amazing things for me, and here I was, wild-eyed, finger-jabbing and virtually holding him responsible for Keep Presenting falling at the first.

He brought me to the hospital at Gloucester and the x-ray results confirmed what I'd suspected: I'd dislocated my collarbone, punctured a lung and broken two ribs. As dislocated collarbones go it wasn't too bad, but the doc told me I couldn't ride for a few days, at least until my lung was all right again.

Chanelle came to collect me from Gloucester hospital and on the way home I had all sorts of mad things going through my head. I was adamant I couldn't miss any days' racing if I was going to ride 300 winners. There are 365 days in a year, I surmised, which only leaves 65 possible days without a winner. It was simply a question of numbers, all other considerations, not least injury, were entirely irrelevant. Single-minded to the point of obsession, I was going to reach the target whatever it took.

Doc Pritchard was firm, though: it would be dangerous for me to ride again before my lung was recovered. He'd always been pretty accommodating of my flying in the face of his medical advice and riding through injuries, so I knew he really meant it.

Rest, he said, get plenty of deep breaths and get yourself feeling good again before you get back on a horse. I shouldn't think about racing again until the middle of the following week at the earliest.

I spent a brooding, anxious and restless weekend thinking about the winners I was missing. Sitting at home while there was racing going on around the country just made no sense to me. On the Monday morning I was still sore and breathing heavily when Dave rang and asked how I was feeling.

'Not good, Dave,' I wheezed. 'But I want to ride tomorrow.'

'I'm glad to hear it,' he said, 'because I've got three or four really good rides at Huntingdon for you if you're up to it.'

Straightaway I rang Doc Pritchard and told him I really needed to ride the next day. There was a weary sigh from the other end of the line.

'OK, I'll tell you what,' he said. 'If you have an x-ray now and it shows things have healed enough, then you can think about riding. But only if things have improved enough.'

He'd barely finished speaking when I was out of the door and on my way to meet him at the Ridgeway Hospital in Swindon. I had the x-ray, the doc placed it on the light box and pursed his lips.

'You're not far away,' he conceded, 'but as things stand, looking at this you really can't ride at Huntingdon tomorrow.'

'Not far away' sounded good to me. Good enough to ride at Huntingdon, in fact.

'When you say not far away . . .' I raised an eyebrow. He sighed again.

'Look,' he said, 'there's a chance you might be OK in the morning but right now it's just not there.'

'What if I had another x-ray later today? Things might have got better by then.'

'They might,' he conceded with a shrug, adding, 'OK, we'll give it a go, but there's no guarantee there'll be any improvement by this evening.'

Furtively, I rang Dave from the corridor and told him he could put me down for the horses at Huntingdon the following day, returned to the hospital late in the afternoon, had another x-ray, and to my delight the doctor took a look, shook his head slowly with a mixture of disbelief and resignation and cleared me to ride.

Three of my four rides at Huntingdon won, so easily in fact that anyone could have been on them, but the pay-off was that my collarbone was absolute agony all day. I'd seen the course doctor before racing and had the usual check-ups and he said I was fine to ride which I suppose strictly speaking I was in a medical sense. I'd even managed to do a few press-ups in front of him. However, by the time I got home that night I was in desperate pain that even the extensive range of painkillers in my bathroom cabinet couldn't temper.

Despite the pain all I could think about was the possibility of riding my 150th winner the next day at Wetherby, where Dave had booked me some more great rides. Although my collarbone had been excruciating, riding those three winners at Huntingdon had only made me more determined. After all, if I'd taken Doc Pritchard's advice at face value and not gone to Huntingdon I'd be three winners down by now. As it was I felt I was properly back on track, making up for the rides I'd missed the weekend after Worcester. In terms of winners I was still three and a half weeks ahead of my 2002 season when I'd broken Sir Gordon

Richards' record and reached my highest ever season total of 289 wins. I have a commemorative print in a frame at home that hangs at the bottom of the stairs and lists all my winners from that season, the names of the horses and the dates. Every time I came down in the morning I was checking how I compared with that season and here I was, nearly a month ahead of schedule and showing no sign of losing momentum as long as I could just keep getting on horses and riding winners.

I got up the morning after Huntingdon, went downstairs, double-checked the 2002 print, and set out for Wetherby where Dave had scheduled four good rides. My collarbone was still very sore but I was in good spirits as my driver Steve 'Scouse' Kelly and I headed for Yorkshire. In the first race I was riding a horse of Jonjo O'Neill's called Goodwood Mirage. He was really keen, a hard puller, a free-going horse that really wanted to get on with it. On a normal day I'd have been in my element on Goodwood Mirage but on this day his enthusiasm had me in absolute agony. With every stride I could feel the pull on my collarbone and the pain shot right through me. With two left to jump I saw a gap in the middle of the field and knew Goodwood Mirage had enough for us to win, and win comfortably. We cleared the last hurdle almost neck and neck with Lightning Rod but the way the horse was motoring I knew it was ours. We were a couple of lengths clear when I picked up my stick to give him a smack and drive him out, but just as I did so I felt my collarbone go pop. I'd dislocated it again. The pain was unbelievable, like an electric current zinging through my upper body. I transferred the stick to my left hand but it wasn't nearly as effective allowing both Lightning Rod and Tidal Wave to come back strongly and we only just held them off on the line. I finished the race, came back into the winner's enclosure wincing and gasping, almost nauseous with the pain, and the first thing I said to Jonjo was, 'My collarbone's fucked.'

Not the ideal way to mark my 150th winner of the season.

I weighed in, and when I went to take my colours off I realised just how bad things were. I couldn't get my silks off. I physically couldn't lift my arm up, it was like it was paralysed. Grudgingly I had to tell Jonjo I was too sore to ride again that day. To add insult to this latest injury, the three other horses I had that day all won; one was even a walkover in a novice chase from which all the other runners had been withdrawn – all I'd have had to do was ride down to the last fence and ride back, as long as I was on the horse it didn't matter. In terms of the jockeys' championship and my 300 it would have been a win that counted the same as the hardest fought short head. Missing out on those three winners absolutely fried my mind. Instead of going home feeling good about reaching 150 wins for the season faster than ever before, I arrived back absolutely in bits at the lost opportunities and the prospect of missing more racing, thanks to my collarbone.

Doc Pritchard had recommended Dr Julian Widdowson to me, the Bath Rugby Club doctor with huge experience of that kind of injury, so I went to see him the next day at his clinic outside Bath. Julian examined me, took another x-ray – my collarbone was being photographed so often at this point I began to worry it might take out some kind of privacy injunction against me – and told me I should rest it for at least a week. I'd been in so much pain with it that when Julian asked me about my broken ribs I realised I'd almost forgotten about them. He suggested a procedure in which he took blood out of my arm and spun it in a centrifuge to separate the white and red cells, leaving plasma in between. Injecting the plasma into the injury stimulates the healing: it's totally legal, they do it with the rugby players, and it did seem to help my ribs heal more quickly. But the collarbone meant I still faced a whole week out. A week of potential winners. A week that pushed the magic 300 further away.

I was back in the saddle again at Exeter on 4 November and managed to ride a winner in my first race, on a horse of JP's called Jollyallan. My joy at returning to action with a win proved to be short-lived, however. My next ride was If In Doubt for Philip Hobbs in a novice chase, the horse's first race over fences. He took the first fine, but there was a large shadow in front of the second fence, ahead of the ditch. If In Doubt decided to come up on the shadow, which was a long way in front of the fence. This meant he breasted the fence itself, landing in the middle of it, stopping dead and catapulting me forward over his head. I speared into the ground with my shoulder and collarbone bearing the brunt of the fall. Gingerly, I picked myself up, put my hand on it and could immediately tell it was absolutely massive. I couldn't countenance missing any more racing so when the doctor came rushing over to see if I was OK I said I was fine, went back to the weighing room, took off my colours and saw my valet Graham's eyebrows shoot up when he saw the state of my shoulder.

'Jesus, that's fucked,' he said. 'Better get you to the doctor.'

'No,' I replied, tight-lipped with pain and determination, 'no doctor. I'm riding in the next race.'

Graham looked at me askance, as if to say, 'your head's gone, mate', and he was right – my head *had* gone. In my obsession to reach 300 winners I'd completely lost it, lost all sense of perspective and all sense of the right thing to do. I was in such bad form, raging against my body for letting me down, raging against the very thought of being forced to sit out any more racing, that the anger replaced the adrenalin and I went out to ride Bobcatbilly in the next race for Ian Williams purely out of temper. Bobcatbilly was a horse on which I'd had a good few wins in the past but that day he finished ninth in a field of twelve purely because my head was completely in the wrong place.

When I got home my head was spinning with the mixture of pain and determination not to miss a single ride. All I could think about was that magical, unprecedented figure of 300 winners.

Chanelle came into the room while I was icing my shoulder.

'My God, look at the state of that!' she exclaimed, horrified, and asked what I intended to do. I think she meant was I going straight to the hospital or was I going to wait until the morning instead. Neither option had even crossed my mind.

'I'm going racing tomorrow,' I replied, tersely. I had a couple of good rides booked at Chepstow and there was no way I was going to miss them.

'Anthony, you're off your head.'

'I don't care,' I snapped, 'I'm going racing.'

Sure enough I went to Chepstow the next day and rode a horse in the first race called Arzal. I finished second and it was an absolutely horrific ride. I was riding Arzal for Harry Whittington who'd only really just started out as a trainer and I felt awful on the horse. I felt bad for Harry afterwards because I shouldn't really have been riding. But my head was wrecked; I was so obsessed with not missing a single day's racing, with trying to ride 300 winners, that I was going to go out and get on a horse no matter what kind of a state I was in.

I ended the day finishing second in a bumper, on Winter Walk, a better ride than I gave Arzal but on another day I'd have won. Clearly I was in big trouble with my injury and even I, in the midst of my self-destructive obsession, had to concede that I couldn't just ride through the pain barrier this time.

I went home via Julian Widdowson's clinic and explained how my already troublesome collarbone had borne the brunt of a heavy fall the previous day and was giving me a lot of pain. He took an x-ray, put the print on his light box and when I saw him practically do a double take at what he saw I knew it must be bad.

'I don't know how you've managed it, AP,' he said, 'but you've broken your dislocated collarbone.'

He kept staring at the x-ray.

'That is almost impossible to do,' he added.

When you dislocate your collarbone, the impact on your shoulder pushes the collarbone out through the joint. The reason it dislocates in those circumstances is because it's almost too strong to break. Either way, you break it or dislocate it, one or the other. Definitely not both.

'I have absolutely no idea how you've managed to break a dislocated collarbone,' he said, shaking his head. 'It should have just dislocated further, pushed further out, not broken altogether.'

Uncommon injury or not, I knew this latest development meant a potentially lengthy lay-off from racing, a realisation that hit me ten times harder than the ground at Exeter. This meant the possibility of weeks away from the saddle. Weeks. Maybe I could have coped with a few days out over the course of the season and still made it to 300, but a long injury lay-off gave me no chance. I travelled home from Bath in a daze, came through the door, barely acknowledged Chanelle, went straight up to the bedroom and cried my eyes out. I felt like the whole world was collapsing around me. That might sound faintly ridiculous in the great scheme of things, but remember that nobody has ever ridden 300 winners in a season. I'd have been the first, and goodness knows how long it might have been before somebody else got there too, years, decades even. That was half my retirement goal, people seeing how good I still was, what I could still achieve and what an achievement that would have been. It wasn't an ego thing, far from it, but riding a triple century of winners at forty years of age would have qualified me to say there you go, I can still do it, thanks for everything, goodbye.

I still had it. Not only that, I was getting *better*. That's why the injury hit me so hard, that's why the self-imposed target of 300 winners had been so important to me, that's why obsession had driven me to the extremes of what I could bear in terms of physical pain. I wouldn't have minded quite so much if I'd missed out simply by not winning enough races, but to be scuppered by an injury, and a freak injury at that, just wasn't fair, it wasn't fair at all. I buried my face in the bedclothes and bawled my eyes out at the sheer injustice of it all. It was over. There was no consoling me.

Looking back now I see that night as a watershed moment. I knew I couldn't reach the target I'd set myself and I knew I now faced an enforced absence from the saddle. I needed to get my head straight and the best way to do that was to put some distance between me and the entire situation. So I took a holiday. I went to Barbados for eight days and got a bit of heat in my bones which was great and helped my recovery immensely. It also gave me a psychological break from racing which, considering the state of my head over the previous couple of weeks, was equally important: I needed to recuperate mentally as much as physically.

Coming back took three weeks altogether, in which time I'd realised there was no point in rushing back into the saddle now I'd had to accept my tilt at 300 had gone. I was up to 152 wins and my nearest challenger in the jockeys' championship was Richard Johnson with seventy-five, so I was far enough ahead to ensure my collarbone could properly heal before putting it on the line again. Thank goodness for that flying start to the season. I still missed a lot of good racing as a result though, including the first big meeting of the season the Paddy Power Open Meeting at Cheltenham, but having that break from racing was unquestionably the right thing to do for my mind and my body.

When I returned to racing after the injury I had a very dry spell: at one stage I only rode two winners in the space of eleven days, a horrible hiccup which put paid to any little glimmer of hope that might have remained of still making it to 300. Earlier in the season Dave had told me that in one week I'd ridden nineteen winners, something I don't think I'd done in my career before, so to ride two in eleven days plonked me right at the other end of the spectrum. I can't say for sure why I had such a barren spell but I think maybe I was struggling for a goal. I'd been so fixated on the 300 that once it had gone I was casting around for a new aim. The jockeys' championship wasn't over but I was so far ahead that even though it wasn't quite mathematically in the bag, another fifty winners or so and it was definitely over. But what then?

I went to Ireland over Christmas feeling a little listless, almost in a kind of limbo. Having the 300 taken away from me had set my retirement thoughts awry. If I'd gone on to ride 300 how could

I not have retired? Without that talismanic figure in front of me I faced four months without a goal, without an ultimate prize to aim for. I had dinner with JP and his son Kieran at Kieran's house in Dublin. Once we'd eaten I pursed my lips, turned to JP and reiterated that I was considering retiring at the end of the season. Even though we'd discussed it briefly the previous spring I think he was a little taken aback. He'd seen I was having a great season and was still riding well so it must have come as a bit of a surprise to learn that I was still thinking of going through with it. My mind wasn't 100 per cent made up at that point, but I was becoming more and more convinced that retiring was the right thing to do. JP in his wisdom said again, see how you feel, you don't have to make any decisions yet, and I managed to put it out of my mind for the next month or so. But the more I thought about it the more convinced I became that it was the right course of action. It got to the stage by the end of January 2015 when I realised that the main thing that was turning over in my mind wasn't whether to retire but how to go about it.

As I drew closer to 200 winners I began to think seriously about whether to announce my retirement in advance or just get to Sandown on the last day of the season and come out with it there and then. Having spent so long mulling over retirement in an abstract sense it felt odd to be weighing it up on a practical level. I rang JP after racing at Kempton on 6 February, where I'd won for him on a really nice horse called Minella Rocco in a novices' hurdle, to sound him out on what was the best way forward. I told him I was considering announcing my retirement when I'd reached 200 winners but wondered whether I might be better off leaving it until the end of the season at Sandown, when I'd almost certainly be presented with the champion jockey trophy.

Perhaps, I said, it might be best for me mentally to reveal that I was retiring and have months of preparation for it rather than being the only person who knew it was coming, nursing this huge secret and having to keep it under wraps. Also, reaching 200 winners is a decent achievement in anyone's book. It's a nice round number, and I'd feel like I was making the announcement on a high as well as heading for retiring as twenty-time champion jockey. In those circumstances I could still go racing while getting used to the idea of having let the genie out of the bottle.

In addition I thought announcing my decision in advance might even be good for the sport. After Cheltenham and Aintree there wouldn't be an awful lot for racing people to talk about or write about: the Flat season wouldn't have got going and the Grand National would be done and dusted. I was concerned that when casting around for things to write about journalists and columnists would notice it was my twentieth year as champion jockey and one or two might start speculating about my future. How long can he carry on? How many championships can he go for? Might he retire? I mean no disrespect to any journalists or broadcasters, I've always had a good relationship with them and know they have a difficult job to do, but I didn't want someone with nothing else to write about filling some column inches with random speculation and then, lo and behold, I pop up at Sandown two weeks later and retire. It might look as if they'd suggested it, they'd put the seeds into my mind and got themselves a scoop, and I couldn't have anyone left with the impression it wasn't entirely my decision. It had to be my decision alone and be seen to be my decision alone, a positive and assertive act, one that would be good for me and might get people interested in racing and talking about the sport I love.

It also struck me that if I did announce my exit in advance then there was absolutely no way I could change my mind. I couldn't arrive at Sandown on the last day of the season intending to retire only to have a great day's racing, get to my last ride and think, you know what? I don't really want to do this, let's give it another year and see how it goes. I knew that was a very plausible scenario. As it happened when I got to Sandown that's exactly how I felt, but by then there was no going back.

At the other end of the line JP listened quietly and patiently to all this, and when I'd talked myself out said he agreed with everything he'd just heard. It would be good for me and the sport to announce my retirement once I'd ridden my 200th winner of the season, he said, adding that I should make sure I was completely happy with the decision because I was going to have to live with it.

Once again, JP had said exactly what I needed to hear and the biggest decision of my life was made. There was no going back.

The next step was actually to tell people, especially those who mattered most. I'd kept my retirement cards so close to my chest that I hadn't even said anything to Chanelle. Given that telling Dave Roberts of such a major decision wasn't something I could do over the phone I asked him to come over to the house for dinner, when I would tell both him and Chanelle together.

It was a Monday evening in early February when we welcomed Dave to the house. I'm sure both he and Chanelle had sensed something was afoot: I must have seemed a little distracted to my wife – even more than usual – and although Dave and I speak every day we see each other only rarely, and even then it's for a round of golf or a meal at a restaurant somewhere.

The three of us had some dinner and when we'd finished

eating both Dave and Chanelle looked at me expectantly. They knew me too well to assume the evening was just a whim of mine.

I took a deep breath.

'Dave,' I said, 'the reason I've got you down here tonight is to let you know before anyone else that I'm going to be retiring at the end of the season.'

He ran his finger around the rim of his wine glass as I explained my reasoning. I don't believe it came as a total shock – if he'd been turning over the possibilities in his mind on his way to the house, retirement was probably high on the list – and once I'd put him in the picture he said straightaway that he fully supported my decision and understood my reasons perfectly.

'J.P. McManus is the only person who knows anything about this,' I continued. 'Even Chanelle is hearing it for the first time here tonight. I wanted both of you to be the first to know officially that I'm retiring from racing.'

They reacted so warmly and with such approval that any last nagging traces of doubt I might have retained disappeared on the spot. I'm sure Chanelle's overriding feeling was relief as much as anything: mine was, after all, a job at which I was literally pursued by an ambulance around my workplace, and it wasn't that long since she'd had to deal with the wild-eyed, 300 winners-obsessed, utterly irrational version of me determined to ride horses whatever the physical risk to myself. Dave, meanwhile, was so kind and gracious. The positive nature of both their reactions vindicated my decision completely.

Hence the reverberations from my bombshell dissipated quicker than I might have expected and we were able to move on to the practicalities, most notably whether I should make a public announcement in advance or wait until I'd ridden my last race at Sandown on 25 April 2015. They both agreed that the latter wouldn't be right, either for me or the sport. Chanelle made the point that there were people around the country who would make a special effort to come and see my last few rides and feel they were giving me an appropriate send-off. Dismounting after the last race of the season, announcing my news and then disappearing into the sunset would deprive them of that. In addition the goodwill and publicity it would create would unquestionably be beneficial to the sport as a whole. Yes, it was definitely the right way to go about it.

Then it was just a question of timing the announcement. I told them that I'd been mulling over whether to do it after I'd ridden my 200th winner.

'I don't want people to think I'm retiring because things are going badly, or I'm sensing the start of a decline,' I said. 'I want to announce it on a high and I want it to come right out of the blue, to be a surprise to people. I thought my two hundredth winner might be the best way to achieve that.'

Dave and Chanelle, the most important people in my professional and personal lives, both thought this was a perfect idea. Everything was settled, then, and it was only after Dave had gone home and we'd gone up to bed that I realised what a tremendous relief I felt having unburdened myself of something that had nagged away at me for so long. I slept more soundly that night than I had in a long time.

TWO

Mr Mole, Newbury
7 February 2015

On the following Saturday I made the short trip to Newbury for a meeting being screened live on Channel 4, arriving at the course on 198 winners for the season. I got changed into my silks and sat in the weighing room thinking, today could be the day. I had some good rides booked and I felt there could well be two winners among them, meaning that by the time I left the weighing room that evening the cat might well be out of the bag and there'd really be no going back.

In the first race, the Betfair Novices' Hurdle, I was riding Qewy for John Ferguson, a really good horse who produced a strong finish that saw us burst through from the middle of the field after the second last and pull away to win by six lengths. That was number 199 and there was still the rest of the card to come.

In the next race I rode Milan Bound for Jonjo and, despite being handily placed with two left to jump he couldn't find the same strong finish as Qewy. It was a similar story in the third on Taquin Du Seuil, when Richard Johnson finished really strongly on Coneygree to leave the rest of the field trailing way behind. Would the announcement come today? I felt the next race held the key.

Mr Mole was a Paul Nicholls ride owned by J.P. McManus, a horse who'd been very temperamental early in his career but who'd really come on, to the extent I'd already had three wins on him in the previous year. I mounted Mr Mole ahead of the Game Spirit Chase knowing he was a really decent shout for my 200th winner. JP had another horse in the race called Uxizandre which I nearly rode, but Paul practically bullied me into riding Mr Mole and I'm glad he did.

The race got off to the worst possible start for Mr Mole when he whipped around to the left as the field set off and for one awful, fleeting moment he looked as if he was going to refuse to race. This was like the old Mr Mole, I thought, as we started a good ten lengths behind the rest, but he soon got into a fantastic rhythm and I knew from early on we were in with a great chance. He jumped the fourth last a nose ahead of Uxizandre, pulled away and went on to win by thirteen lengths.

Two hundred up. I could put it off no more.

After the finish Noel Fehily, who'd finished third on Karinga Dancer, appeared beside me. This time I wasn't going to swear at him.

'Two hundred winners, champ,' he said, patting me on the shoulder, 'well done.'

'Cheers, Noel,' I said. 'Oh, a bit of news for you: I'm going to retire at the end of the season.'

'What?' he said, his eyebrows shooting up.

'I'm retiring,' I replied. 'This is my last season.'

He looked at me a little suspiciously as if trying to work out if I was pulling his leg, but when he saw I'd meant what I said he wished me the best of luck and we made for the winner's enclosure. Now that the 'r' word had come out of my mouth in a racing setting I hoped it would make it easier for me to make the official announcement. Telling Noel had felt a little like a dummy run and also meant I really had to go through with it now. The cat was halfway out of the bag and the genie waist deep in the bottle.

Dave and Chanelle had come to the races that day knowing there was a good chance it would turn out to be a significant occasion, and sure enough Dave was waiting for me as I came off the track. He looked up at me.

'Are you all right?' he asked, seeing me already becoming a little bit emotional.

'I'm OK,' I replied, and was quiet for a moment. I looked at Dave again.

'Do I have to?' I asked.

'Do you have to what?' he replied.

'Retire.' I said. Even at this stage I needed to be sure. I'd just ridden a terrific winner, my 200th of the season, I was all but certain of being champion jockey again, I was enjoying racing and I was riding as well as ever. Dave just looked at me without saying anything, the faintest hint of a smile pulling at the corners of his mouth.

'I'm doing the right thing, aren't I, Dave?' I asked.

The smile spread across his face and he gave my boot a reassuring pat.

'Yes,' he said, knowing exactly what I needed to hear, 'you're doing exactly the right thing.'

We made our way towards the winner's enclosure and I saw Rishi Persad from Channel 4 approaching with a cameraman for what I'm sure he was expecting to be a pretty routine post-race interview. My stomach was churning and I could already feel the emotion building as I tried to get my thoughts in order and work out exactly what to say. I tried to keep the lid on as best I could.

Rishi began by asking me whether I thought Mr Mole was a realistic Queen Mother Champion Chase horse and I answered, 'Sure, why not?' but I was looking away, looking back out across the Newbury course to the hills beyond, trying to prepare myself to make the most important announcement of my life, here, now, and live on television. It would be a total surprise to Rishi and to everyone watching. Only Chanelle, Dave, JP and Noel Fehily had any inkling of what was coming. Even my parents didn't know, they'd be watching at home in Moneyglass and would find out, like everyone else, via the television. All I had to do now was wait for the right question, wait for Rishi to set up the moment.

He said he was going to reel off a stat and informed me this was the tenth time I'd ridden 200 winners in a season then stretched up with the microphone to catch my response. This was the perfect set-up. Thanks Rishi. I swallowed.

'I'm going to tell you something else, Rishi,' I said. 'It's going to be the last time I'll ride two hundred winners.'

I was groping for the right words and still feeling a tangible reluctance to actually say them. A lump was beginning to appear in my throat.

'Having spoken to Dave and JP,' I continued, 'I'm going to be retiring at the end of the season.'

I could see the surprise flash across Rishi's face, as if he thought he must have misheard. Even hearing the words coming out of my own mouth they sounded faintly unbelievable. He blinked a couple of times, still looking up, still holding the microphone up to me

'So,' I said, 'that's a bit of news for you.'

Immediately the wave of relief that I'd felt after telling Dave and Chanelle on Monday night washed over me again. Finally this secret I'd been carrying for so long was out. Rishi asked me why I'd made my decision and the sense of release I felt meant my words just came out in a torrent. I said I wanted to go out at the top, as champion jockey, that I'd spoken to Dave and JP, that Chanelle didn't even know until a few days previously, that my parents didn't know, that they were finding out just then as well – everything that I'd been keeping bottled up for so long tumbled into Rishi's microphone.

I found myself sniffing as I spoke and to this day I couldn't tell you if that was the emotion or the fact it was a freezing late afternoon in February. It had been a struggle initially to get the words out, but as Chanelle said to me later I couldn't have planned it any better if I'd tried. I wanted my announcement to be a suitable occasion: what better than a Saturday afternoon live on television, at Newbury, having won one of the day's big races on one of Jonjo's horses in JP's green and gold to bring up my double century of winners? I wanted it to be a surprise, and it was certainly that. It couldn't really have gone any better if I'd planned it down to the last detail. It was only afterwards that I realised if either winner hadn't come in that day my 200th winner could well have been up at Catterick on the Monday with just about the entire racing world looking the other way. Don't get me wrong, a winner's a winner wherever and whenever it might be, and a win at Catterick counts the same as a win at Newbury or anywhere else, but if you'd asked me to map out an ideal scenario to announce my retirement then, well, it wouldn't have been far off the way it actually happened. Once again I'd been a very lucky man indeed.

There was no time to wallow in the reaction as I was flying to Ireland that night to ride in the Irish Hennessy at Leopardstown the following day. The texts and calls flooded in and I was doing interviews all the way to the airport – it was a relief when I had to switch off my phone as we boarded the aircraft.

Chanelle and I were staying in a hotel in Dublin and having a meal with JP's son Kieran, his wife Marie and another friend called Abi Reynolds, whose father Albert had been the Taoiseach in the early nineties. We took a taxi from Dublin airport and I climbed in behind the driver. He was a typical Dublin taxi driver, a proper northsider with a Dubs GAA pennant hanging from the mirror and who started talking as soon as we got in. He either heard something on the radio or maybe Chanelle had said something about retirement because something prompted him to start talking about me, not realising I was sitting directly behind him.

'Did you hear yer man McCoy, the jockey, is after announcing his retirement today?' he said and before either of us could respond, he was away.

'It's sad news, to be fair, y'know?' he continued. 'He's been around for a long time and done so well, I've won a fair few Euro on him meself over the years. It's a sad day for racing, like, but jeez, fair play to him. Sure, I don't think we'll ever see his like again. He'll be missed, y'know?'

The guy carried on with this magnificent eulogy for my career with absolutely no idea I was sitting right behind him – it was becoming a bit embarrassing and felt a little like turning up at my own memorial service. Eventually he paused for breath and I stuck my head forward between the front seats.

'I'm not fucking dead, you know,' I said, and the poor guy nearly drove off the road. It was a nice thing to hear though, un-prompted and without any kind of agenda, and it was another confirmation that I was doing the right thing. Imagine if he'd said, 'about bleedin' time too' or 'he should have done it years ago'. In fact in a way he helped me relax a little and return my focus to the business of racing, not least with such a big race ahead the following day.

The Irish Hennessy is one of the premier steeplechases in the Irish calendar and always pulls a crowd, but there was a bigger crowd than usual on that crisp, cold sunny day in south County Dublin. I'd never won the Irish Hennessy before but I felt in good form and had a good winner in the race prior on Sort It Out for Eddie Harty. In the Hennessy itself I was on Carlingford Lough, trained by John Kiely. I'd won a Galway Plate on him in the past and a few other races along the way so thought I was in with a chance. As it turned out the race was a thriller for the spectators with plenty of horses still well in contention as we turned for home. I knew Carlingford Lough had a fearsome finish in him but he faced a very strong challenge from Adrian Heskin on Foxrock in particular and by the final furlong it was between the two of us. Fortunately I was able to drive Carlingford Lough over the line by three-quarters of a length to land my first ever

Irish Hennessy win at the very last attempt. The reception I was accorded by the Leopardstown crowd was amazing as I came back in, my first hint of what lay in store over the next few weeks.

After the race I did an interview with Brian Gleeson from RTÉ about my decision to retire, an interview which I assumed was just for television. After a few seconds, however, I suddenly became aware that complete silence had descended on the course. Where normally there'd be the hubbub of the crowds, people walking between the stand and the winner's enclosure, queuing at the betting windows, chatting by the food stands, that kind of thing, the place was strangely quiet. That's when I realised that the interview was also going out over the Leopardstown PA system and everyone in the place was listening. It was almost eerie, all these people, the golden late afternoon sun filtering through the skeletal trees and nobody moving, nobody speaking but Brian and me, the clouds of our breath rising on the breeze. The only sound other than mine and Brian's voices was the faint clop of horses' hooves over in the parade ring. We were on a podium at the back of the grandstand and at one point I glanced up to see all these faces looking down at us from the balcony above. I'd never known anything like it in my life, this rapt attention, this total silence, as if the entire Leopardstown racecourse was holding its breath. It was the first inkling I had of just how big this was and as the realisation dawned on me it was all I could do to keep speaking.

We flew home that evening and in the taxi to the airport Chanelle turned to me and said, 'This doesn't happen to normal people, you know.'

'What doesn't?' I asked.

'You're a jammy fecker, Anthony McCoy,' she said. 'You only

talked to Dave and me about retiring on Monday night, when you still had a few to ride for your two hundred. It just so happened that you rode the final two you needed on a Saturday afternoon live on Channel 4 meaning you got to announce your retirement to the biggest racing audience possible. The next day is your last day riding at Leopardstown and you up and win the biggest steeplechase of the year in front of the biggest crowd, where everyone ends up listening to you talking about your retirement.

'If you hadn't won on Mr Mole yesterday,' she continued, 'you'd have won the Irish Hennessy all right, but with nobody knowing you were retiring you wouldn't have had half the reception you just got, nothing like it. You'd have gone to Catterick tomorrow, ridden your two hundredth and made your announcement to, what, a couple of hundred people in the pouring rain? That just proves it. Normal people don't have that much luck in life.'

I turned to look out of the window, watching the lights of Dublin flash past as we sped to the airport, and thought about what Chanelle had said and about that Leopardstown silence. Chanelle needn't have worried: I knew exactly how lucky I was. I also knew now that nothing was ever going to be the same again.

Extraordinary though Leopardstown had been I just wanted the rest of the season to pass as normally as possible. Indeed, after the whirlwind of that weekend things returned to at least some sense of normality and I slipped back into the old routine. I noticed more people at the races and more requests for autographs and photographs, which was a nice feeling, but other than that the idea of retirement had pretty much gone out of my head. Now I'd stopped mulling over the decision and was able to concentrate solely on my job, in racing terms it was like any other season: the long drives, the boiling hot baths, the mud-spattered goggles, the weighing out and weighing in, all the familiar rhythms and routines: it was as if I'd almost forgotten it was all coming to the end.

The days leading up to the Cheltenham Festival gave me a pretty sharp reminder that the season was far from ordinary, however. Cheltenham has always been very special for me. It's the highlight of the jump racing season and I've had some of my most memorable rides at Cheltenham, so it was natural that the meeting was going to be a major milestone in my last few weeks as a professional jockey. Such was the demand for interviews, in fact, that I ended up having to do a press conference at Oaksey House in Lambourn ten days before the festival. This was totally unheard of: a jockey? Staging a press conference? What's that about? It was Clare, my commercial manager, who'd suggested it and I winced at the prospect. I pointed out that I wasn't a footballer or a rock star or anything like that, I was a jockey. Clare told me the interest in my last Cheltenham had been so great, so unprecedented, that it would be impossible for me to meet every journalist who wanted to interview me, there just weren't enough hours in the day. She said it was the easiest way to try to accommodate everyone and not let anyone down. I felt a bit uneasy as I'm the last person to go chasing the limelight, but it did give me a sense of the impact my retirement was having on the sport – as well as bringing home to me that this really would be my last Cheltenham Festival.

I was looking forward to it very much and determined to enjoy myself. Obviously the key to my enjoyment of Cheltenham always lay in riding winners: Cheltenham is the main stage for jump racing, the highlight of the National Hunt calendar and the place where every jockey wants to win. I had a few horses that were contenders but it took me until day three to break my duck, on JP's Uxizandre in the Ryanair Chase. We led from the off, in fact he pretty much ran away with me for the first mile and a half or so, but was jumping beautifully and I knew once we started coming down the hill that he still had plenty. We won by five lengths. Winning that race – on a horse that wasn't particularly fancied in the build-up – after two barren days was like a release, a big exhalation. Chanelle had noticed that morning that I was in subdued form and wound very tightly but that win restored my mood with an infusion of relief as much as exhilaration. The reception I received from the crowd was like it had been at Leopardstown too, it sent a shiver up my spine. You always get a good reception at Cheltenham whoever you are, the enthusiasm of the crowd there is like nowhere else, but that day it was even better than normal and I practically floated back to the winner's enclosure.

The next day my final ride in the Gold Cup turned out to be a bit of an anticlimax. Carlingford Lough, on whom I'd won the Irish Hennessy, stayed in touch with the leaders most of the way round but I knew fairly early on we weren't going to make it: there'd been a persistent drizzle that day that left the ground too soft for his liking.

A couple of hours after the Gold Cup I had my last ever festival ride, in the very last race of the meeting. Traditionally it's known as the Johnny Henderson Grand Annual, named after trainer Nicky Henderson's late father, but the Henderson family had kindly agreed to Cheltenham's suggestion that for one year only it be named the AP McCoy Grand Annual Steeplechase in Honour of Johnny Henderson. While I was obviously immensely flattered and moved by the gesture I was insistent that Johnny's name still be in there: it would have been wrong to usurp his memory entirely even just for one year. I was on Ned Buntline, a horse I'd ridden a few times before for Noel Meade. I'd seriously considered riding a horse of Jonjo's called Eastlake but felt Ned Buntline had a better chance of winning. People began applauding as soon as I walked out of the weighing-room door, and when I cantered up to the start I was aware of a tremendous roar washing down from the stands as I passed. No one, it seemed, had left early: Cheltenham was still absolutely packed.

I thought we were in with a shout for most of the race, but as we jumped the last in second place I already knew that Ned Buntline wasn't a particularly strong finisher, especially on ground as soft as it was that day. There was to be no big Cheltenham fairytale ending for me, then, as the horse came in fourth: a decent showing in the circumstances and just enough for a place in the winner's enclosure.

I'd been so caught up in the race that I'd almost forgotten it was my last festival ride. Once we'd passed the winning post I congratulated Tom Scudamore, who'd won on Next Sensation for his brother Michael (with Eastlake in second), and was laughing with and chatting to a couple of the other jockeys as we made our way back. All of a sudden I heard this tremendous swell of applause from the crowd as I approached the stands and the emotion surged through me. I waved to the crowd as I passed, that special Cheltenham crowd who had been so incredibly good to me over the years, with tears in my eyes.

I received a terrific reception when I arrived at the winner's enclosure too, which only heightened my emotions: people were cheering for my finishing fourth as much as they were for the winner. I felt a little embarrassed for the Scudamores to be honest, as this was an emotional day for them too: it was a fantastic win for the family, especially as Tom and Michael had lost their grandparents, also great racing people, in the preceding year.

As I stepped up to present the trophy to the winners I felt I had to apologise to the Blandfords, who owned Next Sensation, for all the fuss.

'Not at all,' replied the lady of the family. 'This is our first big-race win and all these people, the media, the photographers, they wouldn't be here otherwise. Everyone would have gone home and we'd have been standing here all on our own. This,' she said, waving her hand at the crowd and the scrum of photographers, 'this is amazing!'

She was incredibly nice about it, but it was something I was going to have to get used to over the coming weeks. I don't seek attention, far from it, and certainly not at the races, so there would be a fair bit of embarrassment and apologising to come before I hung up my colours for the last time. Indeed, there would be occasions where it felt more like the AP McCoy Show than a race meeting, which I often found a bit discomforting. Not because I didn't appreciate people coming to see me ride and taking time to ask me for an autograph or a selfie, far from it, but I worried that the focus was far too much on me to the detriment of anything else. Granted, my last race at Cheltenham was always going to attract a lot of attention given my relationship with the festival over the years, but I'd finished fourth and the last thing I wanted was for my presence to detract from others who really deserved the attention. There was never any resentment from the other jockeys, they're the best bunch of lads and know me well enough to know I'd never set out to be Mr Big Shot: they were laughing and having the craic, telling me to go out early or come in later, to just keep as far away as possible away from them. It was like I had the plague or something.

Also, I had my job to do, of course. I was still a jockey and that was the most important thing: I've too much respect for JP and Jonjo and the other people I was riding for, not to mention my own self-respect, to allow myself to be distracted from that. I had absolutely no intention of easing down towards retirement, quite the opposite, but I did find the attention and trying to accommodate everyone and sign everything while there was a race meeting going on a little awkward at times.

As is customary on the last night at Cheltenham there was a party in the weighing room. There were plenty of lads there I'm very friendly with: Carl Llewellyn, Mick Fitzgerald, Dominic Elsworth and others, but I was racing the next day at Uttoxeter so couldn't stay late. We left at about half-past nine and Chanelle said she was hungry and wanted to stop for something to eat. We had her sister and her husband with us too and they also said they could do with a bite so I brought them to a KFC, my favourite fast food, not far from the racecourse. The place was packed with racegoers refuelling on their way home so we had to eat it in the car: if we'd all piled into KFC in Cheltenham on the Friday night of the Gold Cup it would have been absolute carnage. As contrasts go it was about as far from the hype and the hullabaloo of four hours earlier as I could have imagined: my final memory of my final Cheltenham is the four of us, in the car, in a corner of a KFC car park on the outskirts of

Cheltenham, slurping away at a big greasy cardboard bucket of fried chicken.

Not long afterwards I flew off to Portugal for an annual golfing break with the lads. For the last dozen years or so I've always gone for a few days' golf in Portugal after the Cheltenham Festival with Mick, Carl and Dominic. It's always a great trip and breaks up the season nicely, but in those particular circumstances it was just what the doctor ordered. For the first time since Newbury I was able to properly take my mind off retirement, change the routine and have a decent break. Things carried on as they always did out there, four lads having a great time on the golf course, and it was just what I needed. I came back refreshed, rode again for a few days, and then had another short break, in Dubai, watching the Dubai World Cup. John Ferguson looked after us very well with his racing connections to Sheikh Mohammed. We were invited to the Sheikh's villa to meet him and his wife, Princess Haya, the daughter of King Hussein of Jordan, who were very nice people, and we didn't end up sharing a bucket of KFC there, I can tell you.

I came back in time for Sunday at Ascot, where I rode a winner for Kim Bailey on a horse called Un Ace. It was a particularly satisfying win because jumping the last I was a good ten lengths behind Richard Johnson on Royal Regatta but managed to haul him in with every stride and just steal it on the line by a short head for my 107th – and last – winner at Ascot.

After that I was back on an aeroplane again: J.P. McManus was sponsoring a 'Tidy Up Limerick' campaign, which I was only too delighted to head over and help out with. Paul O'Connell, one of the greatest Irish rugby players of all time, was also there and I spent a bit of time chatting to him about, inevitably, retirement.

I'd met Paul on several occasions in the past as a result of our mutual friendship with JP and earlier in the year I'd bumped into him at Heathrow airport on a Saturday evening after he'd just played for Munster at Saracens. Saracens had absolutely hammered them and he was in understandably bad form. We talked about that in Limerick and he confided that after the Saracens game he'd been genuinely worried he was gone as a player, that he wasn't as good as he once was. Then of course barely a month later he was being lauded as one of the best players in the Six Nations, he had a brilliant tournament, and was much happier when we met again. He asked me about my decision to retire and I told him exactly how it had come about. I could see what he was driving at and told him I thought he should keep going as long as he possibly could while he was still at the top of his game.

JP kindly lent me his helicopter to come back to Berkshire for the Lambourn Open Day, a fantastic annual event which I've attended every year I've been in the country. There are at least thirty racing stables in and around Lambourn, it's second only to Newmarket as a racehorse training centre, and on Open Day most of the yards open their gates and let the public in for a look round. There are races, farrier displays, show jumping, parades, a fair: all sorts of activities staged in aid of stable lads and ex-stable lads in need. The day generally pulls in around 10,000 people, so it raises a good bit of money for a very good cause and is always one of the highlights of the year for me.

Having the loan of the helicopter was fantastic: I had the pilots take us up to the house and took them out for some dinner, and the next day they took Chanelle, Eve and Archie to Haydock for the racing: Archie, eighteen months old, was sitting in the helicopter like he was well-used to this life.

At Easter weekend, with just three weeks to go as a professional jockey, I crossed the Irish Sea to ride in Ireland for the final time. In the Ryanair Gold Cup Novice Chase at Fairyhouse on Easter Sunday I was on a horse of Enda Bolger's called Gilgamboa, a seven-year-old with a good win record who in my view had a really good chance of winning. With four to jump he was having to work very hard just to stay in contention but at the last we jumped level in a trio with Gitane de Berlais and Smashing. As we thundered down the home stages Gilgamboa began to pull away and despite an incredible late burst from The Tullow Tank, who seemed to come flying through from nowhere, Gilgamboa managed to stick out his neck and get us over the line to win.

It was a great race and a particularly good winning feeling as I'd known Enda a long time through his association with JP but never ridden a winner for him before. To break my duck in such a big race and so close to retiring, well, I got more of a thrill out of that than most races in my final season because Enda Bolger is a great man.

In the Irish Grand National the next day I rode Cantlow, one of JP's horses trained by Paul Webber. It rained a lot that weekend, something that had suited Gilgamboa perfectly but wasn't so good for Cantlow. He ran OK but the going had effectively ruined his chances before the start and he finished sixth. The day after the Irish National was my last riding day in Ireland. Unfortunately I didn't manage to ride any winners but the Fairyhouse crowd and the Irish racing community as a whole gave me a heartfelt send-off that stayed with me all the way home. Flying out of Dublin airport at twilight I looked down at the city below as the plane banked round towards the Irish Sea and took in the curve of Dublin Bay, the Wicklow mountains in the distance, and almost directly below, in the west of the city, the vast green expanse of Phoenix Park where this racing story had begun. There are only about a dozen miles between Fairyhouse and Phoenix Park, but my Irish racing journey had spanned a good few more than that in the quarter century since the first time I rode in a race at the old Dublin course way back in 1990. Even then, the first time I'd properly competed on a horse, I was disappointed not to win, a feeling that didn't get any easier over the following twenty-five years, let me tell you.

I was really having to grow used to this relentless succession of 'lasts' and barely forty-eight hours after Fairyhouse I was beginning my last meeting at Aintree. On the first day, the Thursday, I had a really good win on Jezki in the Aintree Hurdle for Jessica Harrington, charging through to win by thirteen lengths, and on the Friday I rode a big winner for Michael O'Leary, the Ryanair boss, on Don Cossack in the Melling Chase. I'd ridden winners for Michael before, but this was my first grade one success for both him and for Gordon Elliott, whom I've known since my time with Martin Pipe and who has done fantastically well for a young trainer.

Michael's some character and I've great time for him. I've won Cheltenham's Ryanair Chase a handful of times over the years, making me quite possibly the only person in the world able to get money out of Michael O'Leary on a reasonably regular basis. He sent me a brilliant letter after that win at Aintree in which he implied that it was about bloody time I'd pulled my finger out to get him some money back. It was very funny, a typical Michael O'Leary letter. Thinking about it, I'm surprised it didn't arrive in a re-used envelope or written on an old scrap of paper, which is what Martin Pipe used to do. I'd say Michael missed a trick there for a man who has a rare gift for saving a penny.

Once racing had finished for the day I could turn my thoughts properly to the following day's Grand National. I'll talk in detail about my relationship with the National later, but obviously it's the most famous horse race in the world and a special day in any jockey's career. When I won on Don't Push It in 2010 it really did change my life; nothing was ever the same again after that. Cheltenham, Ascot, the Derby: there are a whole bunch of fantastic racing occasions in the calendar but the National is the race nobody wants to miss and every jockey wants to win. Like Cheltenham, I was aware of heightened scrutiny with it being my last, which led me to hint that should I be lucky enough to win then I would retire on the spot. I can't say it was something to which I'd given a huge amount of thought and I doubt I would have actually gone through with it, but the press took the faint whiff of a story and ran with it.

My final National mount would be Shutthefrontdoor, one of Jonjo's horses. He hadn't run for a while and Jonjo was struggling to get him sound, indeed I was weighing up the pros and cons of both Shutthefrontdoor and the Gordon Elliott-trained Cause Of Causes, but I suspected all along that Shutthefrontdoor was the right horse for me. He'd won the Irish Grand National the year before, had had some breathing issues that Jonjo had rectified and hence only had one run out during the season, but that was a win in a graduation chase at Carlisle in November so he was in pretty good form. That good form continued into the race, and it felt for a long, long way around Aintree like he was going to win. He jumped brilliantly, absolutely sailing over some of the fences, and raced keenly because he was fresh and hadn't run for a while. When he jumped Becher's Brook for the second time I thought Chanelle might have been right and maybe I was the luckiest fucker in the world because at that stage everything suggested we were going to hit the front and stay there. We by-passed the Canal Turn because Balthazar King had fallen there – Ruby Walsh, who had also fallen there, waved everyone round – and even then I thought he was going to win. A little mistake at the third last cost him and at that point I could feel him begin to tie up. We were still well in touch with the leaders after the second last but faded to finish fifth. At the time I concluded he just didn't stay, but he was a little sore in the weeks after the race so I think he had a little injury that prevented him making a real challenge in the final stages.

Many Clouds went on to win, and I'd walked into the races that morning at the same time as his trainer, Oliver Sherwood, and he was plenty downbeat about his horse's chances at that stage. If I'd been a gambler – and obviously as a jockey you're not allowed to be – and had walked in with Oliver that morning there's no way I'd have been putting any money on Many Clouds. Oliver's a local trainer to me in Lambourn and a man for whom I've ridden a lot of winners so I was delighted he won, and for jockey Leighton Aspell and Trevor Hemmings the owner: it really couldn't have happened to nicer people.

Although I'd been on what some people were calling my farewell tour for a couple of months now, it took a seemingly innocuous incident a few hours after the National for it to really hit home that my career was coming to an end. The practicalities and routines of racing were sweeping me along: I was still riding winners, still having rides booked for me, still heading around the country to different meetings, weighing out, weighing in, all the things I'd done for twenty years – everything was reassuringly normal. Perhaps *too* reassuringly normal, in hindsight.

After racing had finished I went into the owners' and trainers' bar to meet my family. My brother and a few of my sisters had come over from Ireland, Chanelle's sister and brother were there and there were friends of ours too: Chanelle has a shop with a few friends who were also at the racing that day, Emily Hambro and Laura Lopes were there with their husbands Harry and Evvie. At one point we happened to walk past the weighing room and the girls asked if they could have a look. It was a good hour and a half after the last race and everyone had gone so I said, yes, no problem. They weighed themselves on the big scales – you wouldn't be human if you didn't sneak into a weighing room and do that – and I took them through to where all the jockeys get changed. It wasn't as chaotic as it had been earlier in the day, of course, but there were saddle racks all around and a few stray pieces of clothing still hanging on pegs. At Aintree everyone who's ever won the National has a plaque above their saddle rack commemorating their achievement. I was showing them a few of these when one of the girls asked where I sat. I led them over to my peg, the place right by the door where I'd sat for years, and pointed out the plaque above it commemorating my win in 2010.

'There you go,' I said, 'that's where I sit.'

And then it happened.

'No, Anthony,' said Chanelle quietly, 'that's where you *used* to sit.'

That past tense hit me like a train. The room even swam slightly as the enormity of the situation sank in right there, right then. Chanelle was right, of course: now racing had finished this was – and always will be – where I *used* to sit. The Aintree chapter of my racing life was now closed.

I can't explain why it took that moment in particular for the penny to drop. All the 'lasts' I'd had over the previous weeks, Ned Buntline at Cheltenham, my final Irish rides at Fairyhouse: it's not like I'd *forgotten* I was retiring, I was just getting on with racing. Maybe it was being in the weighing room at Aintree where I'd had some of the biggest days of my career. Maybe it was the stillness of the room, normally full of jockeys, the banter, the chatter, the place fizzing with nervous energy, the noise of the beating heart of one of the greatest race meetings in the world. Maybe it was because the illusion-shattering truth had come from my wife, my rock, the one who's been there for me through years of fantastic ups and crushing downs. Whatever the reason, I left Aintree that evening feeling listless and melancholic. By the time I got home I was practically in a trance: it was fortunate that I had a couple of days' break from riding as I couldn't have faced getting up and going racing the next morning.

A similar thing happened a few days later at Cheltenham's April meeting, where I had my final race on the course. I had only one ride, on the Thursday, Milan Bound for Jonjo, but he finished nowhere. I came back in and was getting changed when my two valets, Graham and Craigy, came and sat beside me. We were chatting away, joking around and taking a few pictures together when Graham suddenly looked solemn, was quiet for a minute and said, 'It's weird isn't it? This is your corner, always has been. But after this you'll never be here again.'

'Yeah,' said Craigy, frowning slightly, 'to think that whenever we're in here from now on it'll be, "that's where AP used to sit".'

All three of us sat there in silence.

That day at Cheltenham had been probably the only time I'd driven myself to the racing all season. I'd only had that one ride so I didn't see any point in making Steve go all the way there and back for one race so I'd given him the day off. I pulled away from the racecourse and headed for home, a journey I'd done countless times over the years, and was heading past Birdlip to get onto the A417 when suddenly it just hit me, right there, at the roundabout. I could feel myself starting to cry, thinking, fuck, it really is over. Aintree had been bad enough when Chanelle had used the past tense about my peg, but when the two lads had said it at Cheltenham as well, it represented the two sides of my life, family and professional, like two vast gates swinging closed and about to clang shut. I drove the rest of the way home with cheeks wet with tears.

I flew up to Ayr the next day and rode what turned out to be my last ever winner, a gelding called Capard King for Jonjo in a novices' handicap hurdle. While I'd have preferred to have picked up a couple more winners before bowing out, one thing I'm really glad about is my last win coming on one of Jonjo's horses. That meant something. When I came home from Scotland I decided I wasn't going to ride again until my last day at Sandown, a week later. First of all it would make Sandown more special if I wasn't riding every day in the run-up, I'd be looking forward to it. Also the weighing room mini-meltdowns I'd experienced over the previous week indicated that I had to try and wean myself off racing. After those shattering epiphanies at Aintree and Cheltenham I knew I needed to start preparing for retirement properly, and the best way to do that certainly wasn't to keep racing relentlessly until I passed the post at the end of my last ride – complete cold turkey would make the jolt too great as I adjusted to an entirely new way of life. No, I needed to take a small step back before turning away from racing for ever.

That last week was still hard, of course, as there were horses racing every day on which I could have won, but the break was a good thing for me mentally and gave me the opportunity to get excited about Sandown. After all, I wouldn't have much to look forward to after it.

I was offered plenty of horses for my final day. Again I sounded out Dave and Chanelle and they confirmed what I'd already decided, that my last horses should definitely be JP's. I'd been riding for him for more than a decade and he'd become a close friend and mentor as well as a boss, so saying goodbye to racing wearing anything but the green and gold would have looked wrong and felt wrong. I'd won the National in those colours, the Gold Cup, my 4,000th winner – just about all the great moments of the second half of my riding career had been in JP's colours so I wanted all the photographs that day, all the footage, every-one's memories to have me in the green and gold.

Once that was confirmed the week seemed to drag by at a pace so slow that it was in serious danger of being hit from behind by a glacier. The days seemed endless, no matter how busy I tried to keep myself. Finally, after a restless night, my last day as a jockey kicked off with an early morning appearance on Channel 4's magazine show *The Morning Line*. My old friend Mick Fitzgerald is a fixture on their sofa so I agreed to appear as a favour to him. Somehow he'd also managed to persuade Dave Roberts to appear as well, which may yet turn out to be the greatest achievement of Mick's career as Dave is notoriously publicity shy. So many people in racing speak to Dave all the time but none of them know what he looks like as he's rarely seen out and about. I remember being at a pub in Lambourn once called The Queen's, which was owned by a friend, Tom Butterfield – it must be fourteen years ago now. A few of us had arranged to have dinner with Dave and all his jockeys were there, Norman Williamson, Adrian Maguire, Andrew Thornton, lads he'd known for a long time, for what was a rare public appearance for Dave. We were at the bar waiting to go to our table and Norman, Andrew and I were standing together chatting to Dave when one of the younger lads, Brian Crowley, came over.

'C'mere to me, lads,' he said in his big Cork accent, 'I can't believe bloody Dave Roberts has got us all down here and hasn't turned up himself.'

Dave was literally standing there in front of him and Brian, one of his jockeys, just had no idea because he didn't know what he looked like.

So Dave being on *The Morning Line*, as well as being a scoop for Fitzy, would have been a revelation to many people in the racing world who were seeing Dave's face for the first time. I thought given the day and the occasion the show might not be easy for me: I was a tiny bit concerned that looking back over the years might have made me a bit too emotional in the circumstances, but we spent a really enjoyable time reminiscing about my career and looking ahead to the six hours that was all that remained of it.

Once the gates opened and racing got underway Sandown was transformed into a truly amazing place. The 'sold out' signs had gone up in advance, which is rare outside Aintree and Cheltenham: 18,000 people had bought tickets and absolutely filled the place. Sandown had everything brilliantly organised too, from making sure there were enough well-stocked bars and catering outlets to keep 18,000 people happy to accommodating every family member – including my parents who'd come over from Moneyglass – and friend whom I had wanted to be there.

When you get married people tell you that the big day will whizz by and you'll barely remember a thing. That's pretty much what happened to me at Sandown that day. The racing aside, I'm left with a mental slideshow of images of a day on which my life changed for ever.

I remember seeing my silks hanging up on the peg when I walked into the weighing room. I remember how nice it was to run in to Don't Push It again as I led him around the ring as part of a special parade. I remember receiving a special lifetime achievement award from Sandown Park that was presented by Liam Brady, a lifelong hero of mine, being a Gooner, whose nickname from his playing days, Chippy, I'd given to my first ever pony as a boy back in Moneyglass. I remember presenting the conditional jockeys' championship trophy to young Sean Bowen and Sean pointing out that, with him being only seventeen I'd already been champion jockey three times before he was even born. I remember all the lads from the weighing room giving me a guard of honour when I went out to receive the champion jockey trophy, and seeing two jockeys I respect more than anyone, Richard Johnson and Ruby Walsh, standing there with all the other lads who have been good friends and colleagues over the years. I remember receiving the trophy from Arsenal goalscoring legend Ian Wright. I remember David Casey and Andrew Thornton hoisting me onto their shoulders; I remember the crowd singing 'For He's A Jolly Good Fellow' as I posed with the trophy for the photographers.

Something for which I'm immensely grateful to the British Horseracing Authority is allowing me to keep the champion jockey trophy in perpetuity. Commissioned in 2007, it's been the centrepiece of the big glass dining table in our kitchen at home ever since. It's a beautiful thing, and lists every champion jockey since the competition was inaugurated in 1900. The first name on it is Mr H.S. Sidney: I can't pretend to know much about him but it's pleasing to reflect that I have at least some idea of how he felt about winning that first title as I've been lucky enough to experience exactly the same thing myself. We might be more than a century apart but I bet the feeling was exactly the same. Looking along the list of previous winners is also very humbling in that it's a reminder that I'm just one jockey in an incredible legacy that stretches back more than a century and will continue long after I'm gone. Seeing my name there alongside great jockeys like Jonjo O'Neill, John Francome, Richard Dunwoody and Peter Scudamore is an incredible honour and helps to explain why that trophy means so much to me.

I'd look at it when I came downstairs every morning to remind myself why I was slogging up and down the country in all weathers trying to ride as many winners as I could. That trophy was the reason, its presence on the table the very symbol of what I was trying to achieve. I never wanted it to leave the house because that meant someone else had done better than me and I couldn't stand the thought of that. The idea that someone else could come down the stairs of a different house in the morning and see that trophy gave me the horrors. It was always a strange feeling when, just before Sandown every year, the trophy would be taken away to be engraved and prepared for the presentation. It would almost be a tug of war situation when they came to the house, so reluctant was I to give it up. I'd never fail to feel a pang when I walked into the kitchen to see an empty space where the trophy should be, even though I knew it was still rightfully mine and would be back soon. It made me uncomfortable and I don't mind confessing that I was dreading giving it back at the end of my final year as champion jockey. For twenty years it had been the only thing I'd wanted – Chanelle had even looked into having a replica cast to replace the real thing when it had to finally go back but even that wouldn't have been quite the same – so you can imagine my delight when the BHA told me I'd be able to hold onto it indefinitely. It was a lovely, thoughtful and classy gesture and one for which I'll always be grateful. They say that if the ravens ever leave the Tower of London it means England will fall: I feared something similarly catastrophic would befall me if I was ever parted from that beautiful piece of silverware.

Although many of my memories of that last day at Sandown are a little fragmentary and impressionistic, what I remember most clearly are the two rides I had that day. The first was Mr Mole, on whom I'd announced my retirement after my 200th winner, in a race christened the Bet365 AP McCoy Celebration Chase. Eleven weeks had passed since that day at Newbury, but as I mounted Mr Mole again at Sandown it almost felt like eleven years.

We made our way down the Rhododendron Walk and cantered to the start, hardly aware of the crowd now, just concentrating on the race. Noel Fehily on Special Tiara led for the first few fences and with three to go we were neck and neck, but Mr Mole faded up the hill to come in third as Special Tiara won convincingly.

One race down, one to go. Could I confirm my apparent status as the luckiest man in the world and finish with a win?

The clock seemed to take an age to click round, but finally it was time to go out and race for the very last time. I was focused as I left the weighing room and I must have looked awfully grim-faced to the crowds of people who'd gathered outside to see me walk to the paddock. I signed a few racecards almost on auto-pilot – they were probably the worst signatures I've ever done; apologies if yours was one of them – and there were so many people crowding around that eventually I needed a bit of help to get through them all. I relaxed a bit when I saw J.P. McManus standing there, and then my daughter Eve appeared too. Shortly afterwards Jonjo wandered up, very chilled and smiling his big smile, his hands in his pockets as if this was just another race.

Once I climbed into the saddle on Box Office things began to settle and I could concentrate fully on the job in hand. I had to suppress a few emotions as we cantered past the stand and I heard the cheers of the crowd, but once the flag went up for the start of the race I was fully focused mentally and all other thoughts vanished.

I was on the inside towards the back of the field. Apparently there was another huge roar when I passed the grandstand for the first time but I honestly didn't hear it, I was concentrating solely on the race, biding my time on the inside track. With four to jump I manoeuvred Box Office left across the field to the outside where there was a bit of daylight in front of me and I tucked in behind Brother Tedd at the turn for home. Box Office was in about sixth place at this stage and still only three or four lengths off the lead, but when we jumped the second last and Brother Tedd and Gran Maestro started to put more ground between themselves and the rest of us, I knew Box Office didn't have it.

That was when the voice popped into my head.

This is it. This is the end.

I realised that the approaching fence would be the last I'd ever jump: I must have cleared 100,000 or more in the last two decades, but there would be no more after this one.

There was no question of easing off. There'd be no showboating or waving to the crowd: that's never been my style and that wasn't about to change even in the final furlongs of my racing career. If I couldn't win or come second then I was going to make damn sure I finished third and drove out Box Office right to the line, holding off a couple of strong finishers behind me. Only then did I allow myself to relax a little, to sit down in the saddle as Box Office slowed to a trot, puff out my cheeks and let the tension of the race seep from my muscles and bones. The first face I saw was Richard Johnson's and I congratulated him on a great win. The other jockeys came over: the ritual of camaraderie played out in the hard-breathing aftermath of every race, the familiar faces flushed with the exertion, sometimes spattered with mud, sometimes shiny with sweat, the back slaps and handshakes, the good wishes and commiserations, the smiles and the laughter. Normally there's a sense of 'see you back here after the next one, lads', but of course there was none of that for me this time.

As the adrenalin began to disperse I could feel the emotion beginning to rise in its place. I gave Box Office a good pat and he turned for the winner's enclosure. Then I saw a familiar face: Dave Roberts, the man who has been as responsible for my success as anyone else over the years. We barely said a word, I just reached down and hugged him. We walked past the grand-stand together and the crowd was extraordinary, it was the most wonderful ovation – certainly the best reception I've ever got for finishing third.

I was overwhelmed at the thought that all those people had turned out that day, people who'd supported me over the years and made the effort to come and see me ride for the last time, from the old lads with their roll-up ciggies and a tattered *Racing Post* in their coat pockets to the families, the mums, dads and kids with their 'Thanks AP' banners and – a little alarmingly – cardboard masks of my face (which might have been better saved for Halloween, if you ask me). Looking out and waving at that sea of smiling faces I felt a huge surge of emotion: the tears began to form and the breath began to catch in my throat. I was reassured to feel Dave's hand resting on my riding boot as he walked alongside me in the same way his quiet guiding hand had played such an important part in shaping my career.

I could barely believe this was the last time I'd sit on a race-horse as a professional jockey. It still felt like the most natural thing in the world to me and walking back past the crowds that afternoon a large part of me didn't want it ever to stop. Maybe it doesn't have to be over, I thought, maybe I can come back again under a different name, as somebody else. I wished really hard that I could go back and do it all again, not least because I thought I could do better, ride more winners, use what I'd learnt over the previous twenty years to make me a different, better jockey next time round.

The amazing reception continued as Box Office was led to the winner's enclosure and I don't mind admitting I was having to wipe away tears by this stage. Alice Plunkett ran alongside to interview me for Channel 4 and she could immediately see I was upset. I seemed to set her off a little too: I had trouble hearing her above the crowd but the first thing she said was, 'AP, I can hardly speak.' I was pretty choked up myself, which didn't bode well for a great television interview. In fact I could do little more than just keep repeating 'thank you' to all the well-wishers and acknowledge how incredibly lucky I'd been.

We reached the winner's enclosure, I dismounted and hugged Dave properly this time, then Jonjo appeared, still smiling from beneath that brown trilby, still with his hands in his pockets as if it was just the two of us at his yard, chatting about this and that, and we were immediately swamped by photographers. JP appeared out of the melee and the three of us posed for the last photos ever taken of me in the green and gold, flanked by the two people most responsible for making those colours so special to me.

As the photographers snapped away Nick Luck from Channel 4 had managed to fight his way through the scrum for one last interview before the credits rolled. I managed to gather myself just enough to say how much I'd appreciated everything and everyone over the years but when then he thanked *me*, everything got on top of me and I could barely blurt out a thank you, I was so overcome.

Somehow I reached the weighing room and the lads were all there gathered around the scales spraying me with champagne. Richard Johnson, who'd won the race but been barely acknowledged for it because of me, was standing there and when I'd recovered a bit of my composure I said, 'C'mere, I want a photograph of the two of us, in here, today of all days.' I put my arm round him for the picture and he said, 'Don't be doing that or I'll start fucking crying again.' I didn't realise what he meant at the time; it wasn't until I watched the coverage back at home a couple of days later that I saw Richard's interview with Alice on the way to the winner's enclosure. He'd broken down with the emotion of it all but still managed to say some characteristically kind, modest and generous things. If I couldn't win that last race the fact that Richard Johnson rode the winner was the best consolation I could have wished for. Richard was second to me sixteen times in the jockey's championship and has been one of my best friends on the circuit for many years. He is an extraordinary jockey. He'd be the first to admit that there have been technically better jockeys than both he and I in years gone by: Jonjo, John Francome, Peter Scudamore, Richard Dunwoody, Adrian Maguire, Norman Williamson and Jamie Osborne, for example, and from today's generation the likes of Tom Scudamore and Sam Twiston-Davies. In Ireland you've had Frank Berry, Charlie Swan, Barry Geraghty, Conor O'Dwyer and of course Ruby Walsh, who's as good as we've ever seen, but none of them have ridden as many winners as Richard. He made me achieve a lot of the things I achieved because, as in any walk of life, you need someone to drive you on and challenge you in order to bring out the best in you, and every day of my racing life I felt Richard Johnson brought out the best in me. If I had to single out anyone who made me keep slogging relentlessly up and down the country in search of winners it would be him, because I knew that as long as I rode more winners than Richard then I'd be champion jockey.

While we were the greatest rivals we're also the greatest friends. We sat beside each other in weighing rooms nearly every day for twenty years, he knew me inside out, I knew him inside out, and in my view it was one of the best, healthiest and friend-liest rivalries any two sportsmen could ever have. If I have one abiding memory from my retirement, one that will stay with me for ever, it's when I watched the Sandown TV coverage later and saw Richard Johnson so emotional.

I know that Richard will find incredible success now that I've retired and nobody could deserve it more. I have as much admi-ration for Richard Johnson as I have for any other jockey and I mean no disrespect to any of the other lads in saying that. He won't have it easy because there are a good four or five guys in with a decent tilt of landing the jockeys' championship. The likes of Sam Twiston-Davies, for example, because he's riding for Paul Nicholls and is a good, talented young lad, and Tom Scudamore, riding for David Pipe, is I think the most improved jockey of the last four or five years, but they've long and suc-cessful careers ahead of them. Certainly in the short term at least I hope Richard Johnson gets to know the feeling of being crowned champion jockey because, right now, nobody deserves it more than he does.

Chanelle had organised a fantastic evening for us and our friends when we returned from Sandown that night. Steve drove the two of us and Archie back in the car, but Eve travelled with family and friends on the bus Chanelle had booked to take people to and from the races. A few days later she asked Eve what her favourite part of the weekend was and without hesitating she said, 'Oh mammy, the party bus from Sandown', so it must have been quite a ride. A lot of the adults were having a drink and singing songs, and Eve, seven years old, thought it was the best thing ever.

The bus took everyone back to The Vineyard in Newbury for

drinks and something to eat: Chanelle's brilliant at that stuff and I'm useless. When she's up to her eyes with all the emails and phone calls that go into putting together any big celebration, sometimes I think, why do you put yourself through it, Chanelle? But she's terrific at it, much better at accommodating people than I am, and her hard work never fails to produce an unforgettable occasion. JP came back that night, as did Jonjo and his wife Jackie, Martin and David Pipe and Mrs Pipe, my mum and dad and Chanelle's parents. I was delighted to see a good few of the jockeys there too: Richard, Ruby, Noel Fehily: a few of the older lads I'd been friendly with over the years.

It was the perfect way to round off a day of conflicting emotions. It was wild craic and I had a brilliant time: they even managed to get me up singing at one point, although I reckon that might have just been a ruse to get people to go home. Believe me, if there really are any new career options for me after racing singing is definitely not one of them. Once I'd cleared the place through the power of song we finally got back to the house. It had been a long, unforgettable day and everyone was absolutely exhausted, me included.

However tired I was, though, there was one thing I needed to do before I called time on my last day as a professional jockey. I went over to the kitchen counter, lifted the champion jockey trophy carefully out of its presentation box and placed it back where it belongs: at the centre of the table in the centre of the room in the centre of the house. I have a wonderful life thanks to that trophy and it's only right that it sits at the very heart of things. The room was quiet, the trophy glowed in the dim lamplight and for the first time that day I was alone.

I sat quietly and looked at it while a collage of images from the day flashed across my mind. I noticed the trophy wasn't quite in the centre of the table so I adjusted its position, turning it slightly, causing the lamplight to catch my name on the plinth. I ran my finger back through the years until I reached my first, back in 1996.

Sitting there that night it seemed at once a very long time ago, yet somehow at the same time it almost felt like yesterday.

THREE

Legal Steps, Thurles
26 March 1992

Whenever I see the footage of my first ever win I think, thank God, at least I actually looked like a flat jockey once. I was seventeen years old and carrying 8st 11lb when I rode Legal Steps to an eight-length victory in a twelve-furlong maiden for three-year-olds at Thurles in County Tipperary, and sometimes it's hard to believe it's me on the back of that yoke easing clear of the field with a quarter of a mile to go.

Strange as it might sound for such a significant moment in my racing life, I don't remember a great deal about it. I recall Jim Bolger, to whom I'd been apprenticed for a couple of years by then, telling me the previous day the horse had a good chance but he said that about every horse, and in that race he also had his stable jockey Christy Roche riding Northmaid who started as 4/1 joint favourite. Legal Steps had never raced before and was out at 20/1 by the start so I'm pretty sure no one on the course had me on their minds when making their selections.

WINNER

When I see film of the closing stages I try to put myself back on the horse, back inside my teenage head, but it's been so long now that it's impossible to do. It's like watching a different person. Approaching the last furlong I turn and look first over my left shoulder and then my right, as if I can't quite believe the rest of the field hasn't come with me, but I look calm and assured as I pass the winning post. Like a proper flat jockey.

I know I *felt* like a proper flat jockey after that race, too. It's all very well having rides, and I'd only had a few by that stage, but you compete in a race to win not just make up the numbers, and while that win certainly didn't make me feel as if I'd made it – and not a single winner in my 22 remaining rides that season would have soon disabused me of that anyway – I at least felt that I'd arrived. Travelling back in the lorry that night to Jim Bolger's yard I felt pretty pleased with myself. Maybe there was an oul' fella at the track who'd risked a couple of quid on a rank outsider and was now enjoying a couple of pints from the winnings I'd earned him. Maybe Legal Steps' owner was enjoying a celebratory meal somewhere to mark his horse's winning start. I thought of my parents, watching the race at their local bookmaker's up the road from my home village of Moneyglass, and how proud they'd be. But most of all, sitting in the cab of the lorry that night, the exhilaration of that first win still coursing through me, I watched the beams of the headlights disappearing into the darkness of the road ahead and wondered what the future held. I'd already come a long way, how much further would this journey take me?

Moneyglass is *An Muine Glas* in Irish, which translates roughly as 'the green thicket'. Having jumped a good few of those in my time I suppose you could say it was an appropriate place to grow up. A village in County Antrim not far from the northern bank of Lough Neagh, Moneyglass sits roughly halfway between Belfast and Derry. I'm gone now from Moneyglass a lot longer than I ever lived there, but I'm proud to be a Moneyglass man and always receive a warm welcome when I go back even though I don't get back as much as I should. They put on quite a welcome for me when I visited just after I won the Grand National on Don't Push It in 2010. My eldest sister Anne Marie had organised a pageant and a banquet but she went into labour that morning and missed the whole thing. People still talk about the disastrous pint I tried to pour in Anne Marie's pub The Tumbledown that day as much as the National win itself: I don't drink so the barman's art will always be a mystery to me. That's another thing I've already crossed off my list of possible post-retirement career options.

My family are still in Moneyglass: my parents, my brother Colm and my four sisters, Anne Marie, Roisín, Jane and Kelly, and while I consider Lambourn my home now as I've lived in the area for so many years, I had a great upbringing in Moneyglass and loved living there.

My mother Claire is from Randalstown, half a dozen miles or so down the road, and she married my father Peadar, Moneyglass born and bred, in 1968. They moved into a bungalow my dad had built next door to my grandparents' home. I was born on 4 May 1974 – FA Cup Final day, as it happened – the third of the six McCoy siblings, and once we'd outgrown the bungalow we moved into the family home.

Dad was a joiner and carpenter by trade but he's one of those guys who can pretty much turn his hand to anything and do it well. He came from a big family – there were eight or nine of them, so many that I don't even know for sure – and the extended McCoys all lived nearby so we were always a close-knit family.

My parents are great and I'm hugely grateful to them for the support they've given me over the years, not just in terms of my career but in also giving me such a fantastic grounding as a person. We weren't a wealthy family but we kids never wanted for anything and I certainly couldn't claim to have had a tough upbringing, that's for sure. I had a wonderful, easy-going childhood and I remain very close to Mum and Dad and my brother and sisters even though I effectively left home at fifteen never to permanently return. I'm the only one to have fled the nest, but despite the physical distance we all remain very close. My mother says to everyone that if she had her time over again there's no way she would have let me leave home at fifteen, that's her only regret, but things haven't turned out badly. I may only have been at home for fifteen years but in that time I learned from my parents the life skills and ways to behave with which I could survive on my own despite being so young when I left, and it's thanks to my upbringing that I am the person I am today. I certainly couldn't have done it without them.

If I have one regret about moving away so young it's that I didn't see my youngest sister Kelly grow up. Born in 1986, Kelly wasn't even five when I left so I missed nearly all her childhood as well as her growing into an adult. Having my daughter Eve has made me realise even more what I missed out on with Kelly and it wasn't until she came to stay with Chanelle and me for a few weeks in her mid-twenties when she studied in London that I got to know her. It's a strange feeling only properly getting to know your own little sister when she's a grown woman. Kelly would come over for Cheltenham and I'd see her for an hour or two in the evening then, but it was only when she lived with us while she commuted to London that I spent any significant time with her.

Moneyglass was certainly not a horsey place and there was no history of horses at all in my family. My interest in riding stems purely from my dad. Peadar developed a keen interest in horses when he was a boy and although he didn't ride himself he always dreamed of owning and breeding them one day. So serious was this ambition that when he built the bungalow he also had the foresight to construct stabling for three horses on the land behind the house. It was lengthy foresight too, because it took until 1970 for him to buy his first horse, Fire Forest, a mare descended from a former Grand National winner and in foal to the most sought-after stallion in the vicinity. He paid £300 for Fire Forest, quite a sum back then and I've no idea how he got it past my mother, but it was a pretty sound investment as things turned out: not only did Fire Forest and her colt Apache Pass instil a deep love of horses in me, they also triggered a lifelong rapport between my dad and a trainer from a few miles up the road at Cullybackey named Billy Rock. Billy had heard about the foal, was interested in buying it, dropped by to enquire and thus began a deep friendship that lasted until Billy's death in 2003. This auspicious meeting had wider implications too: Billy Rock would go on to play a key role in encouraging and supervising my first steps towards becoming a jockey.

With the horses being kept behind the house I'd see them every day and became absolutely besotted with them. None of my siblings developed any particular interest; for some reason it was only me. It's odd when you think about it: six children in a house with stables and only one of them developing any kind of interest in horses. In later years when I was riding, the family would come over for the big meetings like Cheltenham and Aintree to see me race but other than that they had and have no interest at all beyond occasionally checking on what I was up to. It's not something that troubles me though, not at all. Racing's always been my thing and just because it was the way I made my living doesn't mean my siblings had to be fans as well. The fact they weren't rocking up at a wet Wednesday evening meeting at Cartmel or phoning me every other day with opinions on my most recent rides didn't bother me in the slightest, I just loved them coming over to support me when they did. My second eldest sister Roisín told me once that even now she's not that fussed about the racing when she comes over but really loves the social side of the meetings. She came to see me in a golf tournament recently, followed me round the course and complained that it wasn't a patch on going racing. Nothing to do with the sport itself, the nature of golf means you have to follow the game around the course, whereas at the races she can hole up in a hospitality box and look up at the TV if she feels like it, which she made very clear was her favoured option.

I was hooked on dad's horses from the moment I set eyes on them. I'm told that I was first placed on a horse when I was about two years old; indeed, there's a photograph at my parents' home of me at the age of two or three sitting on a horse of my dad's called Misclaire, big shock of blond hair on my head and looking absolutely delighted with myself. I was riding, if the picture is anything to go by, with a full length of leg too. Dad looks a little anxious standing there holding the bridle, ready to dive in and catch me if I lost my balance, but you can already tell I'm absolutely in my element with a look on my face of pure happiness.

I was too young to remember this of course; indeed my earliest memory isn't horse-related at all. It did have long-term repercussions for me, though. The first thing I can remember clearly is sitting at home a week after my fifth birthday watching Arsenal beat Manchester United at Wembley in the 1979 FA Cup Final. Even now I can remember the breathless climax: with barely a minute to go after Arsenal had thrown away a two-goal lead in the last four minutes Graham Rix burst down the left, looped over a cross that Gary Bailey in goal could only flap at and Alan Sunderland slid in at the far post to poke home the winning goal. Even now I can see him sprinting away in celebration, his bright yellow jersey almost aflame in the sunshine, perm streaming behind him, face creased with joy. At that moment I thought, that's the team for me, they're winners. I've been a Gooner ever since. I didn't realise it at the time but half the team at Wembley that day hailed from Ireland: David O'Leary, Frank Stapleton and Liam Brady from the Republic; Pat Rice, Sammy Nelson and Pat Jennings in goal from Northern Ireland, as well as the manager Terry Neill coming from Belfast. Big Pat Jennings was an early hero of mine and I remember strong-arming my poor mum into driving me the forty-odd miles each way to the sports shop he'd opened in Magherafelt once, where he signed a ball for me as I stood there speechless and open-mouthed, rooted to the spot – a bit like Gary Bailey, in fact, as Graham Rix's cross sailed over his head.

I enjoyed playing football – soccer and gaelic football, which I still follow closely to this day – and I did a little bit of boxing too in my younger days, but they were only really sideshows to what was becoming my all-encompassing passion: riding horses. I'd come home from school, crash through the front door, dump my school bag in the hall, go straight out of the back door and head for the stables to ride for as long as I could possibly get away with before being summoned back inside. I was besotted with horses, with their sheer beauty: graceful, sleek and with an inherent dignity and class that I found in no other animal (and missing from a fair few human beings too, if I'm honest). The horses became my number one priority and school took a distant second place. Indeed, it wasn't so much that the horses were distracting me from my schoolwork as school was distracting me from riding horses, to the point where my friends started calling me 'Lester' after Lester Piggott.

Dad would sometimes drive over to Billy Rock's stables near Ballymena on a Saturday morning and watch the racehorses exercising. Around the time I started secondary school I began to go along with him and it didn't take long before I realised that I'd rather be having a go myself instead of standing there watching. At this stage it was just the riding I enjoyed – I'd not developed my competitive streak and racing against other lads and other horses hadn't even occurred to me. I just loved the interaction between the rider and the horse, the sense of teamwork, the fact we were learning from each other and about each other. It wasn't like riding a bicycle where the machine was useless without the rider; on horseback it was a meeting of personalities and characters, both of you crafting techniques and developing an understanding with one another. It's a captivating symbiosis and one that remains at the core of me to this day. In jump racing that symbiosis becomes even more important because you're relying on that relationship to keep both of you safe and alive in what is a highly dangerous sport, let alone planning how to outwit and outrun the other horses around you. But all that lay far in the future for me on those Saturday mornings at Billy's, gazing out across the gallops and watching those beautiful, sleek, noble horses being put through their paces before, all too soon, it was time to go home and restart the countdown until the following Saturday.

At that stage, just riding horses was enough for that skinny, fresh-faced kid of eleven. I knew about horse racing of course, and would sit watching it on *Grandstand* and *World of Sport* most Saturday afternoons while waiting for the Arsenal score to come through, but it was the craft of riding itself that fascinated me at that stage. I rode ponies, I even did a bit of show jumping, but it didn't take many Saturdays of watching the racehorses exercising at Billy Rock's before I knew I had to have a go. It looked more fun, for a start: they were much faster than the ponies I was riding and the whole set-up looked much more exciting. There was a thrill, an adrenalin rush about riding a horse at speed, a bug I contracted early on, but it was still out of pure enjoyment rather than a sense of competitiveness. For one thing there wasn't the opportunity to be competitive, they weren't racing when I watched them, and it would still be a good three years yet before I formed any notion of wanting to be a jockey.

Around this time I was given my first pony, who I named Chippy after the nickname given to Liam Brady and his cultured left foot. I'd made it known early on that I wanted a pony and when my dad was satisfied that my interest in riding wasn't a passing childish fad and might actually warrant the expense, he sourced Chippy somewhere through his local contacts. Unfortunately the horse lived up to his name in every sense: he didn't have a great temperament and was very feisty, but that wasn't necessarily a bad thing. Riding Chippy toughened me up in a lot of ways:

I had a lot of falls which, in hindsight, I'm convinced helped me in the long term. My stubborn nature meant that every time he threw me off I'd just pick myself off the ground and get straight back on. No matter how bruised I felt or how winded I was I wasn't going to let the pony win this particular battle of wills. When push came to shove I was just happy to have a pony, any pony, and I knew I was very lucky to have one. But Chippy wasn't the ideal pony for any child; if I had him now would I put Eve or Archie on his back? Definitely not. But in hindsight for me he was a good thing. As well as toughening me up as a rider, Chippy ensured I was never spoilt: I hadn't been given the best pony out there, that's for sure. Chippy was hard work.

Hard work is something I've never been afraid of, indeed, I actively embrace it, but generally it's fair to say that I'm only prepared to put in hard work when I know it's going to directly benefit me in some way. For young Anthony McCoy, that was something that certainly didn't apply to schoolwork. From an early age I was a reluctant scholar, a reluctance that increased in direct proportion to my growing enthusiasm for horses. My dad was away working when I started primary school so it was down to my mum to get me there. The school was only a couple of miles from home but Mum couldn't even get me in the car, let alone through the school gates. I'd try anything not to go: clutching my stomach and moaning in an attempt to feign illness or hiding somewhere in the house. Sometimes I resorted to even more drastic measures: on one early occasion I marched to the bottom of the garden and heaved my school bag over the hedge. One morning Mum had to ask the headmaster, who was a near-neighbour, to help her force me into the car and I bit him on the hand. That was on my second day at primary school.

Eventually I'd attend school regularly, if reluctantly, until I was about thirteen, but once I started riding out at Billy Rock's I had absolutely no further interest in participating in the education system whatsoever. Between Monday and Friday I was barely even going through the motions, just looking out of the window, chewing my pen, not listening to a word the teachers were saying about oxbow lakes, trigonometry or the causes of the First World War, just thinking about horses and counting down the hours until it was the weekend.

You might conclude, given the increasingly single-minded nature of my obsession and the unconventional relationship I had with my education, that I must have been a bit of a loner as a child, but I was nothing of the kind. I had a lot of friends, we'd all get the bus together in the mornings, and we were always in and out of each other's houses. It was just that school wasn't for me, especially from about the fourth year of secondary school. For the first three years I'd come to accept that you had to go to school, that's just the way it was. I didn't like it but I just got on with it, until at the beginning of my fourth year when I was around fourteen I came to the conclusion that I didn't actually have to go after all. I was growing closer to Billy Rock thanks to my weekend visits with Dad and I'm sure he must have seen the wonder in my eyes as I watched and rode the horses. Maybe he saw in me a younger version of himself; maybe he spotted some latent potential in me, I don't know, but when I started taking the odd day off here and there during the week and showing up at Cullybackey, he did little to persuade me of the benefits of knuckling down and getting a few GCSEs under my belt.

By this stage my competitive nature was beginning to emerge and I'd set my heart on becoming a jockey. When I decide something it tends to stay decided and once that particular goal had been set it truly called time on my school career. Becoming a jockey had first occurred to me when I was twelve or so, but from fourteen it became an obsession to the exclusion of just about everything else. I was OK at football and gaelic football, probably not good enough to take it to a high level, but all that went out of the window anyway: I'd decided I was going to be a jockey and that was that.

School was a hindrance to this goal and I didn't do hindrances. I couldn't wait to be free of its shackles and the end of my fifth year couldn't come around quick enough. Time passes much more slowly when you're a kid and the days and months seemed to pass at a glacial speed. My impatience didn't help make the time go any quicker, but as it turned out I wouldn't even make it to the end of my fifth year before I'd hung up my school bag for the last time. By the beginning of my fifth year I'd spent the summer at Billy's yard and once the new term started I genuinely detested school for keeping me from Cullybackey. Billy didn't really help the side of the grown-ups on that score: he'd dangle the possibilities of going in the horsebox to midweek meetings at Fairyhouse or Naas in front of me knowing I'd never say no, and on the rare occasions I'd screw up my face in anguish and mention school he'd say, 'Ah sure Anthony, you don't need to go to school. You're going to be a jockey and you don't need to sit exams for that.'

Billy was a good man. He could be a bit blunt if you didn't know him, that's for sure, but he was a very knowledgeable man both in terms of people and horses. Billy was a Protestant and we were a Catholic family and this was the mid-eighties when the Troubles were still pretty much in full swing. Billy lived in a Protestant area; we lived in a Catholic one and there wasn't a great deal of mixing between the two at the time, even well away from the big cities as we were. He used to wind up my mother around marching season, when the Protestants would have their 12 July parades, and he always used to tell her that he was going to dress me up as an Orangeman and take me out marching with him on the Twelfth. My mum gave back as good as she got, mind. My dad loved him and loved his company. They had a great relationship, something not a lot of people in the North would have had at that time when they came from opposite sides of the sectarian divide.

Although horses were my main preoccupation I was still keenly aware of the Troubles, of course. You couldn't live in Northern Ireland and not be aware of them. We were fortunate in that where we lived was fairly rural and quiet, but there was the odd incident. The local police barracks were blown up one night, and the barracks next to where I went to school in Randallstown were also bombed, but these things were never too close at hand because of where we lived. Also, in a strange way perhaps it was a bit easier for my generation because we didn't know any different, life had always been a drip-feed of bombings, shootings and checkpoints. Unlike my parents I couldn't remember a time when there wasn't the constant backdrop of explosions, abductions and assassinations across the province. Either way the friendship between Billy and my dad – and by extension the rest of the family – showed that good people can always rise above the most prohibitive divisions.

As well as training racehorses Billy was one of the leading artificial inseminators of cows in Northern Ireland, believe it or not. He had about twenty horses in training at any one time, but insemination was actually his core business. Once every three months he'd run a course that farmers would attend from across Northern Ireland. If I was there on those days he'd bring me in and I'd watch him teaching these old lads in their caps and frayed jackets how to bull a cow, all of them pursing their lips, frowning and concentrating hard as Billy demonstrated the right way to do it. When I left to go south to Jim Bolger's, Billy said he'd told Jim I was the best young lad he'd ever had and he should look after me, but he also said that if I didn't make it as a jockey at least I'd know how to bull cows. As far as Billy was concerned not only had he given me a grounding in the world of racing, he'd also given me a trade to fall back on. I think I can remember how to do it to this day: maybe that's another post-retirement option? Twenty jockeys' championships and a dab hand at artificially inseminating cows: not many people can claim that.

Billy trusted me a great deal, and the trade-off was that he helped instil in me a great belief in myself. He had half a dozen full-time staff at the yard when I was there during the summer holidays and often if Billy had to go out for whatever reason he'd tell me what he wanted the lads to do and I'd have to pass it on. I was fourteen years old, these were grown men and he was having me order them around. It was excruciating, I wasn't comfortable with it any more than the lads must have been, but it was part of Billy's way of building my confidence, having me trust myself and believe that I was there purely by right, not some indulgence born out of his friendship with my father.

Billy had a couple of horses that were a bit mad called Dr Jekyll and Joey Kelly. Before they'd race he'd take them to our local course at Down Royal for exercise and to show them around; what they call a schooling day. After racing had finished they'd go out onto the track and school the horses, having some of the jockeys ride them to see what they think of them. Conor O'Dwyer – a brilliant jockey who won the Gold Cup a couple of times – and another jockey called Anthony Powell – God rest him, he was killed a few years later – would ride the horses for Billy, but Dr Jekyll and Joey Kelly seemed a challenge too far. The lads took them out onto the course, came back in and said, 'Look Billy, they're mad, both of them, you can't be expecting us to ride these at the races because we'll be hurled off in no time.'

Billy looked at them and said flatly, 'Well, wee Anthony rides them. He never complains and he's only a kid.' Billy always called me 'wee Anthony', which sounded more like 'wee Auntny' the way he said it.

A month later exactly the same thing happened, Conor and Anthony came back off the track and said, 'No way, Billy, we told you last time, they're as mad as hatters.'

To which Billy calmly replied, 'I told you, wee Anthony rides them both and he's never once fucking complained.'

The two boys, experienced jockeys, having no idea who this 'wee Anthony' was, looked at each other, looked back at Billy and said, 'All right, tell you what, get wee fucking Anthony to come and ride the fucking things then. If wee Anthony's so great, bring him along.'

'I can't,' a smiling Billy called after them as they stomped off to get changed, 'he's only fifteen.'

A good few years later, when I'd probably been champion jockey for ten years or so, we were in Naas for the Punchestown Festival one night and someone asked Conor when he'd first heard about me and he told the 'wee Anthony' story to everyone gathered around the table.

'I heard of AP a long time before any of you lot did,' he laughed. 'I remember raging at Billy, saying that as far as I was concerned he was at the wind up and "wee Anthony" was a figment of his imagination, there was no such person. Well, as it turns out, it's no wonder wee Anthony could ride those fucking horses when the rest of us couldn't because it turned out to be this fella here.'

Billy clearly thought a lot of me and I thought the world of him. My mother became exasperated because nearly everything I said at home began, 'Billy says . . .', but having known Billy for many years by that stage she knew that he was nothing but a good influence on me. She'd have much preferred it if I'd spent more time with my schoolbooks, but if that wasn't going to happen then Billy was the best alternative. It's not as if I was out throwing rocks at the police or smashing up phone boxes or anything: if I was going to be skipping school it might as well be for something positive where I was being looked after and being kept well out of trouble. No one had been on the wrong end of my diamond-hard stubbornness more often than my mum, and with Billy presumably reassuring her as to how well I was doing at the stables she came to accept that I was never going to be an academic and developed a reluctant tolerance of my idiosyncratic approach to education.

So that was the state of play at the start of my fifth year at St Olcan's High School, Randallstown. I'd just finished a second summer spent almost exclusively at Billy's helping around the yard and riding out some of the horses (I particularly recall a lovely, gentle old racehorse called Wood Louse who was a joy to ride) so absolutely hated the prospect of returning to the old routine. The more time I'd spent at Billy's the more pointless school became, and I lasted about a month of regular attendance before gradually gravitating back towards Cullybackey. By October I was missing a day or so every week and as the academic year went on my desk was occupied increasingly rarely until I decided it was probably best I didn't go at all and I began riding out at Billy's every morning.

I should say as an aside, a few years later I was asked back to St Olcan's to speak to the kids. I told them how important it was for them to study hard and get their qualifications, how it was important for their futures to get as many good exam grades as possible. I was pretty convincing too, if I say so myself. However, some of those kids' parents would have been school contemporaries of mine: if the kids went home and told them what I'd said they'd have been on the floor laughing.

I've so much to thank Billy for and I wish he was still around to see what I went on to achieve. The last time I saw him was in 2002 when he came over to an event in Newbury already suffering from the cancer that would kill him a few months later. Billy's funeral was perhaps appropriately on the same day as the Irish Grand National and there was no way I was going to miss it. I flew down to Fairyhouse on a helicopter afterwards.

As well as providing a far more useful education to me than school ever did, Billy gave me a great sense of belief in myself, something that I consider to be the biggest factor in my success over the years. I don't mean in a cocky or arrogant way, he didn't go around telling me I was the greatest or anything, far from it, but he instilled in me an innate trust of myself and my instincts, a sense of self-assurance when it came to making decisions, from major career decisions to split-second ones during races. It was this self-belief that had me criss-crossing Britain in search of winners for all those years, riding through injuries and sweating out the pounds in scalding baths and saunas. It's definitely true to say there was a little bit of Billy Rock in each of my 4,348 wins.

Another of the great things Billy did for me was to send me down to Jim Bolger. Much as Billy liked having me around he knew that if I really was going to be a professional jockey I couldn't stay with him, or, indeed, stay in Northern Ireland where racing is an amateur sport. He always told me that he'd have loved to keep me on, but it would have been wrong: if I was going to progress it would have to be elsewhere.

Perhaps the obvious option would have been The Curragh in County Kildare, the main training centre for jockeys in Ireland on a par with Lambourn and Newmarket in the UK, but Billy knew I was a young kid from a small, quiet place in Northern Ireland; probably younger even than my fifteen years in many ways. He didn't think it was a good idea for me to move straight from little Moneyglass to a place where there were, let's say, distractions. The bright lights of Dublin were only a hop and a skip from The Curragh, an environment where a naïve kid from a quiet village could easily fall in with the wrong crowd and pick up some pretty bad habits. Billy knew that it wasn't simply about my learning the practicalities of being a jockey, he felt a responsibility for me as a person too, not least because of his friendship with my parents. That's why Billy recommended I go down to Jim Bolger's stable at Coolcullen, on the border of counties Carlow and Kilkenny. For one thing Coolcullen is in the absolute middle of nowhere: there was no chance whatsoever of me getting into any trouble there; but equally crucial to my future development was the fact that Jim Bolger was a brilliant trainer who was highly respected throughout the Irish racing community and a long way beyond. This was another thing Billy taught me that I didn't appreciate until much later: to be the best jockey I needed to associate with the best people, and he and Jim Bolger, although very different from each other in most respects, were certainly the best.

When it was mooted that I go south to Jim's my dad was all for it. He could see how much I wanted to be a jockey and this was clearly the best option for me to fulfil my ambition. Especially if Billy said so. My mum was a little less enthusiastic about her fifteen-year-old son abandoning his GCSEs to move 200 miles from home, ride horses all day and live with a bunch of complete strangers. As I mentioned earlier, if it was to happen now there's no way my mum would let me go, but I think she realised there'd have been no stopping me anyway no matter what she tried. She knew me better than anyone and knew what I was like when I'd set my heart on something. Mum had spent years at the thankless task of trying to get me to school – can you imagine what I'd have been like if she'd put her foot down and stopped me going to Jim's? I'd have been absolutely unbearable, I'd probably never have forgiven her. For a start I'd have been out of the door, through a window, up the chimney, whatever, at the earliest opportunity and pretty much walked to Kilkenny if there had been any attempt to stop me.

Moving did make her life easier in one sense, though: over the previous year or so my mother had frequently had to deal with the school attendance officers who would come a-knocking and it was all she could do to keep them at arm's length. Considerable fines could be levied on parents for non-attendance at school, so she had to use all her charm and persuasion to keep us all out of trouble. This way, I told her, she could just tell them I'd left home and gone to southern Ireland, a different country and a different jurisdiction. I was going to be a jockey, she could tell them, and if they wanted me they could come and find me there.

I went for a fortnight's trial at Jim's and loved every minute. From the day I arrived I could tell it was a step up from Billy Rock's: it was a bigger operation, with lorries driving in and out moving horses all over Ireland and over to the UK. There were professional jockeys knocking about the place as well as a bunch of young hopefuls just like me. At Billy's I'd been alone, a young kid among a group of grown-ups, but at Coolcullen I realised there were others like me, who wanted the same things I wanted and they'd come from all over the country to Jim's to get it.

It was my first time away from home but wasn't so bad because I knew it was only two weeks and I'd be going home at the end. I stayed in digs with a lovely, motherly lady called Mrs Delaney in a country farmhouse that was home to about fourteen lads. I shared a room with a lad called Conor Everard, a senior apprentice four years older than me, who became a very good friend of mine. Indeed, some of the lads I met there are still some of my best friends today. It certainly made it easier that we were lads all thrown together in the same situation, all away from home for the first time. It was a young place – even the oldest lads were still in their very early twenties.

Everything went well; it was arranged with Jim that I'd relocate permanently and one day, a few weeks shy of my sixteenth birthday, I packed what little I had into a bag, threw it into the boot of the car, buckled up in the passenger seat and sat there as my dad started the engine, nosed the car out of the driveway and headed south. I twisted round in the seat to take a last look at the house and watched as my mother's face at the window shrank to a speck as we drove away. The journey passed mainly in silence. While I couldn't wait for the car to eat up the miles and whisk me to my new racing life, there was also a slight, really very slight pang of yearning in the pit of my stomach for the life I was leaving behind.

Dad didn't take me all the way to Coolcullen: we were going to Punchestown races where I'd meet with Jim's lads and travel back in the horsebox with them. It was a good day for the Bolger stable: Charlie Swan had ridden Vestris Abu to victory in the Champion Novices' Hurdle so everyone was in great form. I sat quietly, listening to the banter and the laughter, feeling butter-flies of excitement in my stomach and smiling to myself at what lay ahead. I'd made no contribution whatsoever to Vestris Abu's win and the lads in the van didn't really know who I was, but I immediately felt part of a winning organisation and it was a feeling I enjoyed very much indeed.

Excited as I was, knowing this was a permanent arrangement made the first few weeks hard. There was no finishing date now, no circle on the calendar marking the day I'd go home and things would go back to how they used to be, all arguments with my siblings and Mum's magically restocking fridge. I'd lie in bed at night thinking how much I'd like to go home, but it got easier as time went on. It was hard for my mother as well: we'd speak on the phone most evenings in those early days, both trying not to get upset for fear of starting the other off. It wasn't easy to go home for visits either: for the first couple of years when I was too young to drive my dad or Anne Marie would have to drive down to pick me up and then run me back afterwards, and only having every second weekend off and a four-hour journey each way made it incredibly hard to get home to see everyone. I think in the first year or two I only went home once every six months.

Once the homesickness had abated I was certain I'd done the right thing. I mean, there was never any genuine doubt: I had to be here, in a big yard, learning my trade and immersing myself in the world of racing, learning its rhythms and routines, its quirks and traditions. I lay in the dark in my bed at Mrs Delaney's listening to Conor snoring and snuffling on the other side of the room and realised that if I was ever going to be any good as a jockey I'd never live at home ever again. If I ever ended up back in my old room in Moneyglass it would mean I hadn't made it; that I'd failed. Staring up into the darkness I knew that for all I missed its comforts, for all I missed my family, I never wanted to go back home ever again. Things had gone beyond simple ambition to the unforgiving reality of everyday duties in the yard. This was my life now. I'd chosen it for myself, some good people had backed me all the way and I was lucky that I'd come to the best place possible to learn my chosen trade. My destiny was in my own hands and that was exactly how I wanted it to be.

Having expanded my knowledge of racing through reading the papers and watching the television I was well aware that Jim Bolger had a terrific reputation as a trainer. I had no idea what he was like as a person and my first impressions were of quite a scary bloke. Even the way he spoke to you about the most mundane things could send a cold fear creeping up your spine. Jim had tremendous presence, spoke in a very authoritative way and was commanding in everything he did; he watched everything that was going on around him and you could get absolutely nothing past him, but it was all very much worth it.

Jim paid great attention to detail and was very meticulous in everything he did. He couldn't abide scruffiness, for example: he'd tell you to get your hair cut if it was too long and send you off to polish your boots if they weren't immaculate. A big thing with Jim was that you had to look tidy on a horse, you had to look tidy in the yard, and you had to look tidy in yourself. There was absolutely no tolerance of slovenliness in the way Jim did things: as far as he was concerned a slovenly appearance meant a slovenly attitude to racing. His presence and iron sense of discipline meant the yard was very regimented and ran like clockwork. In the mornings there would probably be thirty horses riding out or walking round the middle of the yard so there would be around thirty people there with them: twenty young lads like me and about ten senior jockeys with all the craic and banter that you'd associate with a bunch of fellas brimming with the exuberance and confidence of youth. If Jim walked into the yard though, suddenly all you'd hear would be the birds singing. There was no talking, no laughter, no lads standing about having a cigarette and shooting the breeze, no noise at all beyond what was absolutely necessary to carry out the work. Even the horses shut up when Jim arrived, come to think of it. His was an amazing authoritarian presence; I swear you could sense Jim coming into the yard even if you had your back to him.

The routine was so set in stone I can remember it clearly to this day. You'd get up, have a bit of breakfast, muck out your five or six horses, then ride out one lot between 7.30 and 8.30. You'd have fifteen minutes for a cup of tea and a bit of toast, then have two or three lots up until noon. By then you'd worked up a bit of an appetite, but the yard would have to be spotless before you went for lunch which was taken between 1 and 2, then you'd spend the rest of the afternoon brushing the horses, making them clean and tidy, before you could finally stand down at 5.30. It was the same routine every day, sometimes seven days a week if you'd done something you shouldn't: Jim's regular punishment was to have you in working on the Sunday to teach you a lesson.

I found it too much at first, it felt more like joining the army than being a trainee jockey, but my time there was the absolute making of me. The good habits I learned from Jim were not only just what I needed at a crucial time in my professional development, they stayed with me throughout my riding career. Discipline is so important for a jockey: you can't be successful if you're sloppy in any aspect of your technique, outlook or attitude, and while Jim may have been overly strict at times, occasionally even nasty, I wouldn't have had it any other way. Part of the reason I've no ambitions to become a trainer is that in the modern era I doubt anyone could attain the level of discipline Jim Bolger maintained back then, the kind of discipline that's essential for a young jockey. When I've been back to see Jim in recent years he's told me he doesn't have the same amount of good staff as when I was there, but there are a handful of lads still with him who I knew twenty-five years ago. He confirmed they were still the main cogs in the wheel who keep it all going, but more or less admitted to me that the system of hard discipline he'd always worked to isn't as productive these days because lads who don't like it just get up and leave. They just shrug and say they don't have to put up with it; that they can go elsewhere and be treated better. I'm sure that's the case and maybe some of those lads might still go on to great things, but for me leaving Jim Bolger would be a scandalous waste of a fantastic opportunity. I often think that if my son Archie ever wanted to become

Deciding to retire was the toughest decision I've ever had to make. Sandown, 25 April 2015.

(*left*) I rode my fastest hundredth, on Arabic History, in my final season. Was I becoming a better jockey? Perhaps retiring wasn't such a good idea after all. Newton Abbott, 21 August 2014.

(*above*) I won my 150th winner of the 2014–15 season on Goodwood Mirage, but my injured collar bone was causing me tremendous pain, and the prospect of riding 300 winners in my final season was slipping away. Wetherby, 15 October 2014.

After riding my 200th winner of the season on Mr Mole, I announced my retirement to the world. Newbury, 7 February 2015.

It was a strange feeling going back into the weighing room straight after revealing my retirement plans. Newbury, 7 February 2015.

I came down when riding Goodwood Mirage in the Betfair Hurdle, the race after the big announcement. Newbury, 7 February 2015.

The day after announcing my retirement, I won my first Irish Hennessy on Carlingford Lough at the very last attempt. Leopardstown, 8 February 2015.

The reception I was accorded by the Leopardstown crowd was amazing as I came back in, my first hint of what lay in store over the next few weeks. Leopardstown, 8 February 2015.

My last ever win at the Cheltenham Festival, on Uxizandre. Cheltenham, 12 March 2015.

(*right*) Cheltenham was always very special for me, and saying goodbye was another emotional moment. Cheltenham, 12 March 2015.

(*below*) It wasn't until after riding Shutthefrontdoor, when I was in the weighing room later on, that the penny dropped that I'd ridden in my last ever Grand National. Aintree, 11 April 2015.

(*above*) There was no question of easing off. There'd be no showboating or waving to the crowd: that's never been my style and that wasn't about to change in the final furlongs of my racing career. Sandown, 25 April 2015.

(*right*) As the adrenalin began to disperse I could feel the emotion beginning to rise in its place. Sandown, 25 April 2015.

(*below*) Here I am flanked by J.P. McManus (left) and Jonjo O'Neill (right), the two people most responsible for making the green and gold colours so special to me. Sandown, 25 April 2015.

(*above*) The other jockeys at Sandown
that day gave me a guard of honour.
I'm followed by my agent Dave Roberts.
Sandown, 25 April 2015.

(*right*) Chaired on the shoulders of David
Casey (left) and Andrew Thornton.
Sandown, 25 April 2015.

(*below*) After being thoroughly soaked
by champagne, I wanted a picture with
Richard Johnson. He, perhaps more than
anyone else, brought out the best in me.
Sandown, 25 April 2015.

The crowd at Sandown that day was something else. Sandown, 25 April 2015.

Sharing my final day as a jockey with my family was the icing on the cake. Sandown, 25 April 2015.

a jockey I'd have no hesitation in sending him to Jim because everything's done the right way there, there are no short cuts, it is absolutely the best place to teach a young lad the right way to do things. But make no mistake, it was hard work and there wasn't much chance to let off steam: there were a couple of places locally you could go at the weekend, but you were almost too tired by the time the end of the week came around.

Like all the trainers I've been fortunate enough to work for, Jim was very forward thinking. He was one of the first trainers to have a blood lab in-house, for example, monitoring the horses to make sure they were healthy in ways that might not be visible to the naked eye. He has a very successful breeding operation now, breeding from something like 150 mares, a massive enterprise that makes Jim probably the biggest owner-trainer-breeder in the world. There aren't many of them around – it takes incredible dedication and belief to be a polymath like that – but of all of them I believe Jim is the top man. The only drawback is that if and when things go wrong he can't blame anyone else.

I spent nearly four and a half years at Coolcullen, a period of my life that had a bigger influence on me than any other. I still sense the legacy of my time with Jim in the way I look at things even today. There were times when I hated every minute and it certainly wasn't all plain sailing, but in those days when you became an apprentice jockey you had to sign an indenture that kept you there for three years. If you fell out with the trainer or decided you couldn't take it any more you couldn't just sling a holdall over your shoulder and try the next yard down the road, you were committed to that yard and were prohibited from going anywhere else for the duration of your indenture. If you jumped ship without a very, very good reason your career would effectively be over almost before it had begun unless you appealed to the governing body, Horse Racing Ireland, and went to a tribunal to liquidate the indenture, a course of action that was very rarely successful. It was essentially three years staying put or you could forget being a jockey, it was that simple. It was a hell of a commitment: for a lad of fifteen three years is one fifth of his entire life, and at that age time seems to pass much more slowly than it does when you're older. It could turn into a living hell, and I'm sure there were a few lads who arrived at Jim's, felt the sharp edge of his tongue and thought, what on earth have I done, committing myself to this? While I did become occasionally disillusioned at Coolcullen – you couldn't spend three years there or anywhere without at least one period where you wondered whether you had made the right choice – things never got remotely so bad that I considered jacking it in. Before I signed on with Jim in the presence of my parents after an evening meeting in Dundalk just after my sixteenth birthday, Jim had intimated that he really wanted me there, that he was desperate for me to agree to be his apprentice and go on to be his jockey. Once I'd committed myself to the three-year apprenticeship, however, I sensed things change, that he practically owned me now and I couldn't go anywhere else. There were a few occasions where I didn't necessarily feel that Jim had my best interests at heart and there were a few sleepless, unhappy nights as a result. Even so, if I had my time over again now I would still stick at it with Jim Bolger.

I'd been at Coolcullen for five months before Jim gave me my first ride. I was still a small fella at sixteen and very light so there was never any question of me being anything other than a flat jockey. I'd never considered anything else than the Flat at that stage and I couldn't wait to put on the silks and get on to the track for my first race. That's what the monotony of the routine was all about, that was the carrot dangling in front of you as you endlessly mucked out, rode out, tidied your locker and polished your boots: the thrill of racing. And boy, did Jim make you wait for it. Christy Roche was Jim's stable jockey and he got the pick of the rides, while Willie Supple, as champion apprentice, hoovered up most of the rest. Then there were lads like Conor Everard, Seamus Heffernan, Ted Durcan, Paul Carberry and Calvin McCormack: there was a pecking order and you had to get in line and wait your turn. There was only racing in Ireland three days a week, maybe four maximum, and at the most you might have five or six horses running on any given day, so there wasn't much of an opportunity to keep seven or eight other apprentice jockeys happy. We were like a nest full of baby birds with our faces upturned and mouths wide open waiting for our mother to feed us whatever scraps she had. I felt others seemed to be getting rides before me but I knew that if I just kept on doing what I was doing the call had to come eventually.

At the very end of August 1990 it finally happened. Jim's secretary would ring down to the yard about nine in the morning and ask one of the lads to call up to the office, which meant they had a ride the next day. When the call came you'd all freeze momentarily, trying to act nonchalant but straining to hear the name, hoping against hope that it was you they were after. On 31 August 1990, five months into my apprenticeship almost to the day, it was finally me who got the call. Up I went to the office where I was told that the following day I would be riding a horse called Nordic Touch in a six furlong handicap at Phoenix Park in Dublin. It would be the last race of the day, which would mean a long and nervous wait in the weighing room, but being a Saturday at least it meant my dad and Billy Rock would be able to make it down to Dublin in time to see me ride.

I went to the races in the horsebox and led a horse up early in the day. It might even have been the winner Christy Roche rode in the second race but I can't be sure, it's a long time ago now. Willie Supple was also riding that day and was tasked with looking after me. Willie and I became good friends but he was a bit of a grumpy bollix, so it was with an air of reluctance that he showed me the ropes in the weighing room, how to dress, where I had to go, all the things that soon become routine but which are dauntingly unfamiliar the first time.

The clock took an age to tick round. Jim had a winner in the second race of the day thanks to Christy and I think there were a couple of second places too, until finally it was time for me to change into my colours, purple vertical stripe on a white background, purple and white chequered cap of Jim's wife Jackie, and walk out to the paddock. As he did with all his jockeys ahead of their first race, Jim arranged for a photographer to record the moment. It was a classy touch and I still have the picture of me standing next to my dad. It's hard to tell which of us looks more nervous: we're both trying to smile but you can see in our eyes that smiling is the last thing on our minds. Dad's in a jacket and tie with the top button of his shirt undone behind the knot, binoculars hanging round his neck, and as for me, well, I can't believe how young I look. It's the face of a child looking back at me, the weight of my helmet pushing my ears out like the handles on a trophy. There's definitely a faraway, distracted look in my eyes and no wonder. This was what I'd been waiting for, the moment I'd been leading up to since Dad first put me on a horse,

the culmination of all those falls from Chippy, all those mornings at Billy's and all the months of yard work at Coolcullen.

Jim had walked the track with me earlier in the day and told
me what I should do, the things to look out for, to try and stay
with Christy Roche on Roesboro, and I tried to remember all
the instructions but I was fizzing with nervous excitement and
can't be sure how much I took in. Jim led Nordic around the
parade ring himself, another thing he always did for first-time
jockeys. The horse had six stone eleven so I wouldn't have eaten
too much that morning. I was very light in those days as it was,
six stone four or thereabouts, and the lack of sustenance probably didn't help my churning guts in the minutes leading up to
the race.

Finally, after a day that had felt long enough to span an entire
geological age, the clock ticked towards 5 p.m. and it was time to
line up for the Olympic Extended Handicap over six furlongs. I
was in stall five, I remember Christy calling over to check I was
OK, and then we were off.

After all that waiting, the five months of the same old routine
at the stables followed by the long day of butterflies and nausea
I'd endured since arriving at Phoenix Park, the race itself was
over in a flash. Nordic Touch had started as favourite, somehow
– maybe it was to do with the yoke having finished second in his
two previous races, maybe Billy and my dad had been bigging
me up as a golden prospect in the enclosure – but perhaps not
surprisingly we didn't live up to the odds. A little over a minute
later, barely time for the adrenalin to kick in, we came in seventh, ahead of Christy but exactly halfway down the fourteen
runners. Jim gave me a bit of a bollocking, which was standard
(although he did ask if I'd enjoyed the ride) and before I knew

it we were back in the lorry heading back to Kilkenny. Nordic Touch, incidentally, never won a race in his life. That was some consolation: at least another jockey didn't go out and win on him, and although I was disappointed not to have ridden the favourite to a win I was about as satisfied as I could be with how things had gone. Back in my bed that night I replayed the race over and over in my mind. No matter how many times I did, the result always stayed the same.

If I assumed the rides would come thick and fast after Nordic Touch I was to be disappointed. It was nearly two months before my next one, when I finished second at The Curragh on a horse called Nordic Wind, and I remember being furious with myself that I didn't win that day. Perhaps the dearth of rides had made me hungrier for winners now the novelty of my first race had worn off and I'd spent the following weeks trying to analyse exactly why I hadn't won. When I then went out and finished second behind Willie Supple the disappointment soon morphed into frustrated anger.

The following season, 1991, was quiet too: seventeen rides and two more second places. I wasn't so much hungry for winners as absolutely famished. Hence winning on Legal Steps at Thurles on 26 March 1992 in what turned out to be probably my easiest ever win on the Flat in fact, was a relief and a release. I'd tasted the winning feeling and I loved it. I wanted more. I already knew I hated losing; now I wanted to win all the time and beyond that I wanted to be the best jockey that ever sat on a horse. Winning at Thurles might have made me feel like a proper jockey at last, but I wanted so much more than that. I wanted to be the best and I wanted everyone to see that I was the best.

FOUR

Certain Angle, Stratford
31 May 1996

There isn't really a climactic, defining moment when you win the jockeys' championship; no instant where you cross the line and think, yes, that's it, I've done it, I'm champion jockey. It's not like lashing in a last-gasp winner in a cup final or sinking a putt to win the Masters, there's no adrenalin-fuelled release with the roar of the crowd in your ears, it's generally a question of mathematics, of easing far enough ahead of your nearest rival that it's impossible for them to catch you even if they won every time they sat on a horse until the end of the season.

It might sound an anticlimactic way to confirm the apogee of a year of relentless hard work, vicious self-sacrifice and thousands of miles up and down the country with a few taps on a calculator but, believe me, it doesn't diminish the feeling one iota when someone, usually Dave Roberts in my case, confirms that you are officially the leading jockey in the country and nobody can catch you. It's every jockey's goal to be champion and the manner of its confirmation is largely irrelevant: it's the winning that matters. It matters in every individual race and it matters over the entire course of a season.

When I rode Certain Angle to victory for Philip Hobbs among lengthening shadows in the 6.50 at Stratford on 31 May 1996, the penultimate day of the season, pulling away from Richard Dunwoody on Imperial Vintage and Jim Culloty on Fortunes Course in a handicap chase over two miles and five furlongs, it was my 175th and last winner of the campaign and I already knew I was champion jockey. Not bad for my first season as a professional jockey.

It was relatively close that year – David Bridgwater finished second forty-three wins behind me – so the title was confirmed not much more than a fortnight before the end of the season and I never thought for a minute he wouldn't catch me until it really was mathematically impossible. David was riding for Martin Pipe, and it was well known in the business that whoever rode for Martin had a pretty good shout at being champion jockey. I managed to keep David's challenge at bay, thankfully, and I was fortunate also in that Richard Dunwoody had announced at the beginning of the season that he was cutting back on his riding commitments because he'd had enough of chasing round the country like a lunatic, but to be honest, if someone had told me at the start of the season that I'd be leading rider I'd have laughed at them. I got off to a flying start though which made me start to believe. And when you start to believe in yourself you might start making other people believe in you: trainers, rival jockeys, the racing public, everyone. And when you're believing in yourself and finding other people doing likewise, it's a pretty good indicator that you're doing OK.

When I picked up the Waterford Crystal rosebowl at Market Rasen a couple of weeks after the Stratford meeting I was already focused on the new season that was underway and retaining my title. I was looking ahead, and had little time to reflect on how far I'd come since that first winner at Thurles four years earlier, and how I'd not only moved countries and graduated from the Flat to National Hunt, but almost had my fledgling career curtailed by one of the nastiest injuries I suffered in my entire career.

I've known pain in my time but not much of it has been as frighteningly intense as the day I broke my leg, 2 January 1993. I'd just been home for a brief visit to see in the New Year with the family in Moneyglass but that freezing morning I was glad to be back at Coolcullen, back in the old routine and back on a horse again. Kly Green was a Green Desert colt owned by Maktoum Al Maktoum and I was pretty used to riding him. He was always a keen horse and, having not been ridden out as much as normal over the holidays, he was extra keen that morning. Out on the gallops he was fierce giddy and it was all I could do to keep him under control. He had a fair head of steam up when we reached the farthest part of the gallop where, to my absolute horror, he ran straight into a wooden fence and catapulted me forwards over it. There was nothing I could do, I could barely even brace myself for impact it happened so quickly, and when I hit the frozen ground the sickening snap told me straightaway I'd broken my leg. Barely the span of a breath later the pain hit me, zinging right through every nerve and sinew to my fingertips, a pain so intense I genuinely thought I was going to throw up. I looked down: the lower half of my left leg was pointing in a direction it shouldn't have been pointing. One of the other lads, Seamie Heffernan, had seen what happened and rushed over to me, the blood draining from his face when he saw the state of me.

'My leg's broke, Seamie,' I blurted through the agony, 'go and get help.'

'I'll fetch an ambulance and tell Jim,' he said, and ran off, leaving me alone on the cold and frosty ground looking up at the grey, scudding winter sky as star shells of pain burst in my peripheral vision. A couple of the other lads came down and put blankets over me, leaving only my face visible and as white as the dusting of snow that lay on the ground around me. Later they told me it was minus three that morning, and it would take the ambulance the best part of an hour to arrive. Maybe the cold helped to numb the pain a bit, I don't know, but I'd still never felt anything like it and that was the longest hour of my life. After a while I heard the approach of Jim's jeep, the door open and close, and the crunch of his footsteps on the ground as he walked towards me. I would never have expected any mollycoddling from Jim, but what he said when he saw the mess I was in was still pretty shocking. As I lay there with my tibia and fibia snapped below the knee and my lower leg at a pretty sickening angle, Jim looked down at me and said, 'So, what makes you think your leg's broken?'

Taken aback and blinking up at him through a fog of pain I couldn't summon a response. Wasn't it bloody obvious, even without hearing the snap when I hit the ground?

'You know your trouble, McCoy?' he said. 'You're too soft.'

And with that he walked back to the jeep, slammed the door, gunned the engine and drove back to the stables.

This was my first real introduction to pain. What made it worse was the uncertainty: it was totally different to when you've fallen on the racecourse because you know the ambulance is a minute away at most. But lying there at the bottom of a field in a remote, rural corner of Ireland, draped in blankets with dazzling flashes of pain shooting through you every time you even think about moving, straining to hear the sound of a siren in the distance and having no idea when it might arrive, that was a horrendous and apparently endless purgatory of pain.

Thankfully the paramedics did arrive eventually and the first thing they did was give me gas and air. I've never felt more relieved about anything in my life: the worst of the pain was chased away within a couple of lungs full. One bumpy ride to Kilkenny Hospital later and the obvious was confirmed: I'd shattered my tibia and fibia and faced months of recuperation. I was plastered from ankle to thigh and to be fair to Jim he assured my parents that I'd receive the best medical attention he could arrange. After I came out of the hospital I went home to Moneyglass to recuperate and, thanks to the combination of an unavoidably supine existence and my mum's home cooking for a few weeks, I piled on the pounds. I also had a bit of a growth spurt – whether the knitting of my leg bones inspired the rest of them to have a bit of a stretch I don't know – which meant that by the time I was ready to go back to Jim's I was simply too big and heavy to be a flat jockey. This, it turned out, would change everything.

I was out for four months, all told. I stayed in plaster for two and when the cast came off my left leg had completely wasted away. It was stick thin and milky white and looked ridiculous next to my good right leg. In those days you didn't have access to anything like the facilities and medical care you'd have today to help build your leg back up, and it took as long again as I was in plaster to return to anything like full fitness. The lump on my leg from that break is still there, I can feel it, an everlasting reminder of that freezing morning and my first day of serious pain. Even thinking about it now I find myself rubbing it.

Until that enforced lay-off I had always been light, the perfect build for a flat jockey. I'd never even considered being a jump jockey, but breaking my leg and having all that time to mull things over as I waited for the bones to fuse made me realise that it might well be my only option. Not only was I becoming too heavy – during my enforced lay-off I went from 7st 7lb to 9st 2lb – I realised I wasn't being particularly successful on the Flat and to be honest was also starting to grow a bit bored. For someone with belief I was starting to not believe any more, and breaking my leg proved to be the catalyst for change.

It was early May by the time I went back to Jim's, taller, heavier and more sanguine about the future. Although I managed to get my weight down to around eight-and-a-half stone I realised I was fighting a losing battle on that score. I was nineteen, fully grown, and I was never going to get back down to the weight I'd been the day Kly Green speared me into the ground. My only hope of fulfilling my dream of being a professional jockey now lay in a switch to jumps. I was nearing the end of my three years with Jim and although he was essentially a flat trainer he did have a few jumpers in the stable, but I knew that if I was to switch codes and progress my future would lie away from Coolcullen.

I went to see Jim and told him what I wanted to do. It was probably the first face-to-face conversation we'd had since he'd asked me why on earth I thought I'd broken my leg that chilly morning at the dawn of the year. Predictably, he didn't like it.

'You're never tough enough to be a jump jockey,' he sneered.

'I saw you at the bottom of my gallops that day, screaming and snivelling like a baby. Jump jockeys break their legs like that all the time and do you see them acting the way you did? No, my young friend, you do not.'

Some might suggest this was a ruse to make me determined to prove him wrong, that he was trying to drive me on to success as a jump jockey in order to stuff those words down his throat, but I don't think that was the case. That was just Jim's way, he meant every word. As far as he was concerned I didn't have the balls to make it as a jump jockey pretty much because I hadn't bounced back up off the floor that morning in January still singing 'Auld Lang Syne', hopped the half mile back to the stables, put a splint on my leg using a couple of bits of wood and a length of twine, climbed back onto Kly Green and spent the rest of the morning putting the horse through its paces.

Jim put it to me that I'd be better off staying on with him, that if I just kept my weight in check he would have plenty of rides for me in maiden races, and on horses with high handicaps that would make my eight-pound apprentice allowance work for itself. Jim was – and is – a very persuasive man and by the end of the conversation I'd agreed to stay on for another year with the proviso that he'd take out a jumping licence for me.

I kicked myself a little afterwards. I had managed to prise open a bit of a compromise which not many people can claim to have achieved with Jim Bolger, but I still had doubts as to whether staying with Jim really was the right plan. He had invested three years in me and naturally was keen to see at least some return on that, but I thought I could probably stick it out for another year, especially if I was going to start getting a few rides over jumps. I'd see how it went.

It wasn't all negative: after all, if you could work for Jim Bolger you could work for anyone, and I've always thought he was a great innovator, well ahead of his time. When I left him and came to England and started riding for Martin Pipe, for example, everyone had told me how difficult Martin could be to work for. Richard Dunwoody had ridden for him, David Bridgwater too, and there were a few jockeys who'd said Martin was impossible, but, dear God, Martin was a breeze to work for compared to Jim Bolger.

Jim had you believing anything he said. He could make you feel brilliant, and he could make you feel like the worst person in the world, sometimes in the space of a few seconds. There were days when I liked him and days when I hated him, but he is unquestionably one of the main reasons I was as successful as I was. He taught me to do things properly and not take short cuts. Even towards the end of my career, even to this day, I sometimes look at stable yards and think, Jesus, if Jim Bolger saw this . . . I compare everything to Jim, and I've worked for brilliant trainers: Martin Pipe reinvented the art of training racehorses, Jonjo O'Neill is as brilliant a trainer as he was a jockey, but for me Jim Bolger is still the yardstick. No disrespect to Martin or Jonjo but that's just the way it is.

It took five months before Jim gave me my first ride over hurdles, at Leopardstown on St Patrick's Day – and Cheltenham Gold Cup day – in 1994. I rode Riszard, a horse with a good record on the Flat who'd won the Queen Alexandra at Royal Ascot the previous year but who'd never won over hurdles. We were brought down at the last when motoring pretty well, which of course was completely my fault in Jim's eyes as he bawled me out for being a greenhorn afterwards (the winner of that race, incidentally, was Imperial Call, who went on to win the Cheltenham Gold Cup two years later).

I was lucky enough to ride Riszard again a month later at Gowran Park when he won comfortably to give me my first ever winner over jumps. Before long I'd ridden more winners over jumps than I ever had on the Flat – seven wins against six – and began to get itchy feet. It was difficult to be a young jump jockey in Ireland at the time as some of the senior jockeys like Charlie Swan and Conor O'Dwyer were farming the rides. Add the fact that there were only three days' racing a week and it was clear to me that opportunities to progress would be scarce. England, I realised, was a far better option – there was racing six days a week at that time and a lot more racing meant more opportunities. The more I thought about it the more I reckoned I'd have a far better chance of being successful in England.

Jim wasn't at all keen, of course. He felt he'd nurtured me for more than three years now, taught me how to ride, taught me all these good habits and now I was just going to fuck off and give someone else the benefit of the experience he'd given me. But my mind was made up and wasn't for changing, even by Jim. I wasn't going to back down because Jim didn't think I was tough enough for jump racing. There wasn't even a determination to prove him wrong – at that stage I just didn't care what Jim thought because the long and short of it was that I wasn't doing well enough as a flat jockey anyway and needed to try something else. To give that something else a really good go, I had to go to England.

Jim raged at me, saying he'd put his trainer's licence on the line to let me ride Riszard and now I was buggering off and leaving him. But while Riszard was a good horse for a young jockey to have their first ride over jumps, he wasn't reason enough to have me stick around stagnating, waiting for the crumbs falling from Charlie Swan's and Conor O'Dwyer's tables.

We're still on good terms, though, Jim and me. He'd text me after I'd had a big winner and I'd go and see him in his box at Leopardstown at Christmas, which, when I left Jim's, I never thought I'd do because I nearly hated him and I'm not sure he was that enamoured with me. As time went on, though, I began to appreciate how lucky I was to have worked for him and, let's face it, he got very little direct return from me on his investment.

I'm definitely not scared of him any more, incidentally. I have a suspicion he's mellowed a bit, but maybe that's just because I've known him for a long time now. I'm sure the lads in the yard wouldn't say he's mellowed one iota, but I have heard the odd rumour that he's not as much of an old-fashioned parade ground sergeant major as he once was. But he still has that presence. He's one of those people who has an answer for everything and is usually right, and even if he's wrong he *thinks* he's right, and that's all that matters.

It was all very well deciding to go to England but the practicalities of actually making it happen were something else. A neighbour of ours at home called Paddy Graffin was an amateur jockey well connected in the racing world and knew Richard Dunwoody. Paddy sounded out Richard about the possibility of getting me a job in England, maybe even with Martin Pipe. In addition a racecourse photographer in Ireland called Pat Healy was very friendly with the jockey Norman Williamson and had suggested to Norman that maybe he could try and find me a job with Kim Bailey. I heard back on the jungle drums that there was a good chance Kim had a vacancy for me but they ended up going with another Irish lad, Finbarr Leahy, who had ridden a few winners in the north of England for Jimmy Fitzgerald and thus had an advantage that he was already known in Britain. That, I feared, was the reality: for all I had some half-decent contacts at home, in the UK I was just another fresh-faced kid from Ireland who'd ridden a handful of winners and lads like that were two-a-penny. Paddy didn't really hear much back from Dunwoody or the Pipes at the time and the trail seemed to have gone cold, at least temporarily, until a fella called James McNichol entered the frame. James was from the north of Ireland and had sourced a few local horses for Toby Balding. James had mentioned to Toby that I was possibly looking for a job and although Toby had no idea who I was he'd heard from James that I'd done OK as a young jockey. I was riding for Jim at Wexford one Friday evening when Eddie Harty, who'd ridden a Grand National winner for Toby, Highland Wedding in 1969, appeared in the weighing room and told me Toby Balding was outside and wanted to speak to me.

I swallowed hard. Toby Balding was one of the finest trainers in the sport. He'd trained winners in the National, the Champion Hurdle and the Cheltenham Gold Cup and was renowned for spotting promising young jockeys early and launching them on successful careers. He'd done it with Bob Champion and Richard Linley, not to mention Adrian Maguire. And he was here? In Wexford? Wanting to talk to me?

I went out to meet Toby and he said he'd heard I was looking for a job in England. As it happened he was looking for a conditional jockey. If I was interested then why didn't I come over to his stables near Andover in Hampshire for a few weeks and see how we got on? If things gelled, then we'd give it a go. No commitment on either side, let's just see how things pan out. It sounded like a terrific opportunity, not to mention that at the time it was my only opportunity and the closest thing I had to a solid offer. I left Jim's after the Galway Races in July 1994 and went over to England hoping that I'd do well enough to impress Toby Balding. I didn't know it at the time but I'd never live in Ireland again.

After four years at Jim's, suddenly things seemed to be moving quickly. I'd only been at Toby's for a few days when I had a call from Paddy Graffin saying the Pipes wanted to meet me. Whether they'd been prompted into action after hearing Toby Balding was interested I don't know, but suddenly I'd gone from having no interest in me whatsoever to two of Britain's leading trainers possibly competing for my services as a conditional jockey.

I wasn't taking anything for granted at that stage, of course, but I couldn't help finding myself in a bit of a quandary. Toby had fifty-odd horses on the go and this incredible legacy dating back to the late 1950s, but our arrangement was, initially at least, informal and non-committal on both sides. In addition, the year before I arrived he'd had probably his least successful year ever as a trainer in terms of winners. Now Martin Pipe had set his cap at me too and unless something went badly wrong, was offering me a job. What to do? Should I say nothing and stick with Toby, or say to Toby that the Pipes had offered me a job? Toby's secretary at the time was Shirley Vickery. Her boyfriend was Martin's son so she knew the family well and knew how they operated. Shirley recommended that I speak to Toby and keep everything out in the open, and that certainly seemed like the right thing to do. It was a little awkward: I'd not been there long and Toby and his wife had been very kind to me, yet here I was having my head turned by a rival trainer before I'd even changed the bedsheets at my digs. Toby was magnificent, however, advising me to go and meet the Pipes and see what they had to say. It was very good of him considering the chance he was giving me. I must have seemed very ungrateful, but he could obviously see the dilemma that faced a teenage jockey wanting to make the grade who'd just moved away from everything he knew in an effort to better himself as much as he could.

The following Sunday I drove over to Somerset to see the Pipes and had lunch with them. I liked them immediately and we got on very well. It was an incredible set-up: he was champion trainer, had 200 horses, Richard Dunwoody the champion jockey was riding for him and his conditional jockey had been champion conditional the previous year. This was quite some legacy I'd be joining. If I rode for Martin Pipe with the talent he had and the horses he had there was a good chance I'd be champion conditional, I thought, and who in my position could possibly turn that down? I went back to Toby, told him everything and he told me I was right, I probably would be champion conditional under Martin Pipe, but the following year I'd still be behind Richard Dunwoody in the pecking order and the rides would dry up just as they would have done if I'd stayed in Ireland with Jim Bolger. Short term, he advised me, it would be a good move, but long term he sincerely believed that I'd have more opportunities with him.

I appreciated his honesty and the qualms I'd had about appearing ungrateful for the opportunity he'd given me soon dissipated. He clearly understood and empathised with my position and was being very fair. Toby also played another winning move: he put me in touch with Dave Roberts, who became my agent and went on to become my friend. We first met at Plumpton in August 1994, a Bank Holiday Monday meeting. I knew Dave by reputation: he had all the leading jockeys save Richard Dunwoody, who booked his own rides: Norman Williamson, Adrian Maguire, Mick Fitzgerald, Dave's roster was like a who's who of leading jump jockeys. At Plumpton that day Adrian Maguire won the first five races on the card and Dave remembers me saying, 'Jeez, I'd love to do that,' and sure enough, thanks to Dave, three years later I did it at Uttoxeter. Again I was extremely lucky in having the best people on my side, and Dave is unquestionably one of the best, providing another incentive to stay with Toby. I decided that I owed Toby my loyalty after the opportunity he'd given me and decided to stay on with him. In addition, even taking a detached view it was the right thing to do. He had plenty of horses and no stable jockey, meaning there was likely to be plenty of options when it came to good rides. While Martin Pipe represented a dazzling opportunity, I'd just have been riding horses that only conditional jockeys could ride or yokes that Richard Dunwoody didn't fancy riding, which might not have been the best way forward.

I liked Toby very much as well. It wasn't that I didn't like the Pipes, far from it, but I'd enjoyed the first week at Toby's immensely. He and his wife Caro had both made me feel at home and the staff at the yard were also very likeable; my instinct instructed me to stay put. My instinct paid off too: from having had just seventeen winners the previous year Toby had forty-six in my first year, in which I was lucky enough to be champion conditional jockey and broke Adrian Maguire's record for the number of wins in a season by a conditional in the process.

Adrian, who was effectively racing's Wayne Rooney at the

time and an amazing prospect who'd set the previous conditional record in 1991–92, was also one of Toby's jockeys, which also helped convince me I was in exactly the right place. Toby had given Adrian an opportunity and he'd proved himself and now I had the opportunity to prove myself in the same way. I was also thinking further ahead: in that first year at Toby's I was able to secure rides with other trainers, whereas at Martin Pipe's I could be champion conditional and still be second in the pecking order behind Richard Dunwoody.

Richard was the best, no doubt about it. I was too young to know John Francome, Jonjo O'Neill or Peter Scudamore by anything other than reputation, but Richard was champion jockey and that meant that he was beyond question the best as far as I was concerned. I'm not one for giving much credence to people's opinions, it's statistics that count for me, and there it was in black and white: Richard Dunwoody was the best jockey in the land because the numbers said so. There's no hiding place in a jump season so it's fair to say that whoever is crowned champion jockey thoroughly deserves it. I admired him a great deal, and tried to study him in an attempt to unlock the secret of what made him the best. There were a lot of great jockeys around at the time, the likes of Jamie Osborne, Graham Bradley, Norman Williamson and Charlie Swan, but Richard Dunwoody was the champion and as far as I was concerned being the champion was what it was all about. I watched Richard closely, on television, at the races and even in the races in which we both rode, trying to work out why he was so successful and how I could be like him. I analysed the way he structured his life and the way he rode, the way he conducted himself on and off the track and took a lot from that.

I'll always be a big admirer of Richard Dunwoody, an amazingly tough guy and the toughest jockey I've ever seen. In the light of my broken leg it was watching Richard that taught me if you want to be champion jockey you have to have a high pain threshold. He also taught me the crucial value of stubbornness, of working out what you want and then how to get it. These were all things that didn't necessarily come naturally; I knew I had to do a little bit more than everyone else if I was going to first emulate and then eclipse Richard Dunwoody, and that's what I was prepared to do.

One thing I didn't seek to inherit from Richard, however, was how he wanted to do everything himself. He drove himself to the races and would speak at length to the trainers and the owners about his booked rides. I learned after my first couple of years as champion jockey that I had a better chance of achieving longevity and maintaining a high level of success in the long term if I put myself in a position where all I had to worry about was riding the horses. When I could afford it I hired a driver to take me to the races so I could arrive fresh and looking forward to racing rather than stressed with pent-up road rage and riddled with anxiety about being done by a speed camera. There were days when if I'd had to drive to the races myself I might not have got out of bed in the morning; I'd have thought, I don't want to drive all the way to Hexham and back, but when someone else is driving it's different, less daunting, and you can relax a little bit more and even sleep in the back seat to make the time pass more quickly. I didn't really have any communication with the trainers either, and never spoke to the owners except at the races when I was riding for them. I had Dave looking out for me on that front, and I trusted him implicitly to have that kind of conversation on my behalf.

You could be forgiven for thinking that the opportunity to study Richard up close might have drawn me towards accepting Martin Pipe's offer, but it simply wouldn't have worked out that way. I learned as much from just watching him on the circuit as being in the same stable: for one thing he would have been rarely seen at the stable himself, he would have been away racing most of the time. Hence I learned far more from watching him at the races and seeing him on television than I would have if we'd been stablemates.

Once the whirlwind of that first week in England had died down a little I could take stock and begin to appreciate my new surroundings. Racing in England wasn't much different to Ireland, other than there was a lot more of it, a seven-days-a-week operation. Obviously there was a lot more travel too: I soon had to get used to the endless white lines and junction mathematics of the British motorway system. Also agents have a bigger influence here in terms of relationships with trainers and the kinds of rides you could get, whereas in Ireland you pretty much did all that yourself. Relocating to England felt like a step up in many ways, and I don't mean any disrespect to Irish racing at all in saying that. It's just on a bigger scale with higher stakes and more opportunities for the ambitious jockey.

If the racing world in Britain seemed familiar yet very different, the same was true of Toby and Jim. They both ran yards, they both trained horses to the highest level, but that's about where the resemblance ends. Toby was so laid back when it came to the yard: there'd be lads smoking, the place would be organised chaos and the general discipline level was very different. We're not quite talking St Trinian's level anarchy or anything here, but it was an entirely different set-up to what I'd been used to. It worked, though. It worked like a dream. That's one thing I've found when it comes to training racehorses: as far as I'm concerned there isn't a right way or wrong way to do it. Toby and Jim were total opposites. Jim's yard, the horses, the lads, everything was spotless and there was no chat, no smoking, nothing like that. It was all about discipline, cleanliness and timekeeping. It was completely different at Toby's, there was no chill down the spine when he appeared in the yard, no lads scattering when they saw him coming, no blanket of frightened silence falling at his approach, it was all much more casual and laid back. Yet Toby had trained all those National, Gold Cup and Champion Hurdle winners, so where's the right and wrong there?

I found the easy-going nature of Toby's set up strange at first. You could have a chat with Toby, I felt easy asking his opinion on things and he was a very good sounding board, always ready with good advice. You couldn't really do that with Jim: it was all barked instructions and bollockings. Toby still commanded the same level of respect, though. When I started to ride a few winners I did feel a tangible pride that I was riding winners for Toby Balding because he was racing royalty, a great trainer and a man I liked very much. Toby was a father figure, I used to look up to him almost like a child. He came to the races at Towcester in 2013, barely a year before he died, to see me ride my 4,000th winner even though he was far from being in the best of health. He'd had a stroke a couple of years earlier and his eyesight wasn't great, so it took a great effort for him to be there, which meant a great deal to me. Even then I was still looking up to the man, even after 4,000 winners. He was a big man with real presence yet very kindly and approachable with it.

The way the Baldings made me welcome meant that moving to England wasn't as big a jump as it might have been. I'd already been through the process of leaving home when I'd moved to Jim's, so moving to England didn't present too big a wrench. It was still a big deal though. I came over on the boat with a car packed with my stuff but didn't really have a clue where I was going. I was struggling almost from the moment I drove off the ferry at Holyhead and once I was being swept along the motorway I couldn't work out the junction numbers to save my life. As many cars probably passed me on the motorway that day than pass through Moneyglass in six months. I had to phone the Baldings for help more than once – I'm sure they must have come off the phone, looked at each other and wondered aloud if when I started racing for them I'd be stopping every few furlongs to ask directions. When I arrived I rented a room from a very nice lady called Patricia Box, whose son rode over jumps and whose ex-husband was a jockey as well, so being around racing people helped me settle in, but I knew the best way to make my mark and show that I belonged was to start riding winners as soon as I possibly could.

I didn't know much about Chickabiddy's trainer Gordon Edwards when Dave booked me the ride at Exeter on 7 September 1994 but I discovered he was a blacksmith by trade in a village in Somerset, which sounded like the most English thing ever to a young Irish lad not long in the country. Chickabiddy was a six-year-old mare normally ridden by Mick Fitzgerald, who'd broken his collarbone and opened the way for Dave to give me the ride instead. Chickabiddy was well off in the betting at 7/1 in a six-horse race, but she jumped the hurdles like a dream and I drove her out to win by a length and register my first win in Britain.

I'd finished second at Stratford a couple of times before that, but Chickabiddy was my first winner. I was pleased for Gordon and his wife and Dave was delighted for me, but I didn't dwell on the success for too long. I felt a little more like I'd arrived, just as I had when I'd won on Legal Steps, but winning on Chickabiddy also served to make me even more aware that this wasn't just a great opportunity, it was also my last chance. If I failed now, having come as far as riding my first winner in Britain, the dream would be over and, well, I'd have to face up to going back to Antrim and bulling cows for Billy Rock. Despite an awareness of this Damoclean sword looming over me, however, I never genuinely feared things wouldn't work out. The only person I've ever had to prove anything to is myself, and I felt I was going about things the right way. I'd been lucky enough to fall in with the right people who were giving me the best possible opportunity to be a success. If I failed now, it would be nobody's fault but mine.

I tried not get too far ahead of myself. Right up to when I retired I had always set myself short-term goals, taking things one day at a time and one race at a time as far as I could. Whenever I rode a winner it was gone from my mind almost immediately. Even as I stood having my photograph taken with the owners in the winner's enclosure I was already thinking ahead to the next race, the horse I'd be on, the tactics I needed to employ. The actual winning was all about the moment: there'd be that glorious release as I crossed the line but I certainly wouldn't bask in it or live off it for days. No sooner had my arse hit the saddle again after passing the winning post than I was already weighing up the next race. I'd done my job, done it well and that was it. Next, please.

That's not to say I never felt a thrill when winning, quite the opposite. There's no better feeling than driving out to the line and passing the post, whether it's by fifteen lengths or a short head: that moment is what I lived for; the reason I flogged myself up and down the country at all hours of the day and night to distant courses in front of smatterings of spectators on drizzly afternoons with the wind whipping in across the fields. It was all about that moment, almost a catharsis, a redemption, but it was always fleeting.

A few winners followed Chickabiddy – two weeks later I had my first win for Toby on Anna Valley over two-and-three-quarter miles at Worcester – and I found myself on a bit of a run. It was then I began setting myself goals, landmark numbers of winners, that kind of thing, and once I'd ticked those off I set myself the goal of becoming champion conditional. Not only did I manage to win the conditional jockeys' title, I racked up 74 winners which topped Adrian Maguire's record of 71 set three years earlier.

Again I didn't allow myself to wallow in the achievement. For one thing I had to do well again the following season so I didn't look like a flash in the pan. Some of the racing papers were using phrases like 'rising star' about me but I certainly didn't feel like one. I just wanted to keep winning and show that I wasn't a one season wonder, spending the following years striving and failing to match that conditional season and living with the crushing realisation that I hadn't lived up to my potential.

Every year I won the title there was no dwelling on it. Obviously there'd be a little bit of a celebration, but nothing excessive: as far as I was concerned as soon as the season was over the score was reset to zero again. I was level with everyone else and there was a jockeys' championship up for grabs that I needed to take back. It was the same in my first professional season: for all the talk about my conditional championship I was just another jockey starting on zero again. Being champion conditional cut me no slack, it earned me no winners the following season, it was back to square one just as it would be for the next twenty seasons: knuckle down, work hard, ride hard, and see what happened. When I was confirmed officially as champion jockey every year and presented with the trophy at Sandown on the last day of the season, as far as I was concerned the very next day I wasn't champion any more. As I write this a few weeks after retiring I am still officially the champion, but do I consider myself to be champion jockey? No, I don't. How can I be? I'm not even riding.

I knew it was important to make as good a start as possible to my first season as a professional jockey because there would be eyes on me following my previous success. I worked as hard as I possibly could in the early part of the campaign to give myself a solid foundation to build on.

Then things got interesting.

There had been whispers around the weighing rooms during my conditional season that Richard Dunwoody would no longer be Martin Pipe's stable jockey the following year. Dunwoody himself confirmed it not long after the 1995 Grand National and there was immediate speculation among the lads as to who might replace him. Charlie Swan and Adrian Maguire were names in the frame, but there didn't seem to be one obvious candidate. One evening at Hereford Richard had a bad fall from a horse called James Pigg and although he wasn't seriously hurt he did have to pull out of his rides for the rest of the meeting. The Pipes had a really short-priced horse called Crosula running in a later race and a lot of the senior lads were interested in seeing who would be asked to ride him in Richard's place. Whoever it was, they reckoned, would be Martin Pipe's next jockey. A few minutes passed and Chester Barnes, Martin's assistant at the time, sent for me and asked me if I would ride Crosula. I did. And I won.

The weighing room prediction was a little misplaced, however, because at the start of the next season the Pipes still had no confirmed stable jockey. I started riding a few winners for them, so did David Bridgwater and a few of the other lads, but one day at Uttoxeter at the end of June, when I'd ridden three winners for him, Martin asked me straight if I'd be interested in becoming his stable jockey. It wasn't a question that came out of the blue, I'd been half-expecting it ever since I was asked to ride Crosula that day at Hereford, but I'd tried not to think about it until the situation arose. I wasn't sure that I had enough experience, for one thing: I was in my first season as a fully fledged professional jockey. In addition I was pretty happy with the arrangement as it stood, riding informally but regularly for Martin without necessarily being tied to him. It was still a hell of an opportunity though and I'd already been turning over the pros and cons in my mind.

While there was no retainer with the job, if you were fortunate enough to be Martin Pipe's stable jockey then you were pretty much guaranteed to be champion jockey. Well, if not actually guaranteed, you were at least in the best position possible to secure the title. He had a huge string and some great horses and Richard Dunwoody was quite a legacy to follow. I'd been champion conditional without being one of Martin's jockeys, so who knows what I might achieve if I was part of his set-up?

On the other hand I'd only been in England for a year and was still very inexperienced. I didn't want to be put in the position where one of Martin's big owners came along at Christmas ahead of the King George VI Chase, say, with reservations that I wasn't experienced enough to ride his horse and asking for someone else. I couldn't have stood that. I felt too uncomfortable taking a job where some of the owners might not have backed me fully and there was a chance I could end up as a bit-part stable jockey waiting on owners' approval. I confided my fears in Dave, who said I should just do what I thought was right. He told me he'd been concerned I'd just say yes on the spot and was impressed that I was trying to see the bigger picture.

After considerable reflection and a couple of sleepless nights I decided to keep things as they were. I didn't even turn the job down as such, in fact, I just never gave Martin a direct answer. It came out a few weeks later that David Bridgwater had been offered the job, but I never mentioned to anyone that I'd been offered it for a good fifteen years or so, after I'd left the Pipes and gone to work for J.P. McManus. Sometimes I had trouble deciding if I'd been brave or foolish in turning down Martin Pipe not once but twice in the space of just over a year when I was still a teenager with minimal riding experience. Who did I think I was? I needed my head looking at. It was never an issue between the two of us, though, and I went on to ride plenty of great horses for Martin. We always got on really well and I was riding well for him anyway, but looking back now it really could have gone either way.

The following year Bridgey left Pipe's and Martin immediately rang Dave to tell him that I could ride whichever of his horses I wanted, which was a relief to hear as it showed there was clearly no ill-feeling on Martin's side either. While I was never officially Martin's stable jockey I was absorbed into the post unofficially because he kept putting me on great horses that kept winning. I knew that if I wanted to be successful I had to work for Martin somewhere along the line, but our unspoken arrangement worked well for both of us, without giving me the opportunity to say no to him again.

During that first championship season of 1995–96 however, I rode for Toby, I rode for Paul Nicholls (a champion trainer today but who back then was only really getting started), and also for Philip Hobbs, all three of whom played a big part in my becoming champion jockey the season after I'd been leading conditional. It can't be something that's happened very often in the history of racing, but things did seem to work to my advantage somehow and I thoroughly enjoyed my first full professional season in Britain. I got on well with the lads: the weighing room is a very close place in which there's no room for arrogance or fancying yourself. Jockeys are a close group on the whole: you travel around the country together and see each other every day so there is a strong sense of camaraderie even though you're rivals on the track. The lads were happy for me – well, as happy as they could be about someone else being champion jockey – and that first one was definitely special.

As with the conditional title I didn't want to be seen as a one-season wonder so immediately set out to win another one in order to show it was no fluke. The self-perpetuating cycle was set in motion and wouldn't stop until the day I decided that twenty consecutive titles was a good place to call time on my career. Richard Dunwoody had won three titles and he was the best jockey in the land back then, so once I'd retained my title I aimed to first equal and then beat his figure. John Francome had won seven so I had that in my sights next. Then it was Peter Scudamore's unsurpassed record of eight titles and after that the targets became numerical. Ten, I thought, that would be great. Then it was fifteen, the stakes getting higher with each passing year as the idea of *not* being champion jockey became more and more unbearable. Finally there was twenty and I thought, that's a good number, that's a number worth retiring on, I can finally step off the annual treadmill and exhale at last, looking back at two decades' worth of extraordinary memories and unfairly good fortune.

I'd always hoped I'd be champion jockey, always dreamed it from the moment I decided the jockey's life was for me, but it's not the sort of thing you actually believe is going to happen when you start out. I always believed that I'd do well, that I'd fulfil the expectations I set for myself, but at the start that didn't extend to believing I'd be champion jockey. Success on my own terms could be mine if I worked hard enough.

I found success all right, but if I'd known then the amount of hard work and sacrifice that it would involve, would I have still done things the same way? Well, yes, I probably would, indeed I'd hope I could do even better if I had my time over again. There would definitely be things I'd change along the way, though. Starting with reversing some of the tragedies that littered the way.

FIVE

Gloria Victis, Cheltenham
16 March 2000

Horse racing is a sport almost defined by its unpredictability, more so than any other sport in the world. The long-odds winner coming out of nowhere, the much-fancied favourite trailing in unplaced; it's what keeps the bookies in business, for one thing, but it's also part of what makes racing a unique and extraordinary sport. In racing nothing is certain. Consider how even the very best jockeys in the business lose far more races than they win and can even find themselves losing out to a rookie riding in his or her first race. In what other sport could that possibly happen? Luck plays an enormous part in racing and I'm always keen to acknowledge how incredibly fortunate I was during my racing career, in terms of the horses I rode, the trainers and owners I worked for, my agent, the opportunities I had, even the support of my wife and family.

The trouble with luck, however, is that it goes both ways. People have often said over the years that I've been unlucky with injuries. No I haven't. Quite the opposite. However many bones I've broken or bruises I've suffered, I've always ultimately been able to get back on a horse and go out to do it all again. There are many others I can name who haven't been remotely as lucky as that.

Racing is an incredibly close community. Jockeys see each other every day, week in, week out. We all know each other well, we share the same hopes, dreams, fears and stresses, instilling in us a natural empathy that ensures we all look out for one another. We know the horses too, or most of them at least, by reputation and character even if we haven't ridden them ourselves. So when luck goes the wrong way and tips over into tragedy the reverberations and ramifications spread far and wide throughout the racing world.

While I'm the first to admit that I've been incredibly lucky myself over the years, I've known a great deal of tragedy. The longevity of my career means I probably saw more than most, but none of us go through a racing life without experiencing some kind of heartbreak, grief or loss, both equine and human. On the face of it my career has largely been a relentless narrative of unparalleled highs, but behind all the statistics and records lies another story, one of heartbreak and despair that can often be passed over quicker than it should as the great circus of racing moves from race to race, meeting to meeting and course to course.

By the time the Cheltenham Festival came around in 2000 I was well on my way to securing my fifth jockeys' championship. I'd won the Gold Cup and the Champion Hurdle in 1997, set a new winners' record of 253 in 1998 and three months earlier ridden the 1,000th winner of my career on Majadou in a handicap chase at Cheltenham's December meeting, only the fifth jump jockey ever to reach four figures and in half the time it had taken Peter Scudamore.

Hence I was entering the new millennium high on confidence and knowing that if I kept working as hard as I was then there were more jockeys' championships in the pipeline.

I was also high on the fact that I'd be riding Gloria Victis in the Gold Cup.

Gloria Victis was one of the best staying chasers I ever rode. He was an exciting horse to ride and an exciting horse to watch: he liked to be up at the front from the start and get on with it. Martin Pipe had brought him over from France and in his one season as a novice chaser he was absolutely extraordinary. I rode him over two-and-a-half miles at the Hennessy meeting at Newbury in November and he cruised home by fourteen lengths. Then I rode him at Kempton just after Christmas over three miles in the grade one Feltham Novice Chase and I knew for sure this was a very special horse indeed. A potential superstar, in fact.

There are very few specific races that I can claim to remember well from the early part of my career, but I'll always remember that Feltham in the dying days of the last millennium. Carl Llewellyn was riding Prominent Profile for Nigel Twiston-Davis and I can remember him turning to me after a mile and saying that we must have been crazy going at the pace we were. Jockeys don't talk a great deal during a race so Carl clearly felt pretty strongly about the way things were panning out. The thing was, to me Gloria Victis still felt like he was barely out for a stroll and so far within his comfort zone he was practically whistling a jaunty tune and pointing at the scenery. He ended up winning by eighteen lengths and put up almost as fast a time as See More Business in the King George VI Chase over the same distance just over an hour later, a massive thing for a novice chaser to do. He then won the Racing Post Chase at Kempton in February by ten lengths, although sadly for me I'd earned myself a four-day whip ban and missed that ride. Running against experienced handicappers he won with top weight for Richard Johnson in exactly the same fashion as he'd done for me: jumped off in front and absolutely leathered anything with the nerve to even attempt to keep up with him. Richard was raving about him afterwards; he couldn't believe what a ride he'd had.

After Kempton there were just three weeks until the Gold Cup. Martin Pipe was contemplating running Gloria Victis in either the Sun Alliance Novice Chase or the Gold Cup itself and despite everything I firmly believe even today that running him in the Gold Cup was the right thing to do. I had the option of other rides in the Gold Cup that year, most notably Looks Like Trouble who I'd ridden at Newbury a couple of weeks earlier with the Gold Cup in mind, but when Martin said he wanted to run Gloria Victis I didn't try to dissuade him even though I was down to ride another horse. Looks Like Trouble was a great ride, but as soon as Martin mentioned the possibility of Gloria Victis running in the Gold Cup, even with his relative lack of experience I was more than happy to ride him because I knew this was a horse well capable of winning.

He started well – of course – heading for the front as he always did, and when we were travelling up the back straight he was really motoring. He was jumping well too – he always jumped to the right but it was never a problem – and I knew there was still plenty left in him. There was a tangible thrill in my stomach at the prospect of the kind of finish he might produce and I settled in for the rest of what promised to be a memorable ride.

It was after the third last that I sensed something might be amiss. We were just off the lead when suddenly his engine wasn't running in quite the same way and I felt him coming back under me. I'd never known him do anything like that before, and in the light of what transpired I wonder whether something happened to him in the run to the second last. Whatever it was, as we approached the jump I knew maybe two strides from take-off that he'd gone awry. By then it was too late to make any kind of adjustment, he took the fence all wrong and down we went. It was mystifying at the time: he was an extraordinary horse, one that would never have just fallen like that. He was too clever, for one thing, and too good a jumper.

Gloria Victis didn't get up. I've thought about it a lot over the years and all I can think is that a fracture must have started developing after the third last, been exacerbated by the take-off at the second last and compounded by the landing, causing him to go down.

I knew it was bad as soon as I'd looked up from the turf, and there was no way I could watch the vet put him down. I climbed into the ambulance and drove back to the weighing room where shortly afterwards Martin Pipe's son David came and found me to let me know Gloria Victis had gone.

It was tough to take. I put my head in my hands and cried and that was the end of Cheltenham for me that year. Fortunately it was the last day so I could go home and grieve, and I felt the loss keenly for days afterwards. Every time you lose a horse it hits you hard and you blame yourself, but Gloria Victis was special, he was different. He could have gone on to become one of the greats, as good as Kauto Star and some of the other exceptional horses I rode over the years: Best Mate, Master Minded and Make A Stand. Gloria Victis could even have been the best horse I ever rode. He was extraordinary: handsome, intelligent, fast, the complete package. A few questions were asked about the suitability of running a novice chaser in the Gold Cup but I'm convinced the same thing would have happened if he had run in the Sun Alliance instead. He didn't fall because he was a bad jumper or through lack of experience, he fell because something physical had gone unavoidably wrong with him just before take-off. It didn't make the loss any easier, but there was no reason for Martin to blame himself in any way.

I still think about Gloria Victis now, all these years later. To alleviate the sadness a little I cast my mind back to that day at Kempton when he gave me the most exhilarating ride of my whole career in the Feltham. I will always be grateful to him for that alone, but it still hurts, even today.

The loss of Gloria Victis was the first equine death to hit me hard enough to give me trouble coping with it. Every time a racehorse dies in such circumstances it's a terrible tragedy for everyone, the owners, the stable lads, everyone, and the jockey always feels rotten because whatever the cause there's always a tiny voice in the back of your mind asking if you were responsible. Some equine deaths definitely hit you harder than others and it's hard to predict how the grief will manifest itself, especially at such a high profile event with substantial media scrutiny as Cheltenham. As I would find out.

Two years later Valiramix fractured his shoulder falling under me in the Champion Hurdle. A grey gelding with a naturally quizzical expression, Valiramix was going really well heading into the closing stages and still had enough in reserve for me to believe he was going to win. Then between hurdles about three furlongs from home, and in full gallop, without warning he went down in a flurry of flying legs and tail, dumping me on the turf with him. I rolled over, stood up, saw the race thundering off over the next hurdle, whipped off my helmet and threw it on the ground in frustration as the horse got to his feet. Falling while jumping was bad enough, but between hurdles? In one of the biggest races of the season? It didn't make sense. Some people at the time suggested he might have clipped the heels of Ansar, the horse in front, but from the way he fell I don't think that's what happened. When a horse clips heels it doesn't usually go down, it just breaks its stride, and even if it does fall it generally gets straight up again as right as rain. I've never known any other horse suffer anything like the terrible injury Valiramix suffered as a result of clipping heels.

It was when I saw him heading for the inside rail that I knew something was wrong as he clearly wasn't moving at all comfortably and was becoming distressed. I ran after him, grabbed the reins and tried to calm him down as he was very agitated and I didn't want him hurting himself further.

At first, although there were concerns, the prognosis didn't seem too bad. They were going to take Valiramix to a specialist equine hospital for tests and find out what was wrong. But then the news came through of the shoulder fracture and the inevitability that this magnificent horse brimming with character would have to be destroyed.

The news absolutely floored me. It was like Gloria Victis all over again: a brilliant horse with a brilliant personality that could well have gone on to win the Champion Hurdle that day and still be only hinting at his potential. Valiramix could have gone on to such great things and yet another freak injury had killed yet another horse on the same track two years on. It wasn't fair, it just wasn't fair.

While there were great similarities to the death of Gloria Victis, one key difference for me was that we lost Valiramix quite early in the festival: the Champion Hurdle was only the third race of the meeting. I was absolutely knocked for six and took the horse's death very badly. I was still quite young back then and hadn't yet developed the coping mechanisms required for an emotionally fraught situation like that. I didn't feel as if I dealt with it any differently than I had with Gloria Victis, but two years earlier there had only been two more races left at the meeting so nobody really took too much notice of how I was feeling. But with Valiramix there were still two more days of the Cheltenham Festival to go with every racing journalist in the country within a couple of hundred yards' radius of me the whole time, wanting quotes about this and opinions on that. I wasn't very approachable or chatty, to say the least. I was utterly miserable in fact. Valiramix was playing on my mind and it seemed like I was the only one who cared. As I saw it the Cheltenham carnival carried on as if nothing had happened and I wasn't able to play that game. I took quite a bit of criticism for the Valiramix aftermath. One newspaper even upbraided me for apparently losing all contact with reality. How dare they, I thought, they had absolutely no idea what I was going through. I couldn't believe the complete absence of any kind of empathy for my situation. When I look back now I maybe could have handled things differently, but I just hadn't anticipated the level of unsympathetic scrutiny I'd be under for the rest of the festival. I guess that's one drawback of being at the centre of events: your perspective is different to everyone else's. It's natural, I suppose, but on that occasion in particular I didn't care for it at all.

Many people looking in from the outside neither realise nor appreciate the affinity a jockey has with a horse. They think it's a job in which the horse is merely a tool of the sportsman's trade, like a set of golf clubs or a racing bike. Some don't seem to understand that when a horse dies at the track it's almost like losing a friend. It's a terribly sad process and there's necessarily going to be a period of grieving. Grief isn't an emotion you often associate with sporting events so people are sometimes inclined to ignore it and pretend it isn't there: the races come thick and fast every half an hour and when a horse is destroyed it happens behind the scenes at best or behind screens on the course at worst, out of sight, anyway, by which time the attention of the crowd and the cameras is elsewhere. But it's always a dreadful tragedy for everyone involved and particularly those close to the horse. When you watch racing on the television and a horse falls you see a plunge, perhaps a flying jockey, the commentator's voice ratchets up briefly, but you rarely see the aftermath of the fall because the camera follows the race. Those involved are out of shot almost before they've hit the ground, but the jockey is right there on the spot. You fall, roll, protect yourself from following horses as best you can, make sure you're OK and get up. You look for the horse: thankfully nine times out of ten they're on their feet and absolutely fine, but sometimes you look up and the horse is still on the ground. Sometimes it's trying to get up and can't, it's struggling and in distress, it can't understand what's happening to it and that's the most heartbreaking thing you can imagine. To see and hear at close quarters a horse either dead or dying is one of the most distressing experiences in sport, but when you're not right there, on the spot, and the race has moved on or the fall has happened at the far side of the course well away from the stands, it's easy for people to forget the level of trauma there is for everyone involved. There can be tens of thousands in the stands and millions watching on television yet at that moment, out on the course with an ailing horse, you're in the loneliest place in the world.

Jockeys have a strong relationship with their charges. It's pure teamwork. Riding in a race takes a combination of personalities and a whole heap of mutual trust between you and the animal. When a horse is killed there's not a question of the jockey just getting up, sauntering back to the paddock and mounting the next ride as if nothing has happened. It's not like Formula One, where a driver can have a crash, climb out of the wreckage and walk away without looking back before climbing into a new car next time out. Horses aren't vehicles, they're animals with distinct personalities and character traits and the jockeys love them. I became a jockey for no other reason than I love horses and love the relationship I have with them. It's why I still ride out now, even when I'm retired. Sometimes I even think I prefer horses to people, such is the bond and affinity I have with them.

Whatever the justification though, I didn't handle the Valiramix situation at all well. I wish I could have put on a fake smile and got on with it, talked about my other upcoming rides, gone on *The Morning Line* and given my thoughts ahead of the day's racing, but the grief got to me and I'm not ashamed to admit it. Anyone who believes jockeys, trainers, stewards, valets, stable lads and owners are blasé about the death of a racehorse couldn't be more wrong. Unfortunately equine fatalities happen, and more often than anyone would like. Each one, whether in a high-profile race like the Champion Hurdle or a late afternoon bumper on a small provincial course in front of a couple of dozen spectators, hurts those involved deeply.

Next there was Wichita Lineman, who was a very similar horse to Valiramix in that I think they were both very like me: not the most naturally talented horses, not the best looking creatures, but both of them had a phenomenal will to win. They were racehorses with amazing attitudes who were born winners; you knew from the off that you'd get everything they had. They were unbelievably tough, genuine, honest and straightforward horses, real competitors. I won twice at the Cheltenham Festival on Wichita Lineman, once over hurdles and then in the 2009 William Hill Trophy handicap chase, a race which has been frequently touted as one of the best rides I or anyone else gave a horse. I certainly wouldn't claim that but I do feel strongly that Wichita Lineman himself didn't get half the credit he deserved for that run.

A month or so after that ride in the William Hill at Cheltenham he ran in the Irish Grand National at Leopardstown with awful consequences. He fell at the first fence, just clipping it as he went over, and was absolutely fine, jumping up straightaway. Unfortunately another horse came over the fence, couldn't avoid Wichita Lineman, there was an inevitable collision and the poor horse was left on the ground with a broken back. I'd taken a pretty heavy fall and was a bit sore, but when I saw him distressed on the ground I went over and lay on him in an effort to calm him down and keep him as comfortable as I could until the vet arrived. I knew it was bad and probably fatal, but even so when the vet took a look at him and told me he wasn't going to get up I cried. I loved that horse, it was like I'd lost a mate. Only a month earlier he'd given me that extraordinary ride in the William Hill, one of the great Cheltenham performances, a race in which he was absolutely bursting with life and *joie de vivre*, and now there he was, behind the screens, being put out of his pain and misery on the damp turf of Leopardstown.

The death of Wichita Lineman had a profound effect on me in the same way Gloria Victis and Valiramix did, but probably the worst of the lot was Synchronised. I'm going to talk about my relationship with Synchronised in detail later, but as he was the horse with whom I had the closest bond of them all his death at the 2012 Grand National, just four weeks after his triumph in the Cheltenham Gold Cup, was one of the hardest things I had to deal with in my career. Even today I can't help looking back and thinking 'what if . . .' and the memory of what happened can still move me to tears.

Before the start of the Grand National Synchronised was spooked by a tape, causing me to fall off. He got loose, delaying the start, but didn't get very far. I can't tell you how often I've wished I hadn't remounted, that he'd galloped off, that he hadn't run. I've seriously wondered whether the moment he was spooked it was someone or something trying to tell me something.

In the cold light of day, taking the consequences out of the equation as much as I can, the reality was that he hadn't been stressed by the experience, had only jogged off and not done any excessive exercise so was still in perfect condition to race. After the amazing Cheltenham we'd had I didn't want to take away his chance of running in the National, so I brought him round to the start again and away we went. He jumped the first half a dozen fences beautifully, but the big drop at Bechers caused him to knuckle over and off I came. I was pretty sore as I lay on the ground, but as I could see him galloping off with a few other loose horses I thought, thank goodness, he's all right.

I climbed into a passing jeep with one of the Aintree vets and an ex-jockey and now course commentator called Niall Hannity, who asked if I was all right. I was sore around the ribs but said I was fine, and he said great, and the horse is all right too. If you're going to come off in the National then that's about as good an outcome as it gets. As we got close to the weighing room I could hear some chatter over the vet's radio, saying that such-and-such a jockey was OK but one of the other horses, Synchronised, had been badly injured and would have to be put down.

My stomach turned over. Did I hear that right? Surely I didn't hear that right.

'What?' I said, 'I didn't hear that right, did I? They're not going to put Synchronised down?'

The vet gripped the wheel, turned to look at me and said, 'I'm so sorry, AP.'

I just started crying. It turned out that I'd broken a couple of ribs in the fall but that was nothing to the pain that seared through me as the news sank in. How? How could Synchronised possibly have been mortally injured? He was fine! He'd skipped off with a bunch of other loose horses, I'd seen him go with my own eyes! As I went back to the weighing room in search of news I still nurtured a faint hope that maybe it had all been a terrible mistake, maybe what we'd heard as 'Synchronised' was just someone saying 'euthanised' about another horse. Alas, JP and Jonjo came into the weighing room and the expressions on their faces were enough to tell me my worst fears had been correct.

The room swam in front of my eyes. With Gloria Victis, Valiramix and Wichita Lineman I'd seen they were grievously injured, it was obvious. It didn't make it any easier to bear but at least I knew first-hand what had happened. But Synchronised had got straight up from the fall and galloped off without a care in the world. It turned out that he'd followed the other horses around the course but when he'd jumped the eleventh he'd come down awkwardly and fractured the tibia and fibula of his right hind leg. There was nothing else for it in those circumstances than to put him to sleep.

I got home that night and went straight to bed. No socialising, none of the traditional post-National high jinks, I just wasn't able to. All I wanted was to be alone. I couldn't sleep, either from the pain in my ribs or the grief at the loss of that incredible horse – it was hard to tell which. It was one of the few times in my life that I've felt mentally weak and helpless. I was – and remain – deeply affected by what happened to Synchronised and it took me days to even stop crying. I felt tortured and carried lots of guilt, going through every possible scenario that might have avoided this dreadful outcome: if when he got loose I hadn't caught him, hadn't got back on him. They'd delayed the race while I got him under control again and remounted: what if they'd just said, sorry AP, we've got to start without you? What if one of us had said, he's won the Gold Cup, let's not put him in the Grand National? Sometimes I'll think even today that I wish we hadn't run him. He'd still be here, then. But you can't look back wishing. We'd run him for the very good reason that he was tailor-made for the National and at the peak of his powers. It's one of those moments in life when you wish so hard that it aches that you could go back and change everything, do whatever it takes to alter the outcome, but ultimately you have to conclude that it must have been fated to happen somehow. I try and cheer myself up a little by bringing to mind the incredible ride he'd given me a month before his death, arguably the ride of my career, but in truth I've never got over the death of Synchronised and probably never will.

Sadly there have been human fatalities too, and much as I have enormous love for the racehorses, losing one of them is nothing like as traumatic as losing a friend and colleague. I've been to too many funerals over the years of jockeys who've lost their lives from falls, as well as knowing lads who've been grievously injured in life-altering ways.

Most sports have their dangers, even those that don't outwardly look dangerous. Consider the cricketer Philip Hughes, killed by the kind of ball batsmen face hundreds of times during their careers. Marc Viven Foé is one of a number of footballers who've died on the pitch, and Fabrice Muamba nearly died while playing for Bolton Wanderers at Spurs a few years ago. Other sports are more obviously fraught with danger: Ayrton Senna's was probably the most high-profile death in motor racing, for example, but he's far from alone.

Horse racing is a very dangerous sport, nobody would ever deny that, and we've had our share of fatalities. Some of them have been friends and acquaintances of mine. I wouldn't say any of us are blasé about the dangers of riding, but you try to put it to the back of your mind and tell yourself that it could never happen to you. When a jockey dies, however, you're soon disabused of any sense of your own immortality because it could quite easily have been you as much as anyone else. It wasn't you on this occasion and you hope that it won't ever be you, but there's no doubt that it absolutely could have been.

As long as I live I'll never forget the day Richard Davis was killed. We were good friends, Richard and I: he was also a conditional jockey at Toby Balding's when I arrived in England and though he was a few years older he was a lad very much like me. Richard had been riding for Toby for quite a while by the time I arrived, so in some ways there were good reasons for him not to be particularly helpful to me because here I was, fresh off the boat with the potential to muscle in on his territory. Richard had more experience than me, was better known and more established than me and was doing very well for himself. He didn't really have to give me the time of day in the circumstances, but from the first day I walked into Toby's yard Richard Davis couldn't have been more helpful or accepted me any better than he did. He was just the nicest, warmest, most generous and genuine bloke you could ever meet.

I remember the day he was killed, Friday 19 July 1996, in intense detail. We were at Southwell riding in the first race, the Fisherton Novices Handicap Chase. I was on a horse called Sassiver which started as favourite, Richard was on Mr Sox, his only ride of the day and not a particularly brilliant horse, a five-year-old that had never finished higher than sixth in its life and was way out at 20/1 in the betting. It was one of those races that ordinarily would be completely forgotten about the instant it was over: a low-grade race over two miles four and a half furlongs, only six runners in front of a small crowd on a Friday afternoon in the wilds of Nottinghamshire. Before the race Richard had advised us not to follow him because the horse was so unpredictable, but no sooner had we set off than Mr Sox hit the first fence with his hind legs and plummeted forward in a big cartwheel. I didn't see it myself, but apparently Richard hit the ground and the horse turned over and landed right on top of him and it was immediately obvious to everyone except the other five jockeys haring off up the course that Richard had been badly injured. Paramedics rushed to his aid and were still there with him when we came round on the second circuit. Apparently he was unconscious when they reached him and very pale but before long he was awake and talking and worrying about his dog. He was placed on a spinal board and taken to the ambulance room ready to be transferred to hospital. I went in to see him but was intercepted by a doctor who told me he was conscious but they were taking him straight to the Queen's Medical Centre in Nottingham because there were a couple of things they were concerned about. A few of the lads were going to go and see him at the hospital, but the doctors said there wasn't much point as he'd be going straight in for treatment.

At the hospital they found Richard had suffered massive internal injuries. His liver was torn and he'd suffered serious damage to his vena cava, a large artery that connects to the heart. They tried to operate but apparently he lost eight pints of blood before his heart failed and couldn't be restarted. He was gone.

I was on my way home when the news came through. A mutual friend of Richard's and mine who went by the nickname of Sonic called me when I was sitting at a set of traffic lights in Newbury.

'He's gone, AP,' he told me. 'Dickie's died.'

It took Sonic a couple of goes to get the message through as it just sounded wrong. He couldn't be dead. He'd been knocked about a bit, sure, but last I'd heard he'd been awake and talking. When the news finally penetrated my emotional defences I just froze. I couldn't move. It was like the world had caved in and all I could do was sit there at the traffic lights crying. The lights had changed and people were hooting at me to get moving, not having a clue what had happened, but I just couldn't move. Everything had stopped. Everything.

Richard's funeral in Worcestershire was one of the saddest occasions I've ever attended. Jamie Osborne, Adrian Maguire and Richard Dunwoody were there too, and Richard spoke very movingly at the service. Whenever we jockeys caught each other's eyes there was the same unspoken message passing between us: it could have been me.

Every jump jockey falls regularly. I must have had something close to a thousand falls over my career. You try to brace yourself and land as safely as possible, but there are factors outside your control for which you can't legislate as Richard's death proved. Even the most apparently mundane, run-of-the-mill falls in the most apparently mundane, run-of-the-mill races can prove fatal. You're never completely safe.

Since that black day in 1996 there have been numerous other jockey fatalities. Kieran Kelly died after a fall at Kilbeggan in Westmeath in August 2003, for example, and later that same year Sean Cleary fell at Galway and was in a coma for a week before dying in the Beaumont Hospital in Dublin.

I also happened to be riding in the race in which Tom Halliday was killed, a novices' handicap hurdle at Market Rasen in July 2005. It was a big field and apparently Tom's horse Rush'N'Run was nudged left in midfield by another horse and in trying to correct the imbalance he fell and pulled the horse down on top of him, resulting in massive head injuries. He was only a kid, barely twenty. Every time I went to Market Rasen afterwards I always bumped into his parents. They're a great racing family, his brother James was a jockey and continued to ride even after Tom was killed, and there's a race run every year in Tom's memory at Market Rasen, the Tom Halliday Memorial Conditional Jockeys' Handicap Hurdle.

I didn't know Tom well, I knew him to say hello to around the circuit, but I always make a point of paying my respects to his family every time I see them. I come away thinking how tough it must be for them to go to Market Rasen after what happened there. How his mother deals with that I'll never know, she's the most amazing woman for whom I have nothing but the utmost admiration. There must be times when she feels a searing bitterness because sometimes I'm bitter about friends and colleagues who've been killed, but I can't begin to imagine how you'd cope with losing a son. Mrs Halliday is the most amazing, classy woman you'll ever see and I used to look forward to seeing her and having a chat whenever I rode at Marker Rasen. I hope she knows that Tom, like the others, will never, ever be forgotten by the racing world.

As well as these dreadful fatalities I've also known lads who've suffered horrific, permanent injuries while riding. John Thomas McNamara and Shane Broderick, for example, are both paralysed from the neck down after suffering bad falls. They have very little comfort in life, but I still see them either at the races or at home and never fail to reflect on how lucky I am. By a dreadful coincidence JT's first cousin Robbie McNamara now looks like he could be paralysed from the waist down after a fall at Wexford the day before the 2015 Grand National. Two years after

John Thomas, the same thing happening to the same family. It just doesn't bear thinking about.

But this is a sport in which two ambulances follow you around every day. It's a dangerous game, that's the reality, and the likes of Richard and Tom, JT and Shane, faced unflinchingly the same dangers we all do. And the terrible things that happened to them serve to remind the rest of us just how lucky we are, and what is important in life. Some days you come home from racing in a deep funk after a bad day but then you catch yourself and realise it's really not that bad compared to what some of the lads and their families are going through.

The weighing room becomes a very sombre place when something terrible happens. It takes a long time for people to get over something like that because it demonstrates how it could be any of us. It's the starkest reminder of the dangers that face every jockey in every race, that you can never switch off the risk, not for a single race or a single fence. I'm sure jump jockeys in particular maintain a special bond because of it. There's no room for egos or arrogance in the weighing room because no matter how many winners you've ridden or how good you think you might be, those two ambulances are there for you as much as anyone else, and that takes all the ego and attitude, the sense that anyone is special, completely out of the equation.

Regularly as a jockey you find yourself the evening after racing's finished at some hospital somewhere, bringing a lad's clothes and mobile phone in for him, or helping to get his car home, making sure everything's organised for him because he's got a broken arm or leg or some other injury he's picked up at the races. There are times in his career when every jockey needs the lad beside him and there aren't many other jobs or sports in which you depend on someone who's ostensibly your rival and your opponent to make sure you're all right and being looked after whenever you need it. That's why the weighing room is a much closer place than the equivalent location in any other sport.

Richard Johnson, for example, should have hated my guts because I was in his way for all those years and stopping him becoming champion jockey, but we sat beside one another for twenty years and remain good friends. Both he and I, being longer in the tooth than most of the lads, knew more than anyone the dangers of racing and the tragic consequences – Richard was also riding in Richard Davis's last race, as it happens – and that's why there was such a solid friendship underpinning the rivalry that existed between us on the track: because of the dangers involved. Winning is important, there's no question of that, but there are more important things that ensure any rivalries remain purely on the track, nowhere else.

Having said all that, I can't deny that I found part of the thrill of riding in the danger. It's like James Hunt says in the film *Rush*, 'The closer you are to death the more alive you feel.' When I heard that I smiled to myself and thought, that's absolutely spot on. Much of the thrill and excitement I took from racing came from the risk, it's what gets your pulse racing and the adrenalin pumping. I loved riding, really loved it. It wasn't an everyday job by any means and no two days were ever the same. You might think riding in horse races is pretty repetitive, dull even, but every time you go out it's always different and there's an unpredictability to it that can be intoxicating. It's not like going to an office Monday to Friday, starting at nine and finishing at five with an hour for lunch, and you worry that you might have sent an email to someone you shouldn't have. That's entirely different from thinking, I've got half a dozen rides today and hopefully some of them are winners, or conversely going out on the first horse and falling at the first hurdle and getting injured. It's this unpredictability that gets the blood pumping; that sees you through those endless hours up and down the motorway: the feeling that you're living on the edge and living a different life to any other person because you've no idea what might lie around the next corner.

It's a life that belies complacency and precludes contentment. There were times during my career where I did feel content for short periods of time, maybe occasionally towards the end of a season when I'd been confirmed as champion jockey and was still riding winners, but it was never a regular thing and certainly far from a default setting.

I freely admit that I will miss the danger and the risk of racing, but embracing risk doesn't mean laughing in its face. Quite the opposite in fact, it comes with responsibility. I've definitely enjoyed incredible good fortune in coming through two decades of professional jump racing unscathed save for the odd wee scar and metal pin, but I've never taken that fortune for granted. You can insure yourself against disaster up to a point by avoiding recklessness and knowing just how far you can push the boundaries of risk, but even the most sensible, level-headed jockey knows that you can't control everything. And one day, it could be you.

SIX

Valfonic, Warwick
2 April 2002

Breaking Sir Gordon Richards' record of 269 winners in a season will always be my greatest ever achievement in racing. People might point to the Gold Cups, winning the National or my record in the jockeys' championship and I'm certainly very proud of all of that, but for me passing the season total of one of the greatest jockeys ever to grace the track eclipses everything else. Why? Well, lots of people win the Grand National and the Gold Cup, and plenty of people have been champion jockey. Nobody, however, had broken Sir Gordon Richards' record until I crossed the line on Valfonic in the late afternoon of 2 April 2002.

The record had stood for fifty-five years when I broke it, since 1947. Even for an old-timer like me 1947 seems a long time ago – the war was only two years finished, rationing was still in place and Arsenal were only finishing halfway down the old First Division. Of all the jockeys that had ridden winners during that five and a half decades of flat and jumps racing none of them had even come close to that extraordinary season of Sir Gordon's until I came along. It's the unique nature of that achievement that makes it stand out as my proudest achievement.

Sir Gordon Richards was a remarkable man and a remarkable jockey. Like me he hadn't grown up in a racing town (a village near Telford in Shropshire) and got into horses because his father kept ponies, and like me he was champion jockey in his first full season. Despite our broadly similar beginnings, however, I don't think I deserve to be mentioned in the same breath. Sir Gordon was twenty-six times leading flat jockey – thankfully they weren't all consecutive so at least I've got that on him – despite having had to fight and overcome tuberculosis early in his career. He kept riding professionally until he was fifty and even then only called it a day because of a pelvic injury. In all he rode 4,870 winners in the days before motorways, agents, widespread telephones and all the other advantages I had in modern racing. I never met Sir Gordon, unfortunately, as he died in 1986 but John Francome knew him in his later years in Kintbury and said he was both great craic and a very straight talker.

I went on to ride 289 winners that year – a tally that would turn out to be the best of my career – but it's breaking that record that remains the most memorable aspect of the 2001–02 season and, in my opinion, the finest achievement of them all.

The record had flashed across my mind a couple of times, when I'd ridden 253 winners in 1998 beating Peter Scudamore's National Hunt record of 221 in the process, and then 245 two years later, but I wouldn't say I was setting out to break it at the start of every season because I just wanted to go out and ride as many winners as I could and secure the jockeys' championship. I'd got off to a flyer that year, the first season of summer National

Hunt racing, riding 36 winners by the end of May and topping 50 at the start of July. At Plumpton on 17 September I chalked up my fastest century on Present Bleu for Martin Pipe in a claiming hurdle and the speculation began to build as to how far I could go. I was delighted with the fastest hundredth: summer racing had shifted the calendar round a bit, but this was still two weeks faster than any hundred I'd ridden before.

As someone who prefers to set short-term goals I was trying not to think too much about the record at that stage, even though the Tote apparently had me odds on to beat Sir Gordon's 269 as early as that hundredth winner. I was concentrating on reaching the more modest target of 200 for the third time and then see how things looked from there.

By the end of 2001 I'd reached 195 winners. I had a bit of a scare when the weather closed in and racing everywhere was off for the first week in January, but when we resumed doubles at Fontwell and Leicester on 7 and 8 January carried me up to 199. I had some good rides lined up at Newbury a couple of days later where I thought I might bring up the 200 but instead all I had to show for it at the end was a deep, two-inch-long gash on the back of my head after getting a kick from a following horse after falling on Baclama in a handicap chase. My 200th finally came the next day at Huntingdon on Native Man.

This was the fastest 200 I'd ridden in my career and I'd made it a full 38 days quicker than my previous fastest. It was then I allowed my thoughts to turn towards the record. I was back at Huntingdon on 2 March where I had three rides for Jonjo, all of which came in to take me sailing past my previous best of 253. At the end of the month I'd reached 267, two short of equalling the record, and headed off to Chepstow on 1 April with what

I thought was a decent chance of at least pulling level there: I had five good rides lined up that day and all of them started as favourites. My season had featured a number of doubles and trebles so far and Chepstow looked good on paper at least.

As it turned out I only won once that day, on Carandrew in the first race, which meant the media scrum that had begun to follow me around in pursuit of the record had to decamp to Warwick where I had five rides the following day. The course was a sell-out and there was a sense of great expectation in the air, but to be honest it wasn't a feeling I particularly shared when I arrived at the course that morning. I hadn't been in top form over the previous month (including the disastrous Cheltenham that saw the death of Valiramix) and my rides at Chepstow the previous day had seemed much more promising. Still, all I could do was keep doing what I'd always done: riding to the best of my ability. I knew the winners would come, it was just a question of when. Over-thinking wasn't going to help anyone.

The day got off to a good start when I won on a horse called Shampooed in the first race of the day, hitting the front with three left to jump and coming home by two lengths. That was number 268, one short of equalling the record. The expectation ratcheted up a level but the next race saw disappointment when I trailed in fourth on Sadler's Secret in a handicap hurdle. Next up was Shepherds Rest in the Barford Handicap Chase over three miles, a horse trained by my next door neighbour Charlie Morlock that gave me a terrific ride as we led from the second last and pulled away to win six lengths clear of Richard Johnson on Alpha Gold. Win number 269: I was level with Sir Gordon and on the brink of something historic. The crowd was in great form and gave me a terrific reception when I came back in on Shepherds Rest but the job still wasn't done. I'd equalled the record all right, but I wasn't going to be satisfied until I'd beaten it. Win number 269 was no more or less significant than 268, 143 or 7, it was win number 270 that mattered. I was a little concerned that drawing level only served to put me in a kind of purgatory in which the longer I stayed the more frustrated I'd get. I knew the 270 would come but I wanted it to come quickly, to stop the worry that I might fall and get an injury that would put me out for the season, or cop a suspension, or, I don't know, a freak blizzard to sweep down from the Arctic and knock out racing for a couple of weeks. The sooner I rode the next winner the better.

The sense of anticipation around the course really was palpable as the clock ticked round towards ten past four and the Leek Wooton Novices' Handicap Hurdle. The BBC's racing correspondent Cornelius Lysaght said that after I'd won on Shepherds Rest he had a call from somebody who was mending his car. 'I can't talk about that now,' he gasped, 'I'm watching history.'

I tried to let the hullabaloo wash over me as much as I could and concentrate on the race. The lads in the weighing room wouldn't let me off lightly though: my friend Mick Fitzgerald had the peg next to me and wouldn't let up with the banter, trying to organise a whip-round among the jockeys to get me a bottle of champagne ready for the record. Christ, I thought, I need to win another race soon or that kind of thing would soon become unbearable.

The novices' handicap hurdle was over two miles and my ride was a horse called Valfonic, trained by Martin Pipe and owned by Marcus Reiger, a friend of the jockey Seamus Durack who happened to be lodging with me at the time. Marcus lived in

London and had called me the night before Warwick to ask if his horse had a chance. If it did, he said, he'd drive up to the races but if not then he'd just watch it on the television. I told him not to bother. I genuinely didn't reckon Valfonic had much of a chance: I'd had a disappointing ride on him at Plumpton in January and his two runs since hadn't exactly set the world on fire. No, if I was going to break Sir Gordon Richards' record the chances were it wouldn't be on Valfonic.

When the race got underway I felt I was correct in advising Marcus to stay down south. Valfonic was right at the back of the field and not giving me any indication he was in the mood or form to produce a memorable ride. I'd had instructions from Martin to hold him back in midfield during the early stages but I was having trouble even doing that, especially after he made a bit of a mistake at the second hurdle. But then he really seemed to get into his stride down the back straight and I began to suspect he might just be capable of pulling it off. He travelled beautifully and despite another slight mistake two from home, jumped the last in a line of four horses at the front and pulled away in Warwick's short home straight to win by a length and a quarter.

Oh, and break the record.

The crowd nearly lifted the roof off and gave me a terrific reception when we came in and the applause and backslaps continued all the way to the winner's enclosure and then to the weighing room. There were beaming faces everywhere and people swarmed around me and the horse. Even as I weighed in there was the constant click and whirr of the cameras while I sat on the scales.

Finally I reached the changing room, a smile on my face that mixed a genuine sense of accomplishment and relief that the monkey was off my back. I walked into the room as the man who'd just broken the record of arguably the greatest jockey of them all that had stood for over half a century. When I reached my peg I found my old friend Carl Llewellyn sitting there on the bench, apparently leafing nonchalantly through the racecard. He looked up at me.

'How'd you get on, champ?' he said, with a completely straight face.

That evening a little gang of us went back to The Pheasant in Lambourn for a bit of a celebration: Mick Fitz, John Francome and a few of the lads came for a few drinks but nothing too heavy. I don't drink but I like a hooley as much as the next man, however this wasn't a full-on party at such short notice. Even so I wonder now whether I truly appreciated the enormity of what I'd achieved at the time. It might only be now that I can take in how amazing it really was. That record had stood for more than fifty years, just imagine the number of great jockeys on the Flat and over jumps who came and went in that time. Just to list them would take up an entire chapter, yet none of them had come even close to Sir Gordon's record until I came along and that's something of which to be immensely proud. More than a decade later I can at last look back and truly appreciate what happened that day at Warwick, not least because in my last season as a jockey I moved heaven and earth in an effort to beat it and ended up nowhere near. My record season would remain 289 winners for the rest of my career and will I think remain the record number of wins by a jockey for a good few years to come yet. But it was getting past Sir Gordon Richards' record that will always be my proudest legacy. Nobody else did it. Nobody else got near.

I couldn't have done it without Dave Roberts, of course, the only person who was a constant presence throughout every race of my entire riding career. Dave was actually more obsessed with numbers than I was, an obsession that contributed massively to a career whose measure of success depended almost entirely on numbers. He's a complete anorak and insomniac who got as much satisfaction out of winning as I did. Dave made me very much the winner I was because he continually performed for me, getting me on the right horses and keeping me sane, pretty much doing everything but actually ride the horse itself. He was at Plumpton when I won my 3,000th race and at Towcester for my 4,000th, and rightly so because neither of those occasions would have felt complete if he hadn't been present. My 4,000th on Mountain Tunes in 2013 was tough on Dave because his dad had passed away the day before. I said to him he shouldn't come but he was determined, saying his dad would have wanted him there.

Dave helped to make me a believer, playing a massive part in my breaking Sir Gordon Richards' record and I'm delighted that we became good friends too. Most of all though, that record-breaking year would never have been remotely possible without Martin Pipe. I think I'm right in saying that of my 289 winners that season an astonishing 189 were trained by Martin. I can't imagine any jockey has ever ridden more winners in a season for one trainer than that. Riding for Martin definitely made the record possible and I will always be indebted to him. Indeed, it was Martin who was most responsible for making me aware of the sheer importance of numbers to success in racing. He's always been very wrapped up in his numbers and instilled in me at an early age the importance of being stronger numerically than everyone else. It was probably always there deep down but it took Martin to draw it out of me, and I certainly wouldn't have broken most of the records I did without Martin Pipe behind me.

When anyone looks back at that season they see the number 289. It was the number that won me the jockeys' championship that year and the number that got me past Sir Gordon Richards' record. What Martin helped me realise was that whatever the circumstances each win counts exactly the same, whether it be by fifteen lengths in the sunshine at Cheltenham or a short head in the pissing rain at Ayr. They all count and it's the number at the end that counts most. Ultimately the ride and the occasion don't matter, it's getting past the winning post that's the only important thing. I did that 289 times that season and that's what people will remember. The number.

Here's an extreme example of how every win counts as much as any other from that record-breaking season. On a cold January day at Southwell I was riding Family Business in a novice chase over three miles. He was the favourite in a seven-horse field but I fell off him at the tenth fence. I kept watching as I walked back along the infield and, being a novice chase, these were all inexperienced horses who looked to me as though they were jumping pretty moderately to say the least. I got a lift in a Land Rover to go back to the weighing room and when I got out of the car they'd done a full circuit and three more horses had fallen. This left just three runners going into the final circuit and an idea began to form. The Pipes' travelling head lad had a hold of Family Business and I said to him, 'Just keep him there for a minute because these yokes are jumping terrible.' Sure enough another horse fell, and then there were two. At this point I decided to get back on the horse because now there was prize money at the very least for just getting Family Business round the course. I cantered back to where I'd come off, jumped the fence I'd fallen at because I wanted to make sure I was starting in the right place and set off round the track. Wouldn't you know it, the last two horses both fell at the second last down the back straight and we came round the final circuit completely alone and passed the winning post in about the slowest finish I've ever ridden. It was a strange race, and one that couldn't happen again because you're not allowed to remount any more, but it just shows how a win is a win, because that ride counted exactly the same towards the season's total as a Gold Cup-winning ride would have. It was instinctive, I could see they were all jumping poorly, but it was also a bit of luck that counted as a win at the end of the day. All part of the attitude that Martin Pipe helped me to cement.

I was never his stable jockey in the end, at least not officially, but I had a very good relationship with Martin and always found him very easy to work with and for. Even though I'd turned the job down and still been lucky enough to become champion jockey without him, it was a lot easier riding his horses than chasing them around.

When I started riding for Martin I already knew a lot about him but didn't really know what to expect. I knew he'd had more winners than anyone else and had been champion trainer on numerous occasions (by the time of his retirement in 2006 he'd been champion fifteen times). I knew he was going to be a little bit different from what I'd become used to but had always admired him. How could you not? But it was only through working for him that my admiration grew into genuine affection and I could appreciate at first hand how good he was. People like Martin think differently from the rest. They're always one step ahead and have an uncanny knack for anticipating what's going to happen before it actually does. He's one of the most meticulous people I've ever met, covering every minute detail of every aspect of racing to ensure that nothing took him by surprise. Essentially he was eliminating as much risk and guesswork from his racing operations as possible; there was no guessing with Martin Pipe and his stable was always a very well-oiled and well-run machine.

So, back in 1996, despite having won the jockeys' championship after turning him down I knew that if I was to win further titles I'd have to be on Martin's side. To limit the risk of somebody else getting their hands on the trophy it would clearly be easier to work for him rather than against him, and boy, I'm so glad I did. Martin really drew out of me an awareness of just how important it was to win. If anyone taught me anything about winning it was Martin Pipe: he was obsessed with it and, crucially, very good at it. So strongly did he instil that winning determination in me that I became almost a robot jockey. It got to a point where I just became a machine geared to winning horse races working purely to a yardstick of an ever-increasing total of winners.

Our relationship wasn't purely about winning and numbers however, at least not away from the track and the yard. Martin, his wife Carol and the rest of the Pipes were always very friendly and welcoming to me and still are. We had a couple of rows, instigated by me – I had one very bad row with him over a horse called Courbaril at Cheltenham one year. I completely lost the plot with him and I still wince about it to this day. I must have come across to him like a spoiled, jumped-up wee prick . . . Overall though it was one of the very best relationships of my racing life.

Leaving Martin in 2004 was one of the hardest decisions I've ever made and the drive to the house that evening to tell him that after eight fantastic years I was going to work for J.P. McManus felt like one of the longest journeys ever. Riding for JP was a new challenge, something I felt I needed at that stage of my career, while also as I've said before anyone riding for Martin Pipe was almost a cert to be champion jockey. This meant I always had nagging away at the back of my mind the suspicion that people believed I was only champion jockey because I was riding for Martin rather than enjoying success on my own merits. I certainly didn't feel I was any better than anyone else – as far as I'm concerned he could have picked any one of about ten jockeys and turned them into champion jockeys – but for my own peace of mind I knew that I had to go on and ride for other people and show that my success had at least something to do with me rather than the fact I rode for Martin. It was a risk, but as Sheikh Mohammed once said, the only risk in life is to take no risks. Things didn't turn out too badly all told, but I'll always feel absolutely blessed for those eight years I spent riding for Martin. I still rode a fair bit for him and his son David after I went to work for JP and we remain really good friends. Sometimes when such working relationships come to an end people drift apart but we've always been close and will remain so for the rest of our days. Martin really brought out the best in me and made me a lot of what I am. I wouldn't have beaten Sir Gordon Richards' record without him, and probably the best compliment I can pay him is to say that for most of my riding career I wanted to be like Martin Pipe.

I didn't know an awful lot about Sir Gordon Richards, I must admit. I'd read a bit about him as I've always enjoyed reading about jockeys through the years. One jockey whose story I found fascinating was Sir Gordon's predecessor, Fred Archer, who'd held the record for winners in a season before Sir Gordon with 246 in 1885. Fred was champion jockey thirteen times in a row between 1874 and 1886 and rode 2,748 career winners. He won twenty-one classics including the Epsom Derby five times, a phenomenal record in any era, let alone the nineteenth century. I know Ryan Moore broke Pat Eddery's and Lester Piggott's record for Royal Ascot winners but Fred Archer rode twelve winners at the royal meeting in his time including five in one day, achievements even more extraordinary when you consider he was dead by his own hand before he was thirty.

Fred Archer was tall for a flat jockey, five foot ten, the same height as me, so had a constant battle to keep his weight down. Apparently he was necking all sorts of potions that were supposed to help but God knows what was in them. By all accounts he was a pretty morose character at the best of times, but he fell into a deep depression when his wife died in childbirth and the poor guy ended up shooting himself at the age of 29, two years and a day after the death of his wife. Many people say Fred Archer was the best jockey of all time. Statisticians will tell you it's Sir Gordon Richards, but he only won the Derby once, on Pinza in 1953, the year he became the only jockey ever to be knighted. Fred Archer won five and Lester Piggott's well up there in the pantheon of greats after winning nine Epsom Derbies and with 119 Royal Ascot winners. Will I see a jockey win nine Derbies in my lifetime? I don't know that I will.

In more recent times there have been the likes of Pat Eddery and Steve Cauthen who contested one of the great duels for the jockey's championship on the Flat. Steve was brought over from America to ride in Britain after winning the Triple Crown in 1978 at sixteen (nobody completed the Triple Crown again until 2015) and he arrived having been on the cover of *Sports Illustrated* which is unheard of for a jockey. Pat Eddery is the second most winning jockey of all time with eleven jockeys' championships and 4,633 career wins on the Flat, which is an amazing feat and second only to Sir Gordon Richards. I'm proud that Sir Gordon, Pat and Lester are the only three jockeys to have ridden more career winners than me, and I console myself with the knowledge they were flat jockeys who rode into their fifties, Lester until he was 57.

Many great sportspeople from the past are forgotten, or at least not recognised for who they are and not given the recognition they deserve until the posthumous eulogies and obituaries. It might be something to do with the image people retain of them in their prime, permanently frozen in time in people's consciousnesses as the great sportsperson bursting with youth and vigour. They might not recognise him as the fella with the grey hair and lined face who in his younger days produced some of sport's most breathtaking feats. Additionally others may have come along in the meantime and usurped them in the pantheon of memory, more recent triumphs being fresher in the mind.

That isn't an issue with Lester Piggott.

Recently I was with him at Epsom on Derby Day and everyone was still absolutely in awe of him. You'd hear the whisper go round, 'It's Lester', just the first name. Whoever you are, whatever your field, it's a rare and valuable tribute for people still to know you just by your first name. It took me back to when I was a riding-mad kid in Moneyglass – 'Lester' was the only possible nickname they could have given me back then. That awe, the presence that has stayed with Lester and the respect he still commands is what convinces me there'll only ever be one Lester Piggott. I was in awe of him myself the first time I met him, but now I'm much more comfortable around him and enjoy his company very much. The strange thing is that I find him really easy to understand when he speaks, which a lot of people will find hard to believe. Between you and me, I think he just makes more effort when he has an interest in who he's talking to.

In more recent times there have been great jockeys like Kieren Fallon, six times champion flat jockey in seven years either side of the millennium, and there was also Johnny Murtagh with a great record in the English and Irish classics who is a promising trainer now. Mick Kinane is the most complete rider I've ever seen and every young jockey could do a lot worse than model themselves on Mick. He had a hugely successful career that spanned thirty-four years and featured three Epsom Derby winners among a litany of wins in the classics.

Ryan Moore is the closest I've ever seen to Mick Kinane and is destined to be one of the all-time greats. Ryan is the best jockey in the world, and not many people have a claim on that description. He's the ultimate modern flat jockey, flying around the world riding races and racking up winners, and has a great attitude. By the time Ryan's finished he will be better than Mick Kinane, and I don't think there's much higher praise than that.

Then there's Frankie, of course. Frankie's just . . . Frankie. He's like Lionel Messi, he's different, with a different style to him from anyone else that stems from an unbelievably good sense of balance. Frankie's the biggest name in racing and he's great for the game. He's a brilliant jockey and a great bloke too. He's had a few ups and downs in his time, but I think to ride seven winners at Ascot is an amazing feat and one that speaks for itself.

One of my best mates Richard Hughes has been champion jockey three times, five foot nine and a half and does eight stone seven – he's the modern equivalent of Lester Piggott and Fred Archer: to be champion jockey at that height and weight is a miracle. By the time you read this Richard, who came over from Ireland in 1994, the same year as me, will have retired in order to concentrate on training, going out at Goodwood where he's had some amazing successes over the years. His stylish riding will be missed at courses around the country.

As far as jump jockeys are concerned I can just about re-member Jonjo riding but I'm just too young to remember John Francome. Everyone says Francome was the greatest jockey and he probably was, winning seven jockeys' championships in ten years spanning 1976 to 1985. He's still some rider: recently I saw him taking part in the show jumping at Olympia on the televi-sion and could see that even in his sixties he's more gifted on a horse than anyone else, and certainly more gifted than me.

Peter Scudamore and Richard Dunwoody are two names that dominated racing for many years. Richard in particular I learned many good things from, the toughest bloke I ever met and during my time riding the best jockey around. Richard and Peter brought the standard of riding up to a new level, upping the game with every season they rode and making many of us better too by dragging us up with them. There were also many jockeys who deserve plenty of credit in my time who never got to be champion jockey. JP's racing manager Frank Berry was champion jockey ten times in Ireland, as was Charlie Swan.

Then there's obviously Ruby Walsh, Barry Geraghty and Paul Carberry, who've all been champion jockey in Ireland during the past fifteen years. I also have to mention brilliant riders like Adrian Maguire, Norman Williamson, Jamie Osborne and Graham Bradley, while my admiration for Richard Johnson is well known.

In time I'm sure there'll be jockeys, some of them even mentioned above, who will do some amazing things. I know many of my records will probably be broken eventually and I don't like the idea of that at all, but I don't know if anyone will ever win nine Epsom Derbies again. Frankie's forty-four and he's just won his second, while Ryan Moore has won two by the age of thirty-one so he might pull it off, but I'd be very surprised if he or indeed anyone did. Lester's record seems pretty safe to me and may well prove to be immortal.

Will someone ever ride 289 winners or more in a year? Who knows? They might. I was very lucky because I had such a numerical machine driving me in Martin Pipe and I can't imagine any one trainer dominating statistically as much as Martin did. Without that I think it will be difficult for jockeys in years to come to dominate the way I did. I think the 289 probably will be broken but I don't feel I'm sticking my neck out here by saying it won't be for a good while. I believed for a good ten years that nobody would ever break it, but when I started my final season like a rocket only to be thwarted by injury, I thought to myself that if I was able to get that close at forty – and if it hadn't been for getting injured I absolutely would have done it – it's got to be possible for a younger lad to pull it off one day.

I hope they won't. They'd have to stay well clear of injury for a start. Having an historic opportunity like 300 winners taken away by circumstances beyond your control is the biggest sickener going, and believe me I know just how that feels. If I'd stayed free of injury and suspension and just not ridden enough winners in that last season I might have accepted it wasn't possible, but the way it happened was as frustrating as it was disappointing. For any jockey to reach 300 winners leaves so little margin for error. The last season of my career proved that and it's a sobering thought that the same could have happened to me in 2002 and stopped me from breaking Sir Gordon Richards' record. Thankfully, on that occasion, it didn't. What I wouldn't have given for 2015 to have been equally injury-free.

Imagine going through a season where you ride your fastest 100 and 200 and you get to 250 and you think, I haven't been injured, haven't had many suspensions, the horses are flying and the weather hasn't been too bad. If you get to Christmas and you're on target, it's then you start worrying about getting injured, or the weather turning rotten causing racing to be called off and wiping away the opportunity. But in 2002 I stayed free of injury and other misfortune and it's only now, years later, that I can truly appreciate what I did. Breaking that record is the one thing I'm happy to give myself a pat on the back for because, believe me, it's going to take some beating.

SEVEN

Abutilon, Fontwell
9 November 2007

The 4.10 at Fontwell on 9 November 2007 was a handicap chase over two miles and one-and-a-half furlongs. My ride was Abutilon, a four-year-old horse of JP's trained by Brendan Powell who gave away quite a bit of weight to all but one of the other runners but had been improving enough in his previous rides to suggest this wouldn't be too much of an issue. I held him back for much of the race but he hit the front with three to jump and . . :

Actually, to be honest I don't remember anything specific about that race at all. I've just had to look it up. There is a very good reason for this apparently run-of-the-mill race being awarded important status in the story of my racing life, however. It was a win, of course, and I lived for those. Abutilon gave me another number on the way to my thirteenth jockeys' championship (I didn't know it at the time but I'd record my career lowest season total that year, 140, thanks to breaking two vertebrae in my spine two months later so it was an even more important win than it would have been in other years as it turned out), but there was something extra-special about that day and that race. Something nobody at Fontwell that day would have noticed and only a handful of people in the weighing room would have known about.

Abutilon was the first winner I rode as a father. It also happened to be the first day I'd woken up as a father after the birth of our daughter Eve the previous day. The world suddenly looked a very different place indeed and I was on top of the world when I arrived at the Sussex course that November day. I was also a little daunted: now I wasn't just responsible for myself and Chanelle any more, there was this tiny, beautiful, innocent, defenceless bundle of humanity to consider now, too. She'd been a long time coming, our miracle girl, and the story of how she arrived on this earth is one littered with obstacles, some self-imposed, some not, and which dated back more than a decade to the Punchestown Festival of 1996.

Even before considering the long-term repercussions it had for both my professional and personal lives, 25 April 1996 was a pretty good day for me. I rode three winners which, added to another win a day earlier, were enough to make me the leading jockey of the three-day festival. My first win of the day was on Mayasta in the two-mile handicap hurdle, a horse trained by Frank Berry. I rode Mayasta wearing a set of silks I'd never worn before, green with three golden bands around the middle, colours that belonged to an owner called J.P. McManus, for whom I was riding for the first time. Not only that, Mayasta would one day be the dam of a horse I would meet a few years down the line. A horse called Synchronised.

If the finger of fate had been flexing at the start of the day's racing, that was nothing compared to where it pointed at the end. I'd gone on to win on Shaunies Lady and Have To Think that afternoon, ensuring I would pick up the award for leading rider – not bad considering this was my first ever Punchestown Festival.

I collected the trophy in the parade ring and was about to head back to change when Anna Moore, the daughter of Arthur Moore, for whom I'd won on Have To Think, touched me on the arm and enquired whether she might ask a small favour. There was a group of students at the races that day. She knew a few of them and was trying to ensure that they had as memorable a day as possible and asked if I might join a couple of the other jockeys in just popping in to say hello and talk about life as a jockey for a few minutes. Apparently Richard Dunwoody was supposed to have done it but he'd had to leave early. Having the leading jockey of the festival there would make a big difference, she told me. Why not? I thought. It was only back to the hotel otherwise, and I was in no particular hurry.

'Sure,' I said. 'When you need me just come down to the weighing room and get me.'

A short while later Anna came down to fetch me in the company of her friend who'd organised the trip. When she introduced us I said hello to a student from Galway called Chanelle Burke.

Considering what a humdinger of a day fate was having, it's strange to think that I'd nearly not gone to Punchestown at all that year. The jockeys' championship still had another month to run and although I'd built up a bit of a lead I wasn't quite certain it was in the bag. I'd had my doubts about the advisability of skipping a couple of days' racing in Britain to go to Punchestown, keen as I was to ride there, but in the end I'd looked at the championship, compared it to the calendar and decided that I could probably risk it. In hindsight, I'm pretty glad that I did.

Chanelle was studying finance and marketing in Dublin, where she'd started a racing society at the college, but is originally from Loughrea in County Galway. She has a solid background in racing: her grandfather had been a jockey and her parents had always kept horses. Chanelle's father is a successful vet with links to the racing world, partly through his friend the trainer Dermot Weld, and in the mid-eighties he established Chanelle Pharmaceuticals, for whom Chanelle would work after her studies and continues as Medical Business Director to this day. She had been around racecourses since she was a little girl (and indeed had ridden a winner at the Galway Festival on one of her father's horses in her younger days, funnily enough on a horse called Bamapour on whom I'd go on to win eleven races for Martin Pipe) so was probably the last person in that room full of students who would have been impressed by meeting a jockey. Which was bad news for me as I thought she was amazing and being a jockey was pretty much all I had going for me.

I was instantly attracted to her the moment I set eyes on her, but, with me being me, I didn't exactly make the best opening impressions. Not long after we'd been introduced someone asked me for a photograph and without thinking I just handed the leading-rider trophy to Chanelle, saying, 'Hold this a minute.' I learned later that she'd immediately surmised I was a jumped-up little shit and nearly handed it straight back to me. It's safe to say that I'd given myself a fair bit of work to do if I was ever going to win her over. Well played, McCoy.

The more I saw of Chanelle that day the more amazing I

thought she was and the more I wanted to get to know her. That night we ended up going out as a group to a nightclub in Naas where I spent the entire night trying to chat her up and Chanelle spent the entire night trying to shake me off. At the end I followed her out of the club only for her to basically demand I walk on the other side of the road for fear of someone she knew seeing her with me. My clumsy attempts at wooing may have been falling on stony ground but the more time I spent with her the more I was determined I'd win her over. Chanelle, on the other hand, became increasingly determined that I wouldn't. My odds were lengthening.

Then I went to the Irish Derby in June at The Curragh – purely because Chanelle had said she'd be there, that's how smitten I was – and ended up at a twenty-first birthday party in Wexford where I finally managed to wheedle her phone number out of her. Chanelle made it very clear as she wrote it down that she saw us as nothing more than friends and I shouldn't expect anything more. Being as stubborn as I was smitten I took that as a positive sign that her defences were weakening. When she agreed to come over to England for the Partridge Ball at Toby Balding's later that summer – as a friend, she reiterated – I was absolutely cock-a-hoop. It was probably more to do with her love of racing than any burning desire to see me, but thank goodness for that love of racing because at the time I don't think I was doing it for her. I had Toby's nephew Andrew primed to sing my praises and whatever he said must have worked, because at the end of the night I even got a charity kiss (from Chanelle, that is, not Andrew) and I could sense my odds shortening.

I'd known straightaway that Chanelle was the one. I'd been out with a few girls but nothing serious, and pretty much from that day at the Punchestown Festival I knew I'd met the woman with whom I wanted to spend the rest of my life. Like everything in life I always make sure I get what I want, so whether Chanelle liked it or not it was inevitable we'd be together. Fair play to her, she tried her best to get out of it but it wasn't to be.

It certainly wasn't plain sailing once we got together, however, and there would be a fair few break-ups and hiccups along the way that were, it must be said, mainly my fault. The fact Chanelle was in Ireland and I was in England made things tricky enough, but add in my hectic racing schedule and single-minded pursuit of the jockeys' championship and Chanelle had to make a good few sacrifices on my behalf, something she'd certainly have to get used to over the years. But aside from that there were occasions where I'm ashamed to say that I really didn't cover myself in glory. Considering how much persuasion it had taken to convince her to go out with me in the first place, some of the things I did make me wince when I look back. I wasn't an ideal boyfriend by any means, and I was given the heave-ho more than once in those early days together. We had a huge falling out about me catching her smoking once, at a birthday party at Mick Fitzgerald's house in the summer of 2003. I don't like smoking at the best of times and Chanelle, who was only ever a social smoker, had told me she wasn't smoking at all any more because she knew I didn't like it. So when I found her out the back of the house having a smoke with a friend of ours called Johnny Kavanagh, who's now Jonjo's head lad, I went off like an air-raid siren. I made a terrible scene, insisted we left and drove home. I packed her bags for her and first thing in the morning dropped her at Didcot Parkway railway station with all her luggage. Even sleeping on it hadn't mellowed my position. Chanelle was in tears on the platform, standing there with all her stuff as the train pulled in and do you know what I said to her? Something along the lines of, 'OK, look, I might have overreacted a bit here,' maybe?

Nope. What I said was this.

'OK, I forgive you. Just this once. Get back in the car.'

I look back at that incident now and I'm practically gnawing on my own knuckle. What on earth was I doing? No one would have blamed Chanelle if she'd picked up her bags, got on the train and disappeared from my life for ever. This amazing woman, the love of my life, and I do that to her just over a crafty cigarette at a party? I must have had some level of demons back then, that's the best I can say for myself. After a strained three or four weeks Chanelle told me I wasn't making her happy because I was clearly unhappy and broke up with me. It took mountains of contrition and even a face-to-face sit down with her father to win her back on that occasion. I learned a bit of a lesson from that, having had a bitter taste of what I could have lost, but my single-minded stubbornness still caused occasional ructions. Strange as it may sound I think it made our relationship and our subsequent marriage stronger. For one thing I'd never do anything remotely like that now – admittedly that was a particularly extreme example, but on several occasions I was a very, very lucky boy indeed that Chanelle didn't kick me miles into touch and I gradually learned to appreciate what should have been blindingly obvious: how lucky I was to have her.

Even without me acting the maggot the situation didn't make for a normal relationship. In fairness to Chanelle she knew the demands of my job and she never tried to change me, she just went with it, which is probably a major factor in why we get on so well. She knew the racing game, its rhythms, the sacrifices and commitments you have to make to succeed, and that helped a lot, but she still cut me a hell of a lot of slack when I possibly didn't entirely deserve it.

It's gone full circle now that I've retired, of course. I'm just a yes man in the house with no control over anything, something I have to accept as it's definitely payback time. Chanelle's very busy with the kids, the pharmaceutical company and the shop she co-owns in Hungerford and sometimes I feel I'm just getting under her feet. One day I discovered a book in our downstairs bathroom called 101 *Things to Do With Your Retired Man*. I haven't dared open it yet. Chanelle's certainly earned this turnaround in circumstances, but whatever you do don't tell her I said that.

The years passed and there were a few speculative chats about getting engaged and married, but, as ever, I was worried about what that might do to my career. If I got married, I thought, it might give the impression that I was losing focus and wanting to settle down; that riding wasn't my number one priority any more. These thoughts meant that whenever the subject of marriage came up I'd think, hmm, how can I put this off a little longer? Not because I didn't want to marry her, far from it, but because of this thing I had about losing focus on my career.

For Christmas 2003 I bought Chanelle a very expensive watch. I'd been feeling a bit of pressure to pop the question from a few – female – quarters but I wanted to buy a little more time, so when I handed Chanelle a presentation box for Christmas she opened it to find not a ring but a Cartier watch. She loved it, she thought it was amazing, but she would probably have preferred something to put on her finger rather than her wrist. We went to visit my parents just after Christmas and Chanelle showed off the watch to my mum, who looked at it, looked at her and said,

(*left*) My first professional ride, on Nordic Touch in Dublin in 1990. Phoenix Park, 1 September 1990.

(*above*) I rode my first win on Legal Steps. I'd tasted the winning feeling and I loved it. I wanted more. Thurles, Co Tipperary, 26 March 1992.

My first win over hurdles was on Riszard. Gowran Park, 20 April 1994.

Jim Bolger was unquestionably one of the main reasons I was as successful as I was.

Toby Balding helped me out and showed me the ropes in an almost paternal fashion, showing great kindness to a skinny kid from a small village in Ireland fresh off the boat.

While I was never officially Martin Pipe's stable jockey I was absorbed into the post unofficially because he kept putting me on great horses that kept winning.

Carl Llewellyn (above left), Mick Fitzgerald (above right) and Ruby Walsh (bottom) were three of my closest friends in racing.

Winning the 1997 Gold Cup. Mr Mulligan was a special horse. Cheltenham, 13 March 1997.

Whatever happened in the rest of my career nobody could take away the fact that I'd won the Champion Hurdle and the Gold Cup at the same festival. Cheltenham, 13 March 1997.

The Cheltenham Festival provided some of the other highlights of my career. Winning the 2000 Queen Mother Champion Chase on Edredon Bleu (*above*) and the 2009 Festival Trophy on Wichita Lineman (*below*).

Cheltenham also provided me with some of my lowest moments in racing: the deaths of Gloria Victis (*left*) and Valiramix (*below*) both hit me very hard. Every time a racehorse dies in such circumstances it's a terrible tragedy for everyone involved.

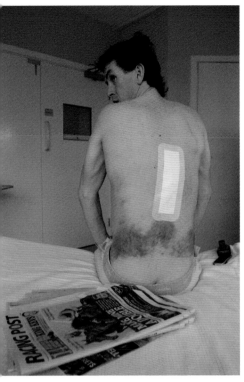

I've suffered some pretty serious injuries during my career, none more so than when I broke my back riding Arnold Layne in 2008.

No matter how bad the injury, I'd do anything to get back racing again as quickly in possible, including the cryotherapy treatment I undertook after breaking my back.

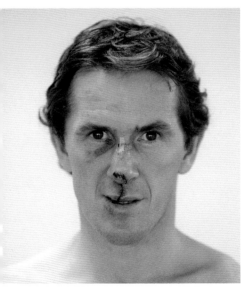

The other injury that got me a wee bit worried was when I was kicked in the face by Mr Watson at Wetherby on 2 November 2012, resulting in 24 stitches. It could have been a lot worse.

Again, it didn't take me long before I was back in the saddle. Kempton Park, 5 November 2012.

I rode my 270th winner of the 2001–02 season on Valfonic at Warwick on 2 April 2002, thereby beating Sir Gordon Richards' record of 269 winners in a season set in 1947. It's the unique nature of that achievement that makes it stand out as my proudest.

'Chanelle, love, it's beautiful, but look at the symbolism. He's literally buying time. I think you should give it back to him.'

My own mother was telling Chanelle to dump me and sure enough she did not long after that, after I'd flatly refused to attend the wedding of a friend of hers for no good reason other than stubbornness. While Chanelle went to the wedding alone to field the 'where's Anthony?' questions, I played golf with the lads. Yes, believe me, I know.

After a few weeks reflecting on how I'd been a little bit stupid to say the least, and not for the first time, I went over to Ireland in an attempt to win her back. Chanelle was having none of it, so I drove to Dublin and bought a diamond at auction. I managed to persuade her that I'd bought it for her as a sign of proper commitment and finally she relented. However she soon made it clear that the diamond had stayed in the safe a little longer than she might have liked, so I made arrangements to have it set into a ring. But how to propose? I consulted Rachel, one of Chanelle's best friends.

'Rachel,' I said, 'there's no two ways about it, I'm going to have to ask Chanelle to marry me. You know Chanelle better than most, how should I go about it?'

The answer came back immediately.

'Venice,' she said, 'it's the most romantic place there is.'

That sounded a bit corny to me.

'Ha,' I chuckled, 'next you'll be telling me I've got to get down on one knee in a gondola and all that crap.'

Rachel looked at me levelly and the chuckle stuck in my throat.

'Oh,' I said, 'that's exactly what you are telling me, isn't it?'

She nodded.

So off I went to book the trip. With the diamond, the ring, flights and a really nice hotel called the Cipriani this engagement thing was turning into an expensive business.

On the second day we had a walk around St Mark's Square and saw a few of the sights, then I said, 'You know what? We're in Venice, let's go for a ride in a gondola.'

Chanelle had an inkling of what was afoot, I'm sure, but we'd been there for a day at this stage and there was no sign of any proposal. She must have been thinking, if he doesn't propose now there's not a hope in hell I'm having him back ever again. I did have a bit of devilment in me telling me not to propose until the plane home, but that would have ruined the trip for her and there was a strong chance we'd have ended up getting off the plane, me walking in one direction and Chanelle in the other. Sensibly, for once, I decided I'd best not risk it.

So we got on a gondola after Chanelle, being a proper west of Ireland girl, had baulked at the price and initially tried to talk me out of it. I got down on one knee, pulled the ring out and asked her to marry me. She said yes. Chanelle asked the gondolier to take a photo and said we'd just got engaged, and as he took the picture he said he pretty much sees the same thing several times a day. So at least I didn't feel like I was alone; I was like every other poor unfortunate so-and-so who'd ever got on a gondola in Venice with his missus and a ring box burning a hole in his pocket.

So ended the McCoy/Burke engagement saga. Chanelle couldn't get away now. Having taken this big step forward in our relationship, I confess that I thought I might be able to get another couple of years out of it if I could stall this marriage lark. It wasn't that I didn't want to marry Chanelle, quite the opposite, but I did genuinely worry that people might suspect I was losing focus when it came to racing. You hear talk of sports-people getting married or having kids and they start to lose their drive and ambition, their edge starts to go, and I was frightened of that happening to me.

Within a month of popping the question, though, the diary kept appearing and the conversation would be steered round to dates. This was the summer of 2005 and I was thinking we could possibly set a date in, you know, maybe 2010? But no, I was overruled and it was decided we would plight our troth the following summer. We had always been inclined towards having a small wedding somewhere abroad, keeping things intimate, just family and close friends. Planning weddings is very difficult, most notoriously in terms of the guest list because where do you draw the line before you're upsetting people? You can't invite this cousin and not that cousin, this friend and not that friend, before you know it the wedding's getting so big it's spanning two postcodes. We still probably did upset a few people in the way we did it, but it was what we wanted and that was the most important thing about the day. In the end we settled on Majorca, where my friend the footballer Steve McManaman had married his wife Victoria. Chanelle went over and looked at a few places with Victoria and we settled on the Residencia Hotel.

I never thought I'd say this about any wedding, especially my own, as I'm not a great one for weddings, but it was a great day, really good fun and very enjoyable from start to finish. For all my talk about buying time and putting it off as long as possible, I felt like a very lucky man indeed when I first saw Chanelle walking towards me on her father's arm that day. She was the most beautiful thing I'd ever seen and she'd been through a lot with me, putting up with things where others might not have stuck around for nearly as long.

There are many things I love about Chanelle. She has a good way about her; she's very easy-going yet at the same time very organised. She's also a very good cook, not that it made much difference to me when I was watching my weight riding, but I'm making up for that now. Most of all right from the start I fancied her more than any woman I'd ever seen, and that's a very hard thing to find. We have very few arguments – I think we got all those out of the way early on, to be fair – and it's rare these days to find us disagreeing over anything. Of course the reason for this is that I've moulded her, that she didn't necessarily come that way, and she shouldn't get all the credit for being perfect. At least, that's what I tell her.

Right from the start I loved everything about Chanelle. She's a beautiful, good, warm and thoughtful person – much more thoughtful than I am. Considering that I'd believed being in a relationship might be a hindrance to my career I actually found the opposite to be true: Chanelle did nothing but enhance my career with her love and support on both an emotional and practical level. She's definitely made me a better person, someone who's more sociable, approachable and less wrapped up in himself which I was pretty much all my life. She made me recognise that it wasn't all about me. At least, these days I pretend to recognise that.

It's also important that she isn't regarded merely as 'Mrs A.P. McCoy', because Chanelle is a very successful woman in her own right. With her father she runs the pharmaceutical company in Ireland that carries her name as well as having a share in the shop in Hungerford with a couple of friends. She works hard, as well as being a fantastic wife and mother. Now I'm retired it frees her schedule up a bit more and she doesn't have to keep quite so many plates spinning. Since I've hung up my silks I've been able to see first hand just how busy and successful she is. Chanelle has always been an ambitious girl but crucially she's a hard worker too, prepared to put in the hours to achieve what she wants to achieve. She could easily choose to just stay at home spending the few pounds I have left but instead she keeps hard at it and if you come to the house during the day you'll usually find her at the kitchen table tapping away at her laptop and frowning.

Being married to a jockey isn't the easiest life. There are the long days away from home, early starts and arriving back at the house at all hours. Then you're away for big chunks of time: Ruby was back and forth to Ireland when he was riding for Paul Nicholls and Barry Geraghty was doing it for Nicky Henderson and will be doing it for JP from now on. It's worse in that respect for the flat jockeys: Ryan Moore has three kids, spends summers here, rides for Coolmoore in Ballydoyle, in November and December he'll be in Japan, then February he's in Dubai, on top of day and evening meetings in England: it's very full-on and pretty relentless. The year-round season means that without a break in the racing calendar family holidays usually had to be snatched at short notice whenever we had the chance. As the only significant breaks from racing I ever took were enforced ones through injury it means that in most of our holiday snaps I've an arm in plaster or my neck in a brace or something. The dangerous nature of the sport also meant that Chanelle lived with the constant fear of receiving a phone call telling her I'd done myself serious mischief. In all, I don't think anyone was happier about my retirement than Chanelle.

She's very close to her family, she had a good upbringing and is a very good daughter and sister as well as mother and wife. She's very good at keeping her family and my family involved in everything and up to date with what's going on which is something I would be absolutely useless at.

She's also an amazing mother to Eve and Archie, neither of whom had the easiest time coming into the world, which meant that Chanelle didn't have the easiest time bringing them into the world either. We'd always wanted children right from the start of our relationship, but despite practising for a while nothing seemed to be happening and we started to grow a little concerned. In the summer of 2002 we went to Oxford to see a doctor specialising in fertility issues called Enda McVeigh in an effort to discover if there was an issue and if so, what it was. We told Enda we'd been together a while but there'd been no progress and he asked us about our diets and lifestyles. Then, hearing that I was a jockey, he asked about my daily routine.

'I start with a hot bath every day for an hour or so,' I said, 'and I spend a lot of time in the sauna too, trying to keep my weight down.'

He nodded in a way that suggested something had just become very clear to him.

'Right,' he said, 'I think we might have a lead on where the problem lies. From what you're telling me your daily routine is basically as good a contraceptive as you can get. The heat of the bathwater and the sauna is killing your sperm. Basically, you're boiling them to death.'

He did a few tests and when he saw the results confirmed his suspicions told us it was a million to one chance that Chanelle and I would ever conceive naturally. We discussed IVF and wondered whether that was the best way forward. Enda agreed while pointing out it wasn't a foolproof solution and there would still be the possibility nothing might happen even via IVF.

I felt crushed. Waves of guilt washed over me and I could barely look at Chanelle. I'd chased her all that time, not made things easy for her, given her a pretty unconventional life thanks to my job, and now this. I knew she really wanted kids, we'd talked about it all along. Yet because I'd been steaming my little swimming boyos into oblivion all these years I might have taken away from her the opportunity to have children. I've never felt guiltier about anything in my life.

Chanelle, of course, was amazing. As we left Enda's consulting room I was in a glassy-eyed daze but Chanelle was already talking about our options, about how if the worst came to the worst there were other routes. We could adopt, for example, and when we got home she was going to look into it. For the umpteenth time since we'd first got together I was reminded what an amazing woman she is and how incredibly lucky I am to have her.

After we married we decided to go ahead with the IVF, give it a try and if it didn't work we'd weigh up our options then. To our delight we were successful pretty much at the first attempt: we began treatment in January 2007 and Chanelle fell pregnant at the end of February.

If we thought we'd done the difficult bit and the rest would be plain sailing, we were wrong. There was one big scare when Chanelle had a serious bleed about six months into the pregnancy. It was a terrifying time and they were preparing her to go into theatre to deliver the baby prematurely when suddenly the bleeding stopped and the baby was fine.

Then, when we were still about six weeks shy of the due date, I was on my way to Cartmel one morning with three lads in the car when I had a call from Chanelle sounding desperately upset saying she was having another bleed and was on her way to hospital. The last time had been bad enough when I'd had the call while schooling horses in Lambourn, but at least that was local. Here I was somewhere north of Manchester and getting further away with each passing minute. I couldn't just turn the car around and head back either, because the three lads had to get to Cartmel.

I'm friendly with the footballer Francis Jeffers and I realised he lived not far from where we were, just north of Manchester. I knew Frannie had a friend called George who ran a taxi firm and, sure enough, one phone call later George was picking me up from the side of the motorway while the lads carried on to Cartmel. As you can imagine I was an absolute mess: it was four hours to where Chanelle was and I've never felt more helpless as I did sitting in the passenger seat as George bombed down the motorway to get me there as soon as he could. Thankfully by the time I arrived Chanelle was fine, they'd done the scans and the baby was OK, but as a precaution they kept Chanelle in hospital for the remaining six weeks of her pregnancy.

Thankfully there were no further problems and our little miracle Eve arrived on 8 November 2007. The next day I celebrated by going to Fontwell and riding Abutilon to my first win as a daddy in my second ride of the day. Had I won on my first ride it might just have been a little too twee in the circumstances. It was a horse of Nick Gifford's called Follow Your Heart.

There was never any question of what our daughter would be called: Chanelle had always loved the name Eve and it was agreed long ago that if we had a girl that's what we'd call her. As it turned out it suited her perfectly and she was amazing. To hold in your arms the child you feared you were never going to have, the child you'd been terrified might not make it, was an indescribable feeling. We were so lucky. So, so lucky.

It wasn't all straightforward though, even though we were over the most difficult part. When Eve was three years old we noticed one of her eyes seemed to be turning inwards. She was referred to a specialist at Moorfields Eye Hospital in London who told us she'd need an operation to correct the problem: my first experience of bringing a child to an anaesthetist. Obviously I was well-used to being put to sleep – I was almost on first-name terms with every anaesthetist in the country – but it's a quite different prospect when it's your child. Eve looked so vulnerable and helpless as she lay there and it was all I could do to tear myself away and leave her once her eyes had closed and it was time for her to go into theatre. After the operation she had to wear a patch on her eye for a few weeks while it healed, then different patches over time to help make the eye stronger. She wears glasses now but she's still absolutely perfect, a beautiful little girl who is everything you could possibly want your daughter to be. We are blessed to have her.

It wasn't too long before our thoughts began to turn to having another child. We tried again naturally but my swimmers were still firmly in the shallow end with water wings so we went back to Oxford to see Enda McVeigh. He told us we could increase our chances of success by putting two eggs in, but with the caveat that we could also end up with twins. Twins might be a bit much to cope with, we reckoned, so we decided to try one and keep everything crossed that we'd get lucky. It was very hard for Chanelle having to inject herself every day until at one stage she thought she was pregnant. We were convinced for a month or so, but when we went back for the next test the baby was gone. It was a hard one to take when you'd built up your hopes and had been planning ahead, and we left it a year before thinking about giving it another go. Were we pushing our luck, we wondered? We'd had our miracle baby Eve, should we content ourselves with what we had and be grateful for that? Maybe it was fate, maybe we were only destined to have one child, but after much soul-searching and many long conversations deep into the night we decided towards the end of 2012 that we'd give it one more shot. Back to Enda we went. This time we'd go with the two eggs: if fate wanted us to have twins, we'd have twins, if we were destined to have one child we'd have one, and if it didn't work we'd always have our amazing Eve. When you looked at it that way we couldn't lose.

Luckily on this occasion the IVF worked like a charm, just as we'd have wanted: one of the eggs survived the process and Chanelle was pregnant again. When Chanelle was expecting Eve we decided we didn't want to know whether we were having a boy or a girl. There are few surprises in life like that. Well, it's not *that* big a surprise, of course, it's going to be one or the other, a boy or a girl, but not knowing gave the wait an extra frisson (although the first time I saw Eve on the screen I remember thinking I couldn't see any bits so it must be a girl).

At this time we were building a new house outside Lambourn and Chanelle wanted to have the room all ready for the new baby. She told me she'd like to know the sex in advance and I said fine, of course, but I still wanted to hold out for the surprise when the baby arrived. Remembering what happened with Eve

I didn't even go in to the actual scan room in case I saw something that gave the game away, but Chanelle kept asking me, do you not want to know what it is? Are you sure you don't want to know? This went on every night for weeks and I kept saying no until eventually she wore me down. Chanelle was desperate to tell me it was a boy. Not that I definitely wanted a boy specifically, I would have been delighted with a healthy child of either gender, but if I'd been given a choice I think I'd have preferred a brother for Eve. In fairness to Chanelle I can see why she was excited to tell me because it is the most amazing feeling knowing you're going to have a little lad to play football with, to go and do father/son things with, and hopefully carry on the family name.

Again there were complications surrounding Archie's arrival and Chanelle had to be induced at thirty-seven weeks after suffering terrible pains in her kidneys. Fortunately he popped out safe and sound even though he was quite premature. The difficulties we had in both conceiving and delivering Eve and Archie really makes us appreciate how lucky we are to have the children. The kids make our lives so much better, so much more enjoyable.

Straightaway when he was born in August 2013 bookies were laying odds on Archie being champion jockey. Personally I'm rather hoping he'll turn out to be a new Rory McIlroy, or Paul Scholes seeing as he has ginger hair, but definitely playing for Arsenal. He's already got an Arsenal kit so is togged out ready, Arsène only needs to give me a call. If Archie did want to be a jockey that would be absolutely fine, certainly rather him than Eve as I don't think race-riding is a job I'd like to see my little girl doing. But if Archie expressed an interest then I certainly wouldn't stand in his way.

As for him being champion jockey, well, we named him Archie Peadar – Peadar being my dad's name – so he's A.P. McCoy too. If he ever does become a jockey and becomes better than me, it'll still be A.P. McCoy up there so I'll be able to live it as much as him. It will also be the same name on the trophy, which is obviously the most important thing. I think his mother's hoping that if Archie does grow into sport it'll be a safer one than horse racing. He sat on a horse recently for the first time, and although I wasn't there I'm told he loved it and was hyper for ages after he was lifted down. He's already physically quite robust and I'd say he'll be more physical than a lot of the lads in his class once he's at school. He likes going on the quad bike and sitting on the lawnmower when you're cutting the grass, and his current thing is tractors. He's mad into tractors and gets very excited whenever he sees one which, considering where we live is very rural, is quite often. Eve has a pony that she rides once a week, but fits it in around ballet lessons and various other things so I'm not too concerned that she has a career as a jockey in her sights at this stage.

Either way she wouldn't receive much encouragement from her mother on that front. Although Chanelle rode a couple of winners for her dad in her younger days as an amateur she wouldn't as much as pat a horse now if you brought it out in front of her. It's just not for her any more; there's no way she'd get on a horse again even if you guaranteed her a lottery win if she did.

Everything was fine with Archie until he was about four months old, when our nanny Sophie noticed he was making wheezy, whistling noises as he breathed which didn't sound natural to her. At first the doctors diagnosed asthma because he only seemed to be having problems breathing whenever he got excited. Chanelle and Sophie weren't happy with what they'd been told, however, so we took him to a specialist in London. After further tests we learned Archie was having problems with his airway, where the arteries around his heart were putting pressure on his airways and making them tighter. It was only getting worse as he got bigger and would only continue to get worse unless something was done.

From there we went straight to the Harley Street Clinic to see a cardiothoracic surgeon called Victor Tsang, who told us Archie needed an operation to help his airway develop normally and it should be sooner rather than later. Naturally we were both very concerned: Archie was a tiny baby and they wanted to operate, but Victor did his best to set our minds at rest. He did two operations a day, he told us, five days a week – three days in Great Ormond Street, two in Harley Street. He really knew what he was doing, he was telling us, and Archie was in the best possible hands. As far as Victor was concerned it was a straightforward procedure and there was nothing to worry about. It was a week before the Cheltenham Festival and as the operation needed to be done as soon as possible Victor booked Archie in for the Friday before Cheltenham.

We took Archie in on the Thursday evening, stayed there the night before and counted down the time until he went down to theatre late on the Friday morning. I was beside myself with worry as I took him down to the anaesthetist. Brian, his name was, and he was keeping me talking, asking me about riding and Cheltenham to try and keep me occupied while he put Archie to sleep. I looked down at our tiny baby, asleep on the trolley, looking so small and helpless and I couldn't bear to leave him. Brian, who must have seen a thousand parents in the same situation, assured me Archie was in the best hands, but I still cried as Brian gently persuaded me to leave him and go back to Chanelle, who hadn't been up to coming in to the anaesthetist's room to see him be put to sleep. I tried to recover my composure as quickly as I could to be strong for her and went back out.

Archie was due to be in theatre for a good four hours, and neither of us could face waiting in the clinic all that time. Chanelle had seen a little chapel nearby and suggested we go there and say a little prayer. We turned out of the clinic and as we walked down the street I recognised a man coming towards us but couldn't for the life of me place him. He was on the phone and carrying a little Selfridge's paper carrier bag, and as he got closer I realised. Fuck, it's Victor!

It didn't make sense at first, seeing him out of context, especially as we'd just seen Archie going into theatre but there was his surgeon, strolling down Harley Street talking on the phone and swinging this paper bag about.

I was about to say to Chanelle look, it's Victor, but immediately thought better of it and shepherded her across the road towards the chapel. I turned round and saw Victor walk into the clinic. It was only then I said to Chanelle she'd never guess who'd just walked past.

'Who?' she said.

'Victor,' I replied.

'Victor who?'

'Victor Tsang!'

'You're fucking joking me, Anthony!'

She was a nervous wreck, as was I, but Victor had assured us Archie was in the best hands so I tried to focus on that. We said a few prayers in the chapel and went back to the clinic. Four hours after Archie had gone into theatre, Victor came out to see us, smiled and assured us that everything had gone well. He'd lifted the arteries away from the airways and he was very happy that Archie would be OK now.

'Ah, brilliant,' I said, relief washing over me, 'thanks so much, Victor. One thing, though. When we left Archie and went for a walk around the block I saw you coming down the street with a Selfridge's bag when Archie was already in theatre. What was that about?'

He smiled in that calm, unflappable way top surgeons do, the kind of smile that puts you immediately at ease.

'Mr McCoy, I have to have my lunch like everyone else, you know!' he said. 'I was facing four hours concentrating on Archie, I couldn't do that on an empty stomach. Archie was still being prepped when you saw me, so don't worry, he was our highest priority from the moment he went into that theatre.

'I know you have a high-pressure job,' he continued. 'I operate on children every day. Sometimes it doesn't go right and I can't sleep for days, it affects me. Most of the time it goes well, like today, and I can come out and give worried parents like you good news. For me operating on a child is like changing a wheel on a car is for you. It's normal to me, and my daily routine is normal too, like any other profession.'

What an amazing man, I thought. The incredible things he does for people and it's just a job to him. Archie was in intensive care for five days after the operation but Victor and the clinic were happy he was stable. He was a little bit agitated as you'd expect, but he was fine. It was a horrific time, though: there were five other units in the intensive-care ward and one day Chanelle was in there with her sister Hilary and a baby died. You can't help looking at the devastated parents and thinking it could have been you.

I was supposed to be riding at Cheltenham a few days later and was seriously contemplating not going. Victor assured me that Archie was out of danger and I couldn't be of any more help to him, so I decided to go. I managed to ride the wrong horse twice in the two big races. I rode My Tent Or Yours for Nicky Henderson in the Champion Hurdle and was beaten by JP's other horse Jezki by half a length. I did the same thing in the World Hurdle on the Thursday, riding At Fishers Cross instead of More Of That, and finished third six lengths behind Barry Geraghty. Normally if I'd picked the wrong horse at Cheltenham I'd have felt like it was the end of the world but that year it was different. I wouldn't say I didn't give a toss but it didn't affect me as much as it might have done. When I was caught up in the actual race and passed the post I was spitting, but as soon as the outside world filtered into my mind again, I reminded myself that the previous Friday I'd been taking Archie into an operating theatre for a procedure that would save his life. Suddenly choosing the wrong horse didn't seem like the whole world was caving in. For the first time in my life I told myself, it's just a fucking horse race.

I never imagined I'd ever think like that in my life, but having kids of your own really helps you keep things in perspective. Before I was a dad I'd hear people talking about how everything was different when you have kids and think, yeah right, but since having Archie and Eve I can absolutely see what they mean, especially as having children hasn't come easy to us.

Archie's flying now, he's a hundred per cent, and the operation

means his early problems won't affect his life in any way. I absolutely dote on him and Eve. It's brilliant to have a bit more time
with them now I've retired. Being a dad has made me a different
person, a better person.

My kids definitely made my racing career better. They made
me happier, they made me come home in the evening able to be
at peace with myself rather than constantly revisiting what had
happened earlier in the day. During my last few months riding
Archie would stand in front of the television and make clip clop
noises with his mouth, and every time he saw someone on a
horse, especially in green and gold, no matter who it was, he'd
get all excited, pointing and shouting, 'Dada!' Eve, being older,
was a little more aware, though she can remember being at the
races for my 4,000th winner very clearly. And of course there
was her favourite thing ever, the party bus back from Sandown
on the day I retired.

At the start of what turned out to be my final season I was
approached about being the subject of a feature-length documentary that would chart my quest to become champion
jockey for the twentieth time. I have to admit I had no interest
in the project whatsoever at first. Then Chanelle pointed out
that Archie will have no memories of me riding and the film
might be something nice to do for him. He'd be able to see the
things I could do and the kind of life I led, something that led
me to make a complete about turn and agree to the film – a
keepsake for Archie, something a bit more significant than him
sitting down and watching the odd race of mine on YouTube
or whatever. He'll have a documentary, with a narrative and a
bit of context rather than old footage in which I'm just a green
and gold figure on a horse. I'm glad I did agree to do the film

too as it's a beautiful piece of work. As I write this it's just been accepted into the Toronto Film Festival, which is a huge achievement for the lads who made it.

I hope Archie and Eve will be proud of their dad when they watch the film and read these words when they're older. If they turn out to be half as proud of me as I am of them, then I'll be a very happy man indeed.

EIGHT

Arnold Layne, Warwick
12 January 2008

When Chanelle's phone rang and she saw Jackie O'Neill's number on the screen her blood ran cold. Although Chanelle and Jonjo's wife are very friendly, this was a Saturday afternoon when I was away racing at Warwick. If Jackie O'Neill was calling on a Saturday afternoon the chances were it wasn't to arrange meeting up for dinner: something must be very wrong. She took a deep breath, pressed 'accept' and lifted the phone to her ear.

'Hi, Jackie.'

It was 12 January 2008 and as Chanelle was taking Jackie's call I was at Warwick Racecourse strapped to a spinal board. I'd been riding Arnold Layne for Caroline Bailey in the prestigious Classic Chase and been going OK when he hit a fence at the start of the second circuit and I hit the ground.

In itself it wasn't a particularly bad fall, and to this day I don't think the damage was done there. Six weeks earlier I'd had a fall at Lingfield from a horse of JP's called Mem O'Rees and been kicked in the back. It felt like I'd broken a couple of ribs, a feeling I know very well, but didn't stop me riding a winner in the next race on Pauillac for the Pipes and David Johnson in a novice chase despite practically crying with the pain. For the next ten days or so I remember going to bed every night in agony, with Chanelle telling me to stop moaning.

This makes me conclude I'd already damaged my back by the time I hit the ground that freezing January day at Warwick, because despite it being a fairly run-of-the-mill fall I lay on the ground and found I couldn't move. Not only that, I couldn't feel anything below my waist, which, frankly, terrified me. It was probably only a few seconds before the sensation began to come back, but believe me, those few seconds felt like a very long time indeed. Where normally I like to get off the ground as quickly as possible when I fall off a horse I knew instinctively on that occasion that I should lie as still as possible until help arrived. The doctors and the ambulance people were on the scene in no time and put me on the spinal board, strapped me down with my head in between blocks so I couldn't turn it, my arms tied to my sides so I couldn't move. I'm quite claustrophobic at the best of times so being lifted onto the board and strapped in was out of the frying pan and into the fire for me, but luckily, after initial reluctance in case I could get back riding again that day, they gave me plenty of painkillers and morphine so I was pretty stoned and not noticing my confinement so much. Nor, equally crucially, was I feeling a lot of pain. By the time I was in the ambulance and heading off up the track to the weighing room I could feel my feet and I was grand again. I don't mind admitting, though, that it was the one occasion in my life that I was scared by the possible repercussions of a riding injury. I was taken to hospital in Coventry, where I was x-rayed pretty quickly and equally quickly a doctor came out to see me.

'I've looked at the x-ray,' he said, 'and it looks like you've broken three ribs. You should be OK to go home.'

Now, I've broken a few ribs in my time so I know exactly how that feels, and this felt like more than broken ribs. This was sore, very sore. I know the difference between being as sore as this and having a couple of broken ribs and there really was no comparison. My PA Gee Armytage was there and by this stage Chanelle had arrived too and both of them shared my concerns. I got them to ring Doc Pritchard.

'He's really sore,' I heard Chanelle telling him. 'He physically can't get off the spinal board, he's in agony, and he's being told he can go home. He can't go home, there's no way he's going home.'

Doc Pritchard arranged for me to stay in hospital in Coventry that night before having me transferred to the John Radcliffe Hospital in Oxford the next morning. Through the haze of morphine I remember Steve McManaman calling in to see me that night – he must have been commentating on a match nearby or something – but it was good to see his friendly face even though I was off my face and probably making even less sense than usual.

At the John Radcliffe Doc Pritchard had asked a surgeon called James Wilson-MacDonald to have a look at me. He x-rayed me and, like the Coventry doctor, said he couldn't really see anything beyond some broken ribs so sent me for an MRI to see if that could identify the problem. From being strapped onto a spinal board to being fed into the MRI scanner it wasn't a great time to be claustrophobic, I can tell you. Thankfully the scan showed up the problem: I'd fractured my T-12 vertebra and smashed my T-9 and T-10 vertebrae. In short, I'd broken my back.

When I think back now to how I'd lost feeling from the waist down when lying on the track and then reflect on the damage I'd done to my spine I realise just how lucky I was not to have seen my career end that day. When I think of what happened to J.T. McNamara and just how much worse that phone call Chanelle took from Jackie O'Neill might have been, it makes me shudder. At the time, though, my only thought was how soon I could get back racing.

James Wilson-MacDonald told me that I faced a long lay-off and the prospect of being in a body cast for three months to protect the spine and allow the bones to fuse again. Even from deep within a haze of painkillers I did the maths like lightning.

'Doc, I can't be out for three months,' I said. 'The Cheltenham Festival is in two months and I have to be there.'

He shook his head.

'It's not going to happen.'

'There must be something you can do,' I pleaded from my prone position. 'I can't be in a cast for all that time, I need to be at Cheltenham in March.'

He let out a weary sigh. I've heard a lot of weary sighs from doctors over the years and that was one of the better ones.

'Well, there is another option,' he admitted. 'I could operate and stabilise the spine with metal but I really don't like putting metal in people's backs. Spines are fragile things at the best of times, damaged spines even more so. I'd rather not operate on yours, to be honest.'

'I'd rather you did, to be honest,' I replied. All I could think about was being back in time for Cheltenham.

James looked at Chanelle. She gave a resigned shrug and smiled.

'Take it from me,' she said, 'there's really only going to be one winner here.'

I had the operation the next day.

It was performed by James and a Croatian doctor named Adi Zubovic, who was mad into racing. They came to see me that day after the op and James Wilson-MacDonald told me it had gone well, indeed he was actually glad he'd operated as it turned out because the bones were further apart than the MRI had suggested and might not have come together again in a body cast.

Then Adi said to me, 'McCoy, you have fucking tough bones. I worked up a hell of a sweat trying to drill through you.'

He went on to tell me the physios would come and see me and teach me how to walk again. I thought, what? I've only been off my feet a couple of days, why would I need to learn how to walk again? I wiggled my toes to make sure and they were fine. Once the docs had decided I could walk the physios came to see me. Great, I thought, I'll show them that I don't have anything to learn from them by walking to the bathroom. They gently lifted me and turned me, and had me sitting on the side of the bed. I went to slide forward and put my feet on the ground – and nothing happened. It was the oddest sensation. I wasn't paralysed, obviously, and I certainly hadn't been flat out long enough to affect the muscle tone in my legs. Maybe it was some kind of neurological instinct to protect the damaged spine, I don't know, but I'd genuinely lost the ability to walk. The physios got me standing and the next day I was walking with a zimmer frame, and before too long I was back to normal again, but it was the strangest sensation.

A month or so before Cheltenham the doc upped the exercise part of my recuperation but was still a little dubious about the advisability of riding at Cheltenham so soon after the injury. There was no way I was missing the festival, though, it was too important. Chances are that even if I'd had the body cast I'd have been at home seeing if I could button up my silks over it in the days leading up to the races.

Then Charlie Brooks, who was a trainer at that time, called me with a suggestion that he said might help speed up my recovery. Charlie had become involved with cryotherapy as a means for helping treat sports injuries and had helped bring it to Champneys health farm in Tring. Cryogenic chamber therapy, to give it its full title, involves sitting for short periods of time inside a chamber cooled through the use of liquid nitrogen at extremely low temperatures. Among other things the low temperatures release endorphins that combat pain, as well as speeding up the recovery time of sporting injuries. It's a fairly new treatment – the first sporting treatment centre was established in 2000 – and had a very good reputation so I thought it must be worth a try. Stephen Purdew, the owner of Champneys, is a racing fan and an Arsenal fan whom I'd got to know quite well and when he kindly offered me a couple of weeks at Champneys having the treatment I was delighted to accept and was looked after incredibly well. My back was still fragile, so although I'd been given exercises to do they were pretty mild and there wasn't much more I could do. It was frustrating, so even if the therapy didn't have much of an effect at least I felt like I was doing something to regain my fitness as quickly as possible.

Two weeks at a health spa sounds like it might be a cushy number, but that's certainly not the case when you're having

cryogenic chamber therapy. The first time I tried it was probably the worst experience I've ever had, worse even than seeing
Manchester United win the Champions League or even losing
to Mick Fitzgerald at golf. Wearing only swimming trunks, clogs
and gloves, you go first into a cold pre-chamber at minus 60 for
a minute, then into the main chamber which is down to minus
120, where you stay for three minutes. It was a contender for
the slowest three minutes of my life, but I stuck it out. I didn't
enjoy it one bit, believe me, but I did it. After three or four days
I began getting used to it and each subsequent time felt like less
of an ordeal. One day I was chatting to Renata, the girl who
looked after the cryogenic chamber, and asked how cold it went.
She told me that the coldest temperature anyone had endured
was minus 145 degrees for four minutes by the footballer Shefqi
Kuqi. Shefqi's a big sturdy lad, six foot four in his stockinged feet,
and I'm a little squirt by comparison, but I mulled it over briefly
before saying to Renata that before I finished the treatment I'd
go in colder than him. She laughed.

'AP,' she said, 'you wouldn't stand it, you're too small.'

'Too small me hoop,' I said. 'I'm telling you, Renata, before I
leave here you'll have seen me in there at minus 150.'

I was as good as my word: I stuck out four minutes in that
chamber at minus 150. I've no idea in hindsight why I did it, especially as I came out badly burnt. All my extremities were burnt,
and I mean all of them, from my nose to my toes and everything
in between, let me tell you: that stubborn streak of mine almost
literally burnt the nuts off me. It was like the worst chafing you
can imagine, times a hundred.

But I'd done it. I said to Renata that I'd do it, and I did. It was
worth it.

Indeed, the whole trip was worth it in so many ways. Most importantly it visibly benefited the injury. When I went in, down either side of the operation scar on my spine was a white line where the blood wasn't getting through to it. After five days of sessions in the chamber that whiteness had almost gone, meaning the blood circulation was obviously improving dramatically. It was only afterwards that I realised how beneficial it was mentally too. I felt like I was taking assertive action to make myself better and fitter, and I was mixing with people helping me achieve what I was trying to achieve. The tangible physical improvements from the start confirmed to me that I was doing the right thing, which was much better for me psychologically than if I'd just been moping around at home doing a few meagre exercises and going stir crazy. I'm an active convalescent, a firm believer in trying anything that might make you better. Cryotherapy was great, it really worked for me and I'd definitely recommend it. Needless to say I was back in time for Cheltenham.

My attitude to injuries, treating them wherever possible as minor inconveniences when most normal people might be sidelined for a long time, must sound strange, unnatural even, but I considered them just part of the job. Different figures are quoted but generally a jump jockey should expect to fall off a horse once in every dozen or so rides. I rode in more than 17,000 races in my career so you don't have to be a mathematician to work out that I had a hell of a lot of falls. Race horses are big, heavy animals jumping great heights and distances at speeds up to 30 mph. The basic physics of that tells you that every one of those hundreds of falls you experience during your career puts you at risk of being injured. Some kind of physical damage is inevitable and I suffered a fair bit of physical damage in my time. Perhaps I was lucky in that I had one of my worst injuries at the dawn of my career, the day I broke my leg at Jim's, fracturing my tib and fib and thinking I was going to die. The pain I felt for that hour waiting for the ambulance was as excruciating as anything I experienced after that so the McCoy pain barrier was set high from that day on: not many injuries have come close to what I felt that cold January morning in the wilds of Kilkenny. Let's not forget also that when Jim came to find me he asked how I knew my leg was broken, with it bent right up under my bum at a sickening angle, and then him telling me I wasn't tough enough to be a jump jockey. It was an awful thing to say but maybe ever since that day I've set out to prove to Jim, and everyone else, but most importantly myself, that I'm more than tough enough to be a jump jockey.

In January 1997 I had my first serious injury as a professional jockey when I had a bad fall on Speedy Snapsgem at the first in a three-mile maiden chase at Wincanton, breaking the clavicle and the scapula in my left shoulder. It was such a bad fall that the poor horse was killed, which made me extra determined not to make a big deal out of my injury as I'd got off lightly by comparison. The pain was utterly searing but even before the medics gave me gas I sensed I was coping with it better than when I'd broken my leg. I missed the best part of a month's racing as a result of that injury, and when I look back the facilities available then were nothing like they are now. There was no cryogenic chamber to climb into in 1997: my recuperation went little further than trips to Andover Leisure Centre for sessions on the exercise bike and in the swimming pool. Twenty-seven days I missed with that injury: in later years with my more developed tolerance of pain and the better facilities I'd probably have cut down that time almost by half.

Six relatively injury-free years followed, until on 21 February 2003 in a handicap hurdle at Kempton a Martin Pipe horse called Neutron mistimed the second fence and speared me into the ground, breaking my collarbone. It was a Friday, the day before the Racing Post Chase, and as soon as I hit the turf and bounced I thought, fuck, my collarbone's gone. The pain was agonising, but I had more good rides booked that day and was having a great season. It was the year after I'd broken Sir Gordon Richards' record and gone on to rack up 289 winners. The thing was, as I lay there wincing on the ground at Kempton I was 21 days ahead of where I'd been during that record-breaking season and I'd be lying if I said the prospect of riding 300 winners that season hadn't crossed my mind. As I picked myself gingerly off the grass I was already offsetting the pain against an iron-willed determination to ride through it. There was no way a broken collarbone was going to get in the way of what I wanted to achieve.

A fence attendant called out to ask if I was all right and I fixed my mask of nonchalance firmly over a face that wanted to wince and grimace.

'Yeah, I'm fine,' I lied.

I walked down the track and as I got near the gate I saw Michael Turner, who was at the time the long-serving chief medical officer of the British Horseracing Board. If you'd asked me who was the last person I'd want to see at that moment it would have been him, no question. As soon as I clapped eyes on Dr Turner I thought, shit, I'm going to have to drop my arm to my side and walk normally.

'All right, AP?' he asked as we passed each other.

'Yeah, fine thanks, doc,' I replied breezily as every casual swing of my arm sent new levels of pain fizzing through my shoulder. It was an act I managed to keep up until I got back to the weighing room where I told Craig Wiley, Martin's head travelling lad, that I'd broken my collarbone and asked him to ring Martin to tell him. Martin asked if I was still able to ride to which I was honest enough to say I didn't know but I'd give it a go.

In the next race I was on the favourite, Wahiba Sands, but we came in third and the pain was excruciating. I had three more rides for Martin that day and although the collarbone was giving me pain I knew I could ride through it. The rides I had were all really good horses, and I wasn't about to wave them goodbye because of a sore shoulder. Next up was Puntal in a novices' hurdle and we came in first by eleven lengths. After that it was another fantastic win, by a dozen lengths, on Deano's Beeno in a valuable three-mile hurdle even though he was kicked at the start and had a very slow first circuit. Withdrawals from the last race of the day left it a straight head-to-head between me on Stormez and J.R. Kavanagh on a horse of Jonjo's called Sudden Shock in which Stormez came home by eleven lengths.

All in all a pretty good day's racing but for the small matter of my broken collarbone. Although I was in terrible pain I took deep satisfaction from the way in which I'd ridden through it, especially on Deano's Beeno who gave me a bit of a hard time on that first circuit until he got properly going. The kick he'd got before the start caused him to lurch a little bit, which almost had me seeing stars with the pain as he pulled at the reins, but riding three winners in the state I was in? I had no complaints whatsoever.

The Racing Post Chase was the next day and I was worried I wouldn't cope with the injury. I went home, took some hefty painkillers and went to bed and although I woke up the next morning in pain I knew I could ride through it. Sure enough, I won the Adonis Juvenile Hurdle on a great little horse called Well Chief, but it didn't happen in the Racing Post Chase on Montreal, in the Pendil Novice Chase on Jaybejay nor on my last ride of the day, Safari Paradise in a Class C hurdle.

Even if I'd ridden another three winners that day there was no avoiding the fact that my collarbone was in a bad way and I couldn't just keep riding. Every time a horse pulled I could feel it moving; there was no way it was going to heal if I just pretended the break wasn't there and kept popping painkillers. The 300-winner target was now in serious doubt, but also there were only a couple of weeks or so to go before the Cheltenham Festival. (When you think about it, it's astonishing how many injuries I had during my career in the weeks before Cheltenham. My telling a doctor, 'there's no way I can be off that long, I need to be at Cheltenham' became almost an annual refrain.) Martin said we should get it x-rayed but I said I didn't want to go to hospital for an x-ray two weeks before the Cheltenham Festival: I wanted to keep this injury under wraps as much as I possibly could. Martin suggested I called in to his place the following morning on my way to the races at Exeter.

'I'll get Ray to x-ray it for you,' he told me.

'OK, all right, grand, see you tomorrow,' I said, but as I put the phone down I suddenly thought . . . Ray? Hang on, Ray's the fucking vet!

Sure enough, the next morning, there I was lying on the kitchen floor at Martin's trying to keep as still as I could while

Ray the vet straddled me while holding an x-ray machine. And people try to tell you being a jockey isn't a glamorous life, eh?

'Yes, your collarbone's broken,' Ray said after a couple of minutes, walking back into the kitchen holding up the x-ray to the light from the window. 'In fact it looks like it's broken where you broke it before.'

'Oh, right,' I said, 'thanks, Ray.'

A few minutes later I was back in the car and heading for Exeter when I thought, hang on, what did he mean 'where you broke it before'? I've never broken my collarbone before in my life. Well, obviously I had at some stage. I'd just been too stupid to realise it.

I told Martin that in the light of the x-ray I couldn't carry on as I was, but still managed another winner at Exeter that day. After that, though, I became vaguely sensible and had a week off, in which I went to Dubai with Chanelle for a few days to let the heat get to it. I came back a few days prior to Cheltenham and made it all the way through the festival, despite a bad fall off Copeland three out when in a close second place in the Champion Hurdle on the first day. After that I managed to survive intact until the end of the last day, two races after the Gold Cup when I had a fall in the Grand Annual off a horse of David Johnson's called Golden Alpha. He fell at the third last fence and as soon as I hit the ground I thought, that's it, it's gone. Doc Pritchard came over.

'It's gone, doc,' I said through gritted teeth, 'my collarbone.'

'I know, I can see that from here,' he said. 'I'll give you some gas and air and we'll get you into an ambulance.'

I walked into the ambulance when it came and we drove to the medical room under the stand to wait for my transfer to hospital. I was lying there, feeling pleasantly half high as a kite from sucking away at the gas and air, when the doc's face loomed into view above me, lips pursed.

'You know what?' he said. 'I think it's better if I put your collarbone back in now, while it's freshly out. It'll make things easier at the hospital if it's in place when you get there. Deep breath and brace yourself.'

I took a big gulp of the gas and air and closed my eyes. Doc Pritchard got hold of my collarbone with both hands and snapped it back in. I was seeing stars and screaming with the pain, but as the pain subsided slightly and my vision cleared, I looked over at the bed beside me to see another jockey lying there looking totally out of it, wired up to so many tubes I thought, fuck, here's me screaming at having my collarbone snapped back into place and this guy's going to die. Then I noticed it was Tony Dobbin and I thought, ah here, he's just a big drama queen. I saw Tony being helicoptered to hospital at Carlisle once but he was back at the course just after the last race with his hand in plaster. He'd been airlifted from the course when there was basically nothing wrong with him beyond a couple of minor broken bones. I was high on the gas and air and the endorphins were racing around inside me after Doc Pritchard's bit of DIY on my collarbone, so I sat up as best I could and just started abusing him, calling him a fucking drama queen and all sorts. Fortunately he was OK: imagine if he really had been at death's door. Oops.

I wasn't in my best form that day, that's for sure. I never am when there's the prospect of a lay-off from racing looming ahead, but I surpassed myself that day. Later that evening I was sitting waiting in A&E with Chanelle for an x-ray – an official one, no lying on a kitchen floor with a vet standing over me this time – and there was someone in a nearby room absolutely screaming the place down, completely hysterical. I asked a nurse what the story was and she said ah, don't worry, she's in here all the time, she tries to commit suicide regular as clockwork. For some reason, and to this day I don't know what it was, I stuck my head round the door and just let this woman have it with both barrels.

'Listen, you,' I roared, 'if you're going to commit suicide fucking make sure you do it properly. Stop being an attention seeker. All you're doing is annoying people and wasting the doctors' time. So if you have actually got the bottle to top yourself, do everyone in here a favour and fucking do it properly.'

Chanelle was absolutely mortified, she wanted the ground to swallow her up. I don't know where it came from. I was having a bad day, all right, I'd had a pretty rotten Cheltenham with only one winner and in sitting in that hospital with a broken collarbone I was effectively kissing goodbye to riding 300 winners, but I'd had bad days before and never reacted like that. I had no idea of that woman's circumstances and the events that led up to her attempting suicide, but when I heard this was a regular thing something snapped inside me. Maybe I imagined I was sticking up for the staff, who do a tremendous job in patching people up often in trying circumstances, but there was still no need for that level of indignation about it.

The following year I had my first broken limb since I'd mashed up my leg on Kly Green at Jim's a decade earlier. I'd had the odd broken bone – the shoulder blade, the collarbone, various broken ribs – but when I came off Kymberlya at the Worcester evening meeting on 18 June 2003 it was the first time I'd had a limb in plaster since Coolcullen. I'd won on the horse ten days earlier on the same course and as we came round the final bend approaching the third last he was travelling really well and I thought we were going to do it again. Suddenly, between fences, down we went. The horse must have suffered a fracture or some other kind of bad leg injury because there didn't seem to be any reason for him to go the way he did. You expect to fall *at* fences, not in between them, so it took me a little by surprise and I went down heavily and heard my arm snap as I landed. As ever, although I knew it was broken I didn't want to admit to myself that I faced a lay-off from racing. I'd grown pretty immune to pain by this stage and every injury seemed to hurt less and less, but once the doctor had given me gas and air I was determined to walk to the ambulance to convince everyone that, despite overwhelming evidence to the contrary, I was all right. As it turned out, even for someone with a badly broken arm, I was far from all right.

It was fairly late in the evening when I arrived at Worcester hospital. They told me it was a bad break that needed more than just setting in plaster, so I stayed in overnight dosed up with morphine and they operated the following morning. I spent another night in hospital after the op before going home on the Friday morning. Everything seemed fine but later on that night I noticed quite a bad pain starting in my arm. I thought nothing of it at first, it was a bad break so of course it was going to be sore. I took a few painkillers at bedtime to knock myself out and thought I'd be grand, but two hours later I woke up absolutely dripping with sweat and with the most horrific pain in my arm. I necked some more painkillers and went back to bed thinking I still might sleep through it but ended up in agony all night. The pain seemed to ease off a little in the morning and I believed I was over the worst of it. It crossed my mind to ring

Doc Pritchard but thought if I call him at the weekend because I've got an arm in plaster that's a bit sore he's going to laugh at me.

As that Saturday wore on, however, the pain seemed to be getting worse, as if my arm was trying to burst through the plaster.

'My arm's horrific,' I said to Chanelle, my face beaded with sweat. 'It's so bad I'm on the point of cutting this plaster off me, I can't stand it.'

Chanelle rang Gee and Gee rang Doc Pritchard, who was at a wedding. The doc told Gee that I should get to A&E straightaway because what she'd told him didn't sound remotely normal. Chanelle took me in and I told the doctors how painful it was, had the arm x-rayed, endured a few tests and within a couple of hours I was on the table in theatre with acute compartment syndrome.

Compartment syndrome isn't an uncommon condition, especially with broken arms, but it is incredibly dangerous. A trauma like a broken bone can cause severe pressure to build up in the bodily compartment where the break is which prevents enough blood getting to the muscles and nerves in the affected region. It's incredibly painful and if untreated for long enough can result in the loss of a limb. My case proved particularly difficult to treat: I ended up in hospital for a week during which I was in theatre four times because they were having trouble cleaning out the wound and closing it up. By the third of the four anaesthetics I was feeling really rotten, in very bad form, and when they told me it was lucky I came in when I did because I could have lost the arm I didn't really take it in. Yeah right, I thought, it can't be that bad.

It actually took until I watched the Paralympics a few years later and saw several athletes there who were missing limbs because of compartment syndrome for me to realise just how serious that injury could have been. It was true, I really could have lost my arm. Once again, I'd been a very lucky man indeed.

There have been a few other bad knocks, the kind of injuries I couldn't just grit my teeth and keep riding through. At the Galway Races in 2006 I broke my wrist coming off Sporting Limerick, a horse of JP's. The wrist was a bit of a mess – I asked how bad it was and the doc said, 'AP, I could get a pair of scissors, cut through the ligaments and bring your hand into hospital, if you want, the bones are that mangled it's only the ligaments keeping it attached.' That was a tough one, not least because I missed out on a winner in the Galway Plate two races later with JP's Far From Trouble on whom Christy Roche deputised. There was one quirky upshot from that injury though: it led to Chanelle and I taking an unconventional honeymoon before we got married, a couple of weeks in Barbados grabbed while we had the chance because I couldn't race. Who'd marry a jockey?

A couple of years earlier I'd broken my cheekbone in three places when Polar Red clipped a fence at Plumpton, threw me out of the saddle and left me clinging on to his neck. It's one of those devil-and-the-deep-blue-sea moments where you don't want to let go because you know you're in for a kicking, but equally you can't hang on to the horse like that for the rest of the race either. So down I went, taking a knee in the face en route to the ground and getting thoroughly trampled when I got there. Blood was pouring from my cheek and I knew it was bad. It's more difficult to have gas and air with facial injuries be-cause when you're inhaling your face puffs up and you could do yourself further damage. They couldn't give me any pain relief on the spot. As was customary by now, this was not long before the Cheltenham Festival. During the week away from racing I had to take to recover I travelled to a college in Blackpool where they make protective face masks for people like me who've suffered injuries that shouldn't necessarily prevent them from competing as long as their face was protected. They'd made a few for some top-flight footballers and Doc Pritchard, knowing how desperate I was to get back riding, put me onto the guys to have one fitted. I wore it for my first few days back in the saddle, winning a Singapore Airlines Novices' Hurdle at Kempton on Eric's Charm looking like something out of *The Phantom of the Opera*. It wasn't so much the risk of another face-first plunge from a horse that was the issue, the mask was more a protection from kickback off the ground. When you're in a race there's always mud and dirt flying up at you from the horses' hooves and occasionally a proper sod of turf can fly up and hit you quite hard. If one of those had thudded into my broken cheekbone I wouldn't have seen the funny side. To this day I still have no feeling on the left side of my face as a result of that injury, along with a little dimple scar on my cheek. It tingles a little bit, like when you've had an injection at the dentist's, but doesn't seem to have affected my rugged good looks too much.

One of the last truly memorable injuries I had was when I fell off Quantitativeeasing in the Barbury International Horse Trials Handicap Hurdle at Cheltenham in April 2013. He made a mistake at the second flight and as he landed must have lifted his head and headbutted me, knocking me high into the air. To this day I'm convinced I was unconscious when I hit the ground. The race replay was inconclusive as to what happens because I was in the middle of the pack: everyone jumps the hurdle safely enough but then suddenly I fly into the air and disappear from view. When you see me briefly on the ground I'm motionless, as if I'm out cold. I was always very good at protecting myself and bracing for the fall, but that day I flew into the air and hit the ground like a corpse being thrown off a ridge. I was conscious soon enough though, and even as I lay on the ground it was already in my mind that with the Punchestown Festival only a week away I didn't want to get signed off with concussion. I was in quite a bit of pain with my ribs but braved the pain as long as I could before eventually going into the ambulance on a stretcher. After five minutes gathering my thoughts and going through a mental checklist I knew exactly what was wrong because it was the same feeling I'd known many times before: I couldn't get a breath, it felt like someone was stabbing me in the side, and this time my sternum definitely wasn't where it should be.

On the way back to the weighing room I bumped into Lisa Hancock, the chief executive of the Injured Jockeys Fund, and she asked if she could come to the hospital with me in the ambulance. Sure, I said, hop in. As we drove through the streets of Cheltenham she watched open-mouthed as I basically told the doctor and the paramedics exactly what was wrong with me.

'I have never seen anyone give as detailed and accurate self-diagnosis in my life,' she told me afterwards.

Once we arrived at the hospital I was convinced I was going home that night, there was no way I was spending the night in the Royal Gloucestershire. My driver had followed the ambulance and had been left under no illusion that if he left me there for the night he was fired. Whatever the doctors said, I was going home. At the same time Chanelle was hinting heavily that if he showed up at the house that night with me in the back of the car, that would also be pretty much grounds for dismissal. The poor guy couldn't do right for doing wrong.

He did keep his job, though, even though it turned out I'd contracted some kind of infection in my lung where I wasn't getting enough air and ended up in intensive care for a week. Chanelle was pregnant with Archie at the time, and when they gave me an epidural it was, as far as I was concerned, the best high I've ever had in my life. I felt nothing, no pain whatsoever, and I told Chanelle that if she complained about giving birth when she had the benefit of this, well, something wasn't right. Lying there, high as a kite, I could have quite happily popped a baby out myself and that would have been absolutely fine.

My week in the Royal Gloucestershire was the longest stay in hospital I ever had, longer even than when I broke my back and longer than when I was struck down with compartment syndrome. Despite this, and the extensive nature of the injuries I'd suffered, I was back riding again within a month – 27 days, to be precise, exactly the same as when I'd been out with that broken shoulder in 1997. If I'm honest it should have been more like 67 days. I came back far too early purely out of stubbornness. For the first three weeks I was back racing there was no way I should have been even near a racecourse, let alone riding horses. I convinced myself that because I could still move despite the broken ribs and shattered sternum I was fine to ride. A broken arm or leg was different because you couldn't hold the reins or get your foot in the irons, but everything else, I'd surmised, was down to the power of the mind. It's different when you break your arm and you can't physically lift or hold things with it, but in my book, anything other than broken limbs were not a good enough excuse to stop riding. Yes, it's going to hurt, but you get used to that. If you can cope with the pain, you're OK to ride. That's not me trying to sound like a hard man, putting myself at risk out of idiotic macho bravado, but the way I see it you can only be successful if you're on the track; you can't be champion jockey if you're sitting at home with your leg up on a chair watching *At the Races*. To attain the success I did during my career wasn't down to talent – there were far more talented riders than me on the circuit; if anything it was down to hard work and the determination not to let injuries get the better of me. Ride through the pain and you've more chance of success. Give in to the pain, you've no chance.

I don't miss any of that now. Far from it. In fact often when I'm sitting at home and I catch sight of a scar on my arm or feel a lump on a bone, I ask myself what made me do that? What made me think that getting in an ambulance every other day of the week was in any way a normal way to live? Maybe it's back to what James Hunt said about how the closer you are to death the more alive you feel. Maybe the pain and the risk was half the thrill. Maybe it was all of the thrill, if I'm honest with myself. I look round today at the lovely house we live in near Lambourn and remember how lucky I am to be there, in one piece. The main reason I became a jockey was because I loved horses and loved riding horses. Then I got to love the habit of winning on them, a love that carried me through the pain barrier and had me covering thousands of miles just for the chance to experience that fleeting exhilaration of winning a horse race. The pursuit of that fleeting exhilaration has given me a very good life and I look around and know that I am blessed to have what I have.

But, bloody hell, the races I rode in when I should by rights have been at home or even in hospital.

The legacy of that quest hasn't taken the physical toll you might expect: I have very few aches and pains despite the way I battered my way through all medical advice and occasionally common sense to make it to the start line in pursuit of the next winner. Sometimes I feel average enough in the mornings and my back isn't great at times, but I'm a lot better than I might have expected to be, or indeed deserve to be. It could have been a lot worse.

I used to see myself as unbreakable. When I broke my back in 2008 and was lying on the ground and not really feeling anything from the waist down, for a fleeting moment I wasn't doing great, but that's the only time I ever got a little scared. My pain threshold got better as I got older, I learned to cope with pain and I was able to get myself in a positive frame of mind whenever I got injured. Here we go again, I'd think, another couple of broken ribs, sure, I know how that feels and it's not too bad. That helped me get back as quickly as I did. If I sustained an injury roughly once every nine months to a year then I reckoned that was normal, an acceptable level of physical risk. If I could ride in 800-odd races and in that time have one bad fall where I broke an arm or some ribs I thought that was about right, a fair ratio, a deal I was happy to make with the racing gods.

When I retired people made a great deal of my injury record – there were pictorial graphics published in newspapers that looked like chaotic games of 'Pin the Injury on A.P. McCoy' – but I don't feel I was any more unlucky with injuries than any other jockey. The longevity of my career probably meant that I had more injuries than most, but the ratio was about the same.

Indeed there were stages of my career when I didn't have any bad injuries at all. For example between my broken shoulder in 1997 and 2003, when I broke my arm, I didn't have a single injury serious enough to stop me riding. That was incredibly lucky, in hindsight. After that things seemed to go in more regular cycles and I came to accept that my bones would be broken and I'd be confronting pain again before too long. As long as I could keep the pain at bay through the strength of my mind then I would remain pretty much unbreakable. I used to find injuries easier to deal with than Chanelle did, or Mum and Dad, because as far as I was concerned I was in pain but it would only be for a short period of time and then I'd be right as rain again. Everyone else had worst case scenarios permanently at the ready, and it must have been awfully worrying.

If I'm honest, aside from those frightening few seconds on the ground at Warwick in 2008 there was one other occasion when I was a wee bit scared. It was at Wetherby on 2 November 2012 and I was bringing Mr Watson round to the start of the first race of the day. He was a bit keen and before I knew what was happening he'd dropped me and kicked me in the face as he was getting rid of me. Even as I write this I can see his hoof coming towards me in slow motion. He sent me flying backwards, I got off the ground and the blood came gushing out. It felt like my face had been pushed into the back of my head. If I'd been eight inches closer to him when he lashed out I reckon he would have killed me. I don't know if I jerked back out of sheer reflexes or I was just lucky to be just far enough away, but I do think that kick could well have been the end of me. He broke all my front teeth and left me needing 24 stitches in my face, but compared to the possible alternative I'd take that any day of the week. Even as I lifted my head and felt the blood was pouring out of my face I half-smiled to myself and thought, fuck me, that was lucky. My face was a mess, my teeth looked like a bombed graveyard, but I felt like a very fortunate man indeed. That was definitely one that I got away with.

Generally though, injuries are something you get used to and that some people cope with better than others. As some jockeys get older injuries become a bigger deal, they get weaker, it takes them longer to come back and maybe they lose their bottle a little bit waiting for the next fall, but I found that I was able to cope better the more I was injured and the older I got. I saw it as part of the job, like weighing out or driving for hours to a remote course: it was all part of the deal that got you winners in return. The trick was to just get yourself treated and get on with it.

Although every time I was injured I'd convince myself that would be the last one, for the first time in my life, now I've retired I've accepted there shouldn't be any more ambulance rides or x-rays. My old bones are safe now, there'll no more hearing the snap of breaking limbs or the crunch of ribs going yet again. Lucky as I've been, there are a lot of lads who aren't as privileged, which is where the Injured Jockeys Fund comes into its own. It's an amazing organisation that provides rehab for jockeys, both physical and mental, and they're very supportive of lads whose careers have been ended by injury and been dumped out of the sport with no qualifications and no idea what to do next, or jockeys with families who find themselves with no income and no other means of support.

My relaxed attitude to injuries was definitely helped by the fact medical care is much, much better today than when I started out and the IJF is at the forefront of that, too. The standard of medical care couldn't be better and we're very lucky to have that safety net. Health and safety is so much better in racing these days too: the helmets, body protectors, plastic running rails, the standard now is much better than it ever has been.

If you go to the John Oaksey House in Lambourn or the Jack Berry House in Malton you'll see just how amazing the facilities are. These places have helped jockeys in general become more like other professional sportspeople because they now have the right facilities to treat them the right way, and let's face it, a jockey is injured more often than any other sportsperson so good treatment and rehabilitation are absolutely essential.

There's continuous research and development going on to make racing better and safer, it never stands still, but whatever improvements are made to make the game safer, you're never going to lose that element of risk entirely. Racing is, in many ways, an extreme sport so it's very difficult for it not to contain any danger at all. The speed and the nature of the sport means there'll always be a danger – it wouldn't work otherwise – but it's fair to say that while racing has become less dangerous some sports have become more so. Rugby for example: the players have got fitter, faster, bigger and more physical, the impact has become greater and the professional game is arguably more dangerous now than it ever was. Horse racing isn't like that, rather it's becoming safer every year thanks to the advances that are being made and the valuable work of the Injured Jockeys Fund.

The IJF supports not only the injured jockey but their family as well. When Brian Toomey had a really bad head injury at Perth in the summer of 2013, for example, the IJF flew his family over from Ireland, put them up, and looked after them financially while they were at Brian's bedside. Not everyone can afford to just up sticks and fly off when they receive a call like the Toomeys did, so that's one of the things the IJF is very good at. It's a fantastic organisation and one I'm proud to support.

During my career I was very lucky in terms of the doctors looking out for me. Philip Pritchard, who was an amateur jockey in his day and trained a few horses as well, was brilliant at looking after me and kept me together, quite literally. He was also very good from a personal point of view in that he was always on call, always on hand and willing to make sure I was receiving the best possible treatment, from being in the most appropriate hospital to sorting out the best surgeons. When I broke my back it was Doc Pritchard who arranged for me to see James Wilson-MacDonald and Adi Zubovic at the John Radcliffe, for example, and Julian Widdowson at Bath Rugby Club in my final season. He was fantastic at identifying the best people for my specific needs at the drop of a hat. When I had my teeth kicked out by Mr Watson at Wetherby Doc Pritchard got me in to see a dentist he knew at nine o'clock that Friday night. He was great at that kind of thing and I owe Doc Pritchard a huge debt of gratitude for patching me up and sending me out again the way he did. Every sports person, especially a jockey, needs a Doc Pritchard to do those things for you. I had him tearing his hair out at times, but he played a big part in my career and was a key part in my keeping going as long as I did. He's a good friend of ours now and we still keep him busy: it's Chanelle that annoys him at inconvenient times these days though, because every time there's something wrong with Eve or Archie, Doc P gets the call.

I look down at my body now that I've retired and see scars

here and lumps there, but overall I think I did pretty well. The scars are fading and if all goes to plan there won't be any new ones either. If I do find myself injured in the future, falling off a ladder with a paintbrush in my hand, say, or turning my ankle over on the golf course, I expect I'll be a little more relaxed about convalescing. Recovering from injuries takes time, and these days time is a commodity I have a little more of than I used to.

NINE

Don't Push It, Aintree
10 April 2010

You know pretty early. By the time you've got over the first couple of fences you have a good idea of what kind of shape you're in and what kind of thinker the horse is. That's crucial in any race but especially in a race like the Grand National, because no matter how good a jockey you are, if the horse doesn't fancy it you won't get him round. In those early stages of the race it's all about getting into a good position, about following the right horse that might be a good, safe jumper, even though there's probably no such thing in the National. You have to give yourself the best possible options and the best possible chances of getting round: as Martin Pipe used to tell me, just get over the first and concentrate on the rest after that. After the third I was pretty happy and when I got to Becher's I knew Don't Push It was liking it as well because he'd got into a really lovely rhythm. It was as if the occasion was absolutely lighting him up.

Once you've completed the first circuit you can have a look

around, weigh things up, see how you're doing and see which horses are going well and which aren't, and by the second circuit I was pretty happy I was on the right horse. You have to believe that you're going to win the Grand National. It's easier to convince yourself of this before the start than it is when you're thundering around the course, but there were times during that race when I genuinely believed I was going to win it. Maybe, at the fourteenth time of asking, this was going to be my year.

I'd known Don't Push It for a long time. Indeed I'd ridden him in his very first outing, a two-mile National Hunt flat race at Warwick at the end of 2004 when he finished third. As a young horse he was very, very good, and I considered him a hugely exciting prospect. I rode him over fences in a novice chase at the Cheltenham November meeting in 2006, ahead of which I'd said to JP, this horse is the business, this horse will win. I'd ridden him to a couple of wins over the previous year at Stratford and Haydock and genuinely regarded Don't Push It as a proper horse. Sadly he was beaten by half a length by Denman that day – at the time I couldn't work out how he lost that race and spent days afterwards mulling it over to no avail, but he was after all bested on that occasion by a horse that became one of the best chasers of the modern era.

Then I rode him in the Arkle at the 2007 Cheltenham Festival where he was going pretty well all the way round until he fell at the second last at the bottom of the hill beside Ruby Walsh on Twist Magic. There's a well-known photograph of Ruby and I trudging back together and you can clearly see how gutted I am because I was convinced Don't Push It would win that race.

After that I felt he became a bit of a timid horse who didn't have the same confidence he'd once had. We'd hoped he could be a Gold Cup horse, but after that fall in the Arkle it took Don't Push It a long time to get back to anything like his old self. He won the odd race but he lost his way after that Cheltenham fall and was probably never as good a horse again, which makes you wonder just how good he could have been.

In 2009 we took him to Aintree where he won the race before the National, the John Smith's Handicap Chase over three miles and a furlong, battling hard to win by nearly four lengths, but a month before the 2010 Grand National Don't Push It ran in the Pertemps Final at the Cheltenham Festival and pulled up at the last when well out of contention. Although I wasn't riding him that day it was a big disappointment and left me with a hard decision to make about my National ride. The other contender was a horse of Jonjo's called Can't Buy Time, who'd won at Cheltenham on New Year's Day and shown a bit of form. Right up until the first day of the Aintree meeting on the Thursday I still didn't have a clear idea of which horse I was going to ride, but in any case didn't think either horse had a great chance. Can't Buy Time had the best recent form whereas Don't Push It was probably a better horse but had clouded the issue by pulling up at Cheltenham a few weeks earlier just when he'd been showing signs of fulfilling his early potential again. Whichever horse I rode, it really needed to pull out all the stops on the day.

Dave Roberts rang me on the Thursday morning and asked which horse it was to be.

'I've still no idea, Dave,' I said. 'But sure, it doesn't really matter anyway, does it? Neither of them is going to win. We might as well just let Jonjo decide.'

Dave said he'd speak to Jonjo, then my phone rang and there was the man himself on the other end.

'Just spoken to Dave, there,' he said. 'So which horse do you want to ride, then?'

'I really have no idea,' I replied.

'Well, I've no idea either.'

'OK, why don't you toss a coin?'

'OK, hang on.'

There was a brief silence on the other end of the line punctuated by a bit of rustling.

'All right,' I said, 'which is it?'

'Don't Push It,' said Jonjo.

'All right, Don't Push It it is, so.'

That was it, decision made. Not in the most scientific way, but there didn't seem to be a scientific solution. Whether Jonjo really did spin a coin or had just decided I'd ride Don't Push It I'll never know, but I didn't feel particularly animated about the horse's prospects either way.

When National day arrives you can't help getting a bit excited no matter how many times you might have ridden in the race before. It's the Grand National after all, the highest profile race in the country if not the world, the one everyone watches, the one that has your office running a sweepstake and your granny handing you a crumpled fiver and asking you to put on her only bet of the year for her. For jockeys, the closer it gets to Grand National day the more the butterflies start and you think, yeah, I am going to fucking win this. I'd thought this every year, of course, fourteen times in all, and as had become widely known at that stage it had never happened for me. I'd had better feelings about the race and better horses in the past than I did in 2010, but on the day I started to think winning might well be on the cards.

Mind you, if you didn't go into the Grand National thinking you had a chance of winning then there wasn't really much point in being there at all. Jonjo and JP always told me to go out and enjoy myself and see how things went, but the only way I was ever truly going to enjoy myself in the Grand National was by winning the thing.

That day I remember walking around at the start with David Casey on Snowy Morning, who pointed over at the big screen and said, 'Jesus, AP, look at the price on Don't Push It'. Two weeks before Aintree he'd been out at 50/1, then he was 33/1. On Grand National morning he'd come down to 25/1. Now, just before the race, I looked up at the screen and saw he'd been backed down to 10/1 joint favourite. I couldn't believe it. There was no way this horse was a favourite for the Grand National.

David gave me a nudge and grinned at me.

'So, how are you going to cope with getting beat on yet another Grand National favourite, then?' he said, with a wink. 'People are starting to get bored of it, you know.'

We had a laugh about it but as I walked around at the start part of me couldn't help thinking, here we go again.

As everyone knows by now, that day, for the first time ever, I wasn't beaten on the Grand National favourite. On the second circuit I tried not to get too excited but the horse was absolutely loving it and I knew that if I kept it simple and stayed out of trouble then he had a great chance of winning. After jumping the last alongside Denis O'Regan on Black Apalachi I did think, just before we got to the elbow, fuck me, this horse is really going to win.

If you're in that kind of position when you clear the last and embark on the long run-in to the finish at Aintree you don't hear the roar of the crowd until you've passed the winning post in first place. Back in third you hear it all the way up. That day I didn't hear a thing until I knew I'd won, then I was up in the irons, roaring with delight and pumping my fist. I'm not normally that emotional when I cross the line, and I'm a bit embarrassed at how that moment has become probably the best-known photograph of me, it gets used everywhere, but the release I felt was extraordinary. It was probably the first time I'd ever such felt an overwhelming sense of relief after a horse race.

The Grand National is the biggest race in the world and one of the biggest sporting events in the world. It's an amazing race to win and gave me a very different feeling from breaking Sir Gordon Richards' record or riding my 4,000th winner. For a start, now I could stop trying to invent excuses. Before 2010 I'd tried to reassure myself that there were better jockeys than me who'd never won it either: John Francome, Peter Scudamore, Charlie Swan and Frank Berry. Jonjo O'Neill never once even got round the course. There you had five jockeys who'd probably won forty jockeys' championships between them yet couldn't point to a single National win. On the other hand the racing writer Marcus Armytage, who co-wrote my newspaper column for a long time and is a good friend, won the National as an amateur on Mr Frisk in 1990. When I was in danger of brooding on my lack of success in the National I'd sometimes think, well, if Marcus can win the National clearly anyone can. I said to him recently, tongue firmly in cheek, I'd watched him ride and I wouldn't let him sit on my front gate let alone a horse, yet he still tells me Mr Frisk holds the course record for winning the National (I countered that Don't Push It carried a lot more weight so actually has a better record than Mr Frisk in *real* terms).

I rode in that race for twenty years – I missed it in 1997 because I was concussed – which is the record for a jockey in the Grand National, albeit a record Richard Johnson is certain to break, so it would have been a bit of a blot on my record to have ridden in more Grand Nationals than anyone else and never won the bloody thing. My career strike rate wasn't exactly great when viewed as a whole, but at least I won it once. It would have been a big gap in my riding CV if I hadn't.

For all my slagging Marcus, the National really is a big deal when you win it. The fact that I won the BBC Sports Personality of the Year award that year demonstrates how big a deal because I'd never have even been in the frame if I hadn't won the National. My profile with the general public was suddenly much higher after that race. Jockeys aren't like footballers: even though racing is the second most televised sport in the country it remains a minority sport and I'd never for one moment felt that I was famous. I'd be invited to sporting events and functions with heroes from other sports and turn up genuinely assuming people wouldn't know who I was, feeling almost embarrassed to be there alongside some of the big names in sport.

Sports Personality of the Year is a wonderful accolade to win and it was a terrific honour, but I am always quick to point out that 2010 was a pretty rotten year for British sport in general so it's not like I was fighting off a host of other claimants. Nobody won anything in that year: Andy Murray didn't win Wimbledon, Lewis Hamilton didn't have much of a season and England were dumped out of the World Cup in pretty shambolic style. To be fair the golfers won the Ryder Cup and I guessed one of them might be in with a chance. Lee Westwood was world number one at the time and Graeme McDowell sank the winning putt, but otherwise there weren't many standout achievements that year, luckily for me. The key factor was that the racing public really got behind me. There was a co-ordinated voting campaign which made me a little bit embarrassed, but I really appreciated all the effort people had gone to and to this day feel very lucky to have won it. It was a good thing for the sport, too. I have a great life as a result of being a jockey so I try to give something back by promoting the sport wherever I can; I hope being the first jockey to win Sports Personality of the Year had a wider effect that benefited more than just me.

It paled in comparison to winning the Grand National, however, for me that was the biggest deal of all – not least because I'd had fourteen goes at it. People with no interest in horse racing know about the Grand National, the kind of people who when they hear you're a jockey ask if you've ever won the National before they ask anything else. After fourteen years of saying no, now I could actually say yes. As well as a personal accomplishment I felt I'd given other people a great deal of happiness too: Jonjo, obviously, and Jackie and the McManuses who were responsible for producing a Grand National-winning horse, my family, Chanelle's family, a lot of the other families involved, but also the people who'd backed me, the people who'd been backing me for years. It made me happy to think I'd given so many people a day to remember.

That feeling had certainly been a long time coming, though. Was I superstitious about it? Did I worry when people talked about me having some kind of Grand National jinx? Not really, no. The only time I'd ever consider that I might never win the National was when I'd walk out of Aintree on the Saturday evening after I'd fallen or finished third or whatever and I'd be in a rotten mood. Then I might wonder if it would ever happen. But that was the only time and it soon passed; indeed by the time the National came around again the following season I'd be thinking, yes, this is my year.

I don't remember a great deal about my first National ride, on Chatam in 1995. I got the ride pretty late and it was my first for Martin Pipe in a big race. Chatam was a very good horse in his day and had won the Hennessy Gold Cup in 1991, but his best years were well behind him by the time the 1995 National came round and he wasn't one of the fancied horses. That's why I, still a conditional jockey, was riding him rather than one of Martin's more likely horses, but being on such an experienced ride was definitely a good thing in my first National even if he did fall at the twelfth. It was a good feeling to have cleared Becher's first time around, a fence that would come back to haunt me in years to come, but at that stage of my career it was more about experience than winning, even though on the day I'd obviously have loved to win.

A year later and I was not only a professional jockey but leading the jockeys' championship as well. My ride Deep Bramble was a good horse and for the first time I felt I had a genuinely good crack at winning. He was going well after the first circuit and with five to jump I was really starting to believe I could win the Grand National in my first year as a professional jockey, but he got injured crossing the Melling Road and I felt him coming back under me and pulled him up. He wasn't a particularly good jumper and I remember a lot of people saying he wouldn't have been the sort of horse they'd have been looking forward to riding, but he actually jumped very well and I got a very good ride off him.

Ah well, there's always next year.

But there wasn't, as it turned out. I'd hit my head in a fall at Uttoxeter riding a horse called Strong Tel a couple of weeks before the 1997 National and was stood down for three weeks. It was the year of the IRA bomb scare when the whole place had to be evacuated and, as I wasn't riding, I was at the course doing a bit of work for the BBC. I was probably the only jockey in Liverpool on that Saturday night that had clothes – the lads had all changed into their colours when the order to evacuate came and none of them had anything with them. I think it might have served a few of the young lads well with the ladies of Liverpool that night, even if they did look more like they were on a stag do than professional sportsmen there for the biggest race in the calendar.

If I hadn't been out with concussion I would probably have ridden Belmont King for Paul Nicholls that year. He got very upset during all the hullabaloo of the bomb scare, and when the horses were moved to Haydock Park he became very worked up. By the time the race was eventually run on the Monday Paul felt the stress had taken too much out of the horse and pulled him out of the race. It was a tough thing to do as he'd been aiming for the National all year, but he kept him back instead for the Scottish National the following Saturday when I was back from my enforced lay-off and able to ride Belmont King to victory. So something good came out of the disruption in the end.

My return to Aintree the following year went about as badly as it possibly could, falling at the first on Challenger Du Luc. I'd genuinely believed he was tailor-made for the National as well, and if I could have picked any horse to ride that year Challenger Du Luc would have been my first choice. He was a big preening ponce of a horse, a right poser, and I would have thought he was the one horse that would have taken things carefully rather than get stuck right in straightaway. Instead for some reason he took off at the start like his arse was on fire. Whether the occasion got to him I don't know but as he got closer to the first he was getting faster and faster. So fast in fact that he didn't so much jump the fence as try and head butt his way through it. Being a gymnast, he did a rather elegant somersault and dumped both of us on the ground on the other side of the fence. I ended up watching more of that race than riding in it. There's nothing worse than getting yourself excited about riding in racing's biggest spectacle of the year in front of a global audience of hundreds of millions and for it to be all over in about thirty seconds leaving you with a muddy arse and spitting out a mouthful of grass.

By 1999 not only had I never won the National I'd never once even ridden the race to a finish. Nobody was talking about jinxes yet, however, and I felt I had another good horse that year in Eudipe, owned by the Johnsons. He'd finished second in the Sun Alliance Chase, was a very good horse, and was travelling well when he knuckled over at Becher's the second time around. I was OK but poor Eudipe was killed. Those were the days of the old Becher's before the 2005 rebuilding of the brook and the changes made in 2011, and it was a hard one to take. I still believe Eudipe had a good chance of winning that day. It was tough, not nice, and there's no doubt the changes made to the Grand National course in recent years have made it far more horse friendly which is definitely a good thing.

My first National of the new millennium saw me fall off Dark Stranger at the third, meaning that I arrived at Aintree in 2001 still waiting just to complete a Grand National, let alone win one. But the horse I was riding gave me serious cause to believe that I was about to crack it.

Blowing Wind was probably the one horse other than Don't Push It that I'd have said would definitely win a Grand National. He was brilliant and had enough speed to win the County Hurdle at Cheltenham in 1998 (of which more later). Whenever Martin Pipe had a lot of runners in the National I'd go over to the gallops and ride them all to see which one I liked. That year we had ten horses lined up for the race and Blowing Wind was obviously the best horse of the bunch.

He jumped brilliantly on the first circuit and when we embarked on the second there were only seven horses left in the race after a big pile up at the Canal Turn caused by a loose horse called Paddy's Retreat. One of the seven was Beau who made a bad mistake at the first fence on the second circuit and lost his reins, effectively leaving only six horses in contention. Ruby Walsh was on the previous year's winner Papillon, I was on Blowing Wind and there was also Smarty, Red Marauder, Brave Highlander, Unsinkable Boxer and Beau. Going past the winning post the first time round I saw Chester Barnes, Martin Pipe's assistant, standing inside and I shouted, 'I bet you can't believe I'm still here,' as I went past. I was growing in confidence with every fence, as Blowing Wind was giving me a really great ride. Then at the nineteenth a couple of loose horses ran across the front of the fence, causing Brave Highlander to unseat Philip Hide, Papillon to turf off Ruby, and Blowing Wind to have me on my arse too. And that appeared to be that.

Ruby and I picked ourselves up, dusted ourselves down and noticed our two horses among half a dozen other loose animals up in the corner at the back of the previous fence. On the big screen we saw the reinless Carl Llewellyn finally unseated by Beau at the next fence, meaning there were just two horses left in the Grand National. Ruby and I looked at each other, looked back at the screen, looked at each other again and said, let's give it a go. We ran over to the horses and I suddenly thought, hang on, which one's Blowing Wind? I think I would have spotted him but luckily enough in the National they had names as well as numbers on the horses. We remounted, kicked the horses into action and off we went. When we jumped the sixth last fence it was obvious Papillon was pretty knackered, so I said to Ruby we'd go easy and help one another until the last fence and have a race then. Red Marauder won and Smarty was second, then some time later I came in third on Blowing Wind with Ruby the last to finish on Papillon. It makes for quite a good story now but at the time I was desperately disappointed by the way the race turned out. I'm convinced that under more normal National circumstances, Blowing Wind would have gone on to win that day. He's a horse that definitely should have won a Grand National and that should have been his year. Finishing the race for the first time was no real consolation to me in the circumstances, especially as if it happened today I wouldn't have finished because you can no longer remount after a fall, because that horse should have won.

I rode Blowing Wind again the following year and came in third again, in more conventional circumstances this time, but he was well off the pace and well beaten. His time had gone. Right from the start he didn't feel the same as he had the previous year and I knew it wasn't on. At least I'd found myself a safe conveyance around the Grand National course and I was able to finish, if nothing else, but it just made the previous year's race even more frustrating. That was his race, his time, and it was taken away from him by the luck factor that weighs so heavily on the Grand National, good and bad.

After a fall and a pull-up in the next two Nationals, I rode Clan Royal in the 2005 race. He was very keen all the way round the first circuit, pulling very hard from early in the race even though his saddle had slipped. He wasn't the cleverest horse I've ever ridden but he was a good jumper and going well, and as we started out on the last circuit I was convinced he would take some beating. There were a few loose horses around him so before Becher's I went out wide in an effort to get away from them. Unfortunately a couple came with me and as we got closer to Becher's two of the loose horses turned with me and they carried him out.

I was absolutely gutted and felt like crying. It was the worst I'd ever felt at the Grand National as I'd really believed he could win. Looking back now I'm not so sure he would have done because Hedgehunter was a very good winner and a very convincing winner, but certainly at the time I was sure he'd been in with a chance. I came back in spitting and said to Jonjo that it was the worst day ever, the worst thing that could ever happen.

Jonjo was quick to pull me up.

'No, it isn't,' he said. 'That's not the worst thing that could ever happen, not by a long way. Believe me, the worst thing that could ever happen is lying in a hospital bed waiting for the doctor to come in and tell you whether you're going to live or die. That, my friend, is the worst day ever. I should know. I've been there.'

I'd been so wrapped up in the terrible injustice that had befallen me that I'd completely overlooked the fact that Jonjo had beaten cancer a few years earlier. It was a jolting reality check, one that worked instantly and taught me a valuable lesson about how to cope with setbacks. Whatever happened to me at the races it could always have been a lot worse.

Even so, being carried out at the Grand National is always extra-frustrating because it's caused by factors outside you and your ride. Falling isn't so bad in comparison, because that's between you and the horse. If you make a mistake it impacts on the horse and vice versa, either way the responsibility stays in-house. It's frustrating and galling of course, but when you're taken out of the race by factors entirely out of your or the horse's control it's a pretty rotten feeling. If you fall of your own accord, well then you weren't meant to win that year, but when you're carried out by another horse or horses it's proper bad luck.

I rode Clan Royal again the following year but it was essentially a repeat of the Blowing Wind situation: his time was gone. No excuses like being carried out this time, his chance had just gone. Third behind Numbersixvalverde and Hedgehunter was no disgrace but a year earlier, maybe, and no loose horses forcing us out and we might have had a winner together. He stayed in contention until the second last fence and whenever you're still among the leading bunch at that stage of the National you know you're in with a shout. It's between the second last and last that the winners are separated from the losers and you know whether you're going to make it or not. The dream stays alive all the way around but it's at that stage the reality sets in. It happened that year on Clan Royal, he just didn't have enough left, and the same thing happened on Shutthefrontdoor in my last National in 2015.

I got round again on L'Ami the following year, coming in tenth out of twelve finishers. L'Ami was trained for JP by François

Doumen in France and was a decent horse. I hadn't ridden him much but Mick Fitzgerald had been on him quite a few times and had said he was a brilliant jumper who'd give me a great ride at Aintree. I hadn't particularly liked watching him because I always found him a bit straight-backed but Mick was right, I did get a very good ride off him. Just not good enough. The following year Mick was down to ride him and asked me what I thought.

'He's brilliant, Fitzy,' I said, 'I can't see you getting a better ride than him.'

Sadly he fell at the second, and Mick sustained a terrible back injury that led to him hanging up his silks. He never rode again. When it happened all I could think about was the look in his eyes the previous year when he was telling me what a great ride L'Ami was and seeing the same look when I told him the same thing a year later.

I rode Butler's Cabin in the next two Nationals, falling at Becher's the second time around in 2008 and getting a better ride off him the following year but, yet again, the horse had missed his chance.

In 2011 I rode Don't Push It again, hoping lightning might strike twice. It was a strange feeling walking into Aintree and not having everyone wondering whether finally this would be my year. At last there was the little plaque over my peg that every National winner has in the Aintree changing room. But we couldn't repeat the previous year's triumph and, despite Don't Push It running a great race we came in third. He jumped really well but it was probably the weight that beat him, in hindsight.

The next year of course saw the tragedy that befell Synchronised and after that I attempted to exorcise the terrible memories on first Colbert Station and then Double Seven. Colbert Station had won the Paddy Power at Christmas before the 2013 National. He was a decent horse but I knew from a long way out that he wasn't going to win and although he was usually a very good jumper he unseated me at The Chair. Very few horses fell that year but he was one of them. He'd started the race as one of the leading fancies, and I would certainly have bet on him if I was a punter, but then again on National day I'd have bet on every horse I rode.

Double Seven started the 2014 National as joint favourite. If you'd said to me earlier in the year Double Seven was going to be my ride in the Grand National I'd have laughed at you. If you'd said he was going to be joint favourite in the National I'd have laughed again because I didn't think he was anywhere near good enough. As it turned out, though, he ran an unbelievably good race to come in third despite picking up a little injury on the way round.

While I have a number of Grand National memories filed away in my head, obviously Don't Push It is the one that stands out. A great horse who truly rose to the occasion to give me one of the most memorable rides of my career. Winning the National became for me a bigger deal than it probably should have done with the fourteen-year wait I endured before riding a winner. It's a race that deserves its place among Britain's premier sporting events, but for me it's not the top race of them all. The Grand National witnessed the heartbreaking end to the horse that won the top race of them all for me when, a month before the 2012 race, Synchronised won the Cheltenham Gold Cup.

TEN

Synchronised, Cheltenham
16 March 2012

Jonjo felt the horse had a chance, but he wasn't necessarily expecting great things from Synchronised going into the Lexus Chase at Leopardstown at the end of December 2011. He'd had a couple of good wins at that stage, the Midlands Grand National in 2010 and the Welsh Grand National in January 2011 after it was put back a couple of weeks because of the bad weather, but 2011 was proving to be an anticlimactic year after those two promising wins. His win in the Midlands National was his first in a race of any note and the first real indication that he was a proper racehorse, while his Welsh National victory had been his most assured, accomplished run yet.

Yet after that he didn't really perform. After the Welsh National he ran the Midlands again but with a big weight, a 16lb increase, and on drier ground than when he'd won the year before. It was only his second race over fences in a year, and at one stage he was so far out of contention it even crossed my mind to pull him up.

When Grand National day arrives you can't help getting a bit excited, because it's the highest-profile race in the country if not the world, the one everyone watches. But it's a notoriously difficult race to win, and I had my fair share of disappointments over the years: I twice finished third on Blowing Wind, in 2001 and 2002 (*above*), and I was carried out by two loose horses at Becher's Brook when in contention with Clan Royal in 2005 (*below*).

When I finally did win the race, on Don't Push It in 2010, the release I felt was extraordinary. It was probably the first time I'd ever such felt an overwhelming sense of relief after a horse race. Aintree, 10 April 2010.

Peter Kay presented me with my trophy. Aintree, 10 April 2010.

Winning the Grand National was as much for the people who have supported me, none more so than Chanelle, as it was for me. Aintree, 10 April 2010.

The best horses win the Gold Cup and that makes it the best race of them all as far as I'm concerned. Cheltenham, 16 March 2012.

I've felt close to countless horses over the years but Synchronised was truly special. Cheltenham, 16 March 2012.

The Gold Cup is the true barometer of National Hunt racing and the yardstick by which to judge racehorses. Cheltenham, 16 March 2012.

I was adamant that I wanted to ride my 4,000th winner on one of JP's horses. I wanted to look back at the photographs and see myself in the green and gold, the same colours I'd been wearing on Don't Push It, Synchronised and in all the other great moments of the second half of my career. Riding Mountain Tunes, Towcester, 7 November 2013.

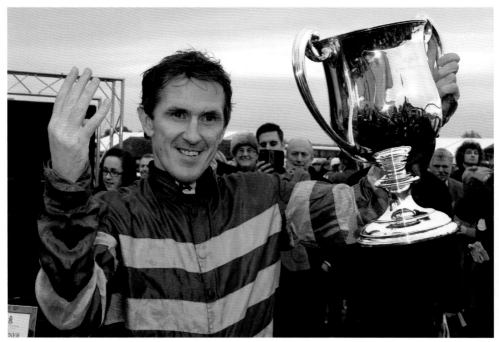

One day, now I'm out of the way, someone may well break my record of 289 winners in a season. I'm pretty convinced, though, that no jump jockey will ever ride 4,000 winners again. Towcester, 7 November 2013.

One of the positives of retirement is that I will get to spend more time with my family. (*Above from left to right*: Colm, Roisin, Jane, me, Ma (Claire), Dad (Peader; and below), Kelly, Annemarie.)

I absolutely dote on Eve and Archie. Being a dad has made me a different person, a better person.

But from five out something seemed to click and he produced a thunderous finish to come in third, a finish so committed and exhausting that he nearly collapsed coming off the track. That underlines just how tough a horse he must have been because that could have been the end for many horses.

Five weeks before the Lexus he ran over hurdles at Haydock but came in third, and that followed a disappointing run at Aintree in a Pertemps qualifier in October, but at Leopardstown something clicked. He ran with a combination of stamina and class, powering away after the final fence to win by almost nine lengths. Winning the Lexus was a big step up for Synchronised, and to do it in such style and so convincingly made Jonjo wonder whether he might be a Gold Cup horse rather than the National contender he'd had in mind all along.

What to do? The Irish Hennessy in mid-February would be the perfect barometer of his Gold Cup credentials but there was a problem. Synchronised was a horse that needed time to get over his races and definitely ran better when he'd had a good break after his previous run. It took the horse an awfully long time to get over the Lexus and Jonjo found himself struggling to have him ready in time for the Irish Hennessy. In the end he took the decision to withdraw him in order that he be fresh, keen and ready for the Gold Cup. It was a gamble, all right, but this was a special horse.

The Gold Cup of 2012 had a fairly open field, with Long Run, who'd won the King George VI Chase, the favourite. Other contenders were the The Giant Bolster and Burton Port, and the fact that Kauto Star had been a bit under the weather in the run-up to the race led to talk he might not be at this best. I'd heard rumours he might have had some kind of fall at home, either way the word was that he wasn't in top condition, but although this was encouraging news for the rest even a slightly out of sorts Kauto Star was a match for most horses. There were some excellent, evenly matched horses running and stiff opposition for Synchronised, yet aside from Long Run winning the King George none of the other main contenders had been in any better form than he had in the run up to Cheltenham. He may have missed the Irish Hennessy but the Lexus, being a grade one, had been an excellent dry run and meant he would be fresh and well into the bargain. Certainly on the face of it, Jonjo and I thought none of the other contenders had more outstanding claims than he did and were quietly confident he could do well.

Synchronised went into the Gold Cup in good shape and Jonjo was glad he'd pulled him from the Irish Hennessy. If he'd run him at Leopardstown there was no way he'd have been in the kind of form to take on a Gold Cup field. In fact Jonjo was only truly happy with Synchronised in the last week before the festival, which cut it fine enough. As things stood though, when the Friday of the festival dawned I looked down the list of Gold Cup runners in the racecard and knew we had a pretty decent chance.

Synchronised wasn't a slow horse, far from it, but it did take him a while to get warmed up when racing. He was the sort of horse that if he ran three miles and then had to run a fourth, he'd run that fourth mile faster than any of the previous three. The further he ran the quicker and keener he got. As we lined up at the start I knew it was just a matter of keeping him in contention, keeping him in touch enough over the first couple of miles that he could power through and win in the later stages. It proved trickier than I'd anticipated as for the first half of the race he seemed to be really struggling. He was off the bridle, only just hanging onto the back of the field, able to just about hold his position and even then it felt like a struggle. But knowing Synchronised as I did I was aware that as long as he held his position he was far from out of the race. Still, even going out on the final circuit, once Ruby had pulled up Kauto Star early in the race he was probably going the worst of all the runners. If you were watching the race you wouldn't have given Synchronised a hope in hell. Jonjo told me later that he was watching the race in a box with a bunch of people who didn't know a huge amount about racing. They were shaking their heads saying he was too far behind, he'd lost it, he had no chance, and Jonjo was trying to explain to them that no, this is how he runs, this is the kind of horse he is, he's still close enough, watch him go, just watch him go.

Gradually, bit by bit, I felt Synchronised start to pick up, a surge of excitement rising in my stomach as I sensed him building momentum. With five to jump he was still at the back of the group and still not giving off any signs of a potential winner but I knew what was coming. The only people at the races who had an inkling of what was about to happen were Jonjo in the stands and me on the horse. When we reached the top of the hill there were still five horses in with a chance and Synchronised was the last of them behind Time For Rupert, Burton Port, The Giant Bolster and Long Run. He was hanging onto the back still about four lengths adrift with three to jump, but knowing Synchronised I was convinced he was still close enough. When he got round the bend I knew for sure he was close enough because I could feel him picking up, feel his momentum building with every stride, and although I was racing as hard as I ever had in my life I felt a calmness fall across my mind, as if subconsciously I somehow knew what was about to happen.

As soon as he started to meet the rising ground he started going up through the gears. When he passed Burton Port between the second last and the last I could almost hear Jonjo's voice in my head telling everyone that nothing was going to stay up the hill faster or better than Synchronised. I could feel him getting stronger, reeling in the other horses, and in the last furlong up towards the finish it was almost as if the others were standing still, he just surged further ahead with every stride. Synchronised was still getting faster as he passed the winning post after a brilliant, brilliant performance in which he peaked at exactly the right time. If it was a thrilling finish to watch, just imagine how it felt to ride.

In many ways Synchronised was still more of a Grand National horse than a Gold Cup horse, but to win the Gold Cup you need a ride that stays and no horse stayed like Synchronised. Especially that year, because the 2012 Gold Cup was a real stayers' race. It's a gruelling contest for a horse at the best of times, physically and mentally, because it's run at flat-out pace from start to finish: there's no let-up and absolutely no place to hide, which is tough on the horses. In fact, for me the Gold Cup is just as gruelling a race as the National. The National gets the headlines – ask anyone their opinion on Britain's toughest horse race and they'll all say the National – but for me the Gold Cup is just as demanding because it's the best horses in the land bringing out the best in each other at the fastest pace. The Grand National may be the most famous race in the world but the Gold Cup will always be for me the peak horse racing contest of them all. The best horses didn't always win the National, the Desert Orchids, the Kauto Stars, the Arkles, some of the greatest National Hunt horses, but the best horses won the Gold Cup and that makes it the best race of them all as far as I'm concerned.

The National is worth a lot of money and it's the most famous race in the world. Everyone, not just racing fans, has heard of the Grand National but not everyone knows the Cheltenham Gold Cup. That makes it more of a race for racing people too, which might be what makes it extra special. Everyone in racing is intrigued to know who'll win the Gold Cup because then they'll know the best horse to have raced that year. The Gold Cup is the true barometer of National Hunt racing and the yardstick by which to judge racehorses.

The Gold Cup doesn't suit all horses, even some very good ones, but it suited Synchronised better than most. He gave me the most amazing ride that day and that's the main reason why when I'm asked to list my favourite horses Synchronised is always there at number one. Winning that race is obviously the main reason behind that but there's more to it than just the Gold Cup. I've felt close to countless horses over the years but Synchronised was truly special. We had a bond that went back to before he was born, even: you might remember that the first time I won for J.P. McManus back on 25 April 1996 at Punchestown, the day I met my future wife, I'd won on his dam, Mayasta. That day will always be special to me for personal and professional reasons, so to think that almost exactly sixteen years later I was to win the Gold Cup on Mayasta's son really was something very special. It was also Jonjo's first Gold Cup win as a trainer and JP's first as an owner. Not only that, Synchronised was home-bred, sired by the great Irish flat horse Sadler's Wells. The huge irony was that JP had spent years trying to buy a Gold Cup winner and in the end his wife Noreen managed to breed him one right on the doorstep. Synchronised being a McManus horse to his very bones gave that 2012 Gold Cup win another layer of emotional depth and there was such a confluence of so many good things about that race and that horse that day that you would almost wonder if the stars were aligned and it was pre-destined.

Synchronised was, I felt, very like me. He wasn't the most naturally gifted horse and he certainly wasn't the best looking horse, but he had that cast-iron will to win that outgunned any perceived shortfalls in talent or ability. Synchronised showed that if you have that determination to succeed embedded at your very core it can take you a very long way indeed, even if the other odds aren't exactly stacked in your favour.

Everything came together that day. Call it happenstance, call it serendipity, call it what you like, but whenever I think back to the 2012 Gold Cup I always find myself marvelling at how everything about that day was, well, synchronised.

One unexpected consequence of winning the Gold Cup that year was that I ended up in Las Vegas. On the Tuesday of Cheltenham Jamie Moore, a lad I've known since he was a child, managed to get himself suspended for seven days. Once he'd finally stopped moaning about it he decided he was going to use the break to get away to Vegas and was going around the weighing room trying to rope in some of the other lads. After three days of constant badgering still he had no takers. I'd heard enough about this Vegas thing by then so I said to him, 'Jamie, if it'll shut you up, I'll bring you to Vegas myself if I win the Gold Cup, OK?'

After that no one at Cheltenham was cheering louder for

Synchronised than Jamie Moore, and funnily enough one of the first things to cross my mind when I passed the winning post was, shit, I can't go back on my word now, I'll have to bring Jamie to Vegas. Carl Llewellyn decided he'd go too and we fixed a date for the middle of September and booked the flights. A guy called Mike Hunter, through Carl, very kindly booked us a hotel in Vegas, a fantastic three-bedroom suite at the Vdara Hotel beside the Bellagio. Jamie's dad is the racehorse trainer Gary Moore. A few weeks before we went Jamie said that one of his dad's owners had got wind we were going to Vegas and wanted to come too. This owner, a man called Jerry Hynes, was just getting divorced for the second time and as he was in need of a bit of cheering up had asked Jamie to see if we minded if he came along too. It was fine with me and Carl so there we were, four of us heading to Vegas. Then three weeks ahead of the trip Jamie said that one of his best friends from Brighton, a guy called James Pennock, a tattoo artist, wanted to come along too. His girlfriend was an air hostess and could get him a cheap flight if we were happy for him to join us. No problem, I said, I don't mind him coming at all. Fast forward to a Wednesday morning in September and the gang of us all met at Gatwick airport. Carl and I were there first, then Jamie arrived with Jerry, who is a really nice man. At the last minute James Pennock wandered up, just as we were starting to wonder where he'd got to. He introduced himself and my first thought was that he was everything Carl Llewellyn doesn't like in a bloke. James had a rucksack over his back, a pair of shorts on, flip-flops, this scruffy T-shirt, his hair's all over the place and he's unshaven. Carl is always one for the grooming, he's very particular about that, so the sight of James must have been something out of his worst nightmare. What also made you hate James was that he's about as good-looking a bloke as you'll ever see in your life. He dropped his bag and headed off to the toilet, whereupon Carl turned to me open-mouthed and said, 'Look at the state of that scruffy so and so.'

Anyway, off we went to Vegas and James and Jerry turned out to be brilliant, really nice lads, and we all hit it off great. On the first night we went to a nightclub where we first witnessed the Pennock Effect: from the moment we walked in every woman in Las Vegas seemed to be looking at James. Carl, being single, thought this was the best thing that had ever happened to him, standing next to this guy as the entire female population of the city was drawn to James like moths to a flame. 'I'll stick by him and happily oblige if he needs a bit of help,' he told me. That's Carl, utterly selfless, always thinking of what he can do for other people.

By four o'clock in the morning James had, after a rigorous selection process that broke many hearts, narrowed down the field to a Mexican girl called Tania who lived in San Francisco, and the two of them disappeared off into the breaking desert dawn together. Jamie, Carl, Jerry and I gravitated to the casino in the Bellagio and by half-past seven in the morning when we called it a night there was still no sign of Pennock.

At lunchtime the next day Pennock arrived back at the hotel, dealt with the predictable inquisition like a gentleman but said he didn't think he'd see her again.

At four o'clock the next morning the five of us were making our way to the Bellagio when we saw Pennock on the phone. He saw us looking at him, put his hand over the phone and mouthed the word, 'Tania'. And that was pretty much the last we saw of him until it was time to go home after what had been a fantastic few days.

A month or so later, Jamie collared me at the races and said, 'You remember Pennock, right?'

'Of course I do,' I replied. 'How is he?'

'Well,' said Jamie, 'he's only gone and finished with the girl-friend, the one who worked in the travel industry, and is heading out to San Francisco to see Tania.'

I couldn't believe it! So much for what plays in Vegas stays in Vegas.

Six months later I was racing at Fontwell, which isn't far from Brighton, and Jamie came up to me in the weighing room and said Pennock was outside and wanted to see me. I popped outside and sure enough, there he was. Not only that, he had someone with him.

'Hi, AP,' he said. 'You remember Tania, from the Vegas trip?'

Of course I did. It turned out that Tania was over in England studying at a college in Brighton, which was great for Pennock and, well, quite the coincidence . . . The next thing I knew, in the summer of 2014 a wedding invitation landed on our doormat requesting the pleasure of Chanelle and my company at the wedding of Pennock and Tania in San Francisco, where he lives today as a happily married man.

On top of everything else Synchronised had been indirectly responsible for a marriage and an emigration. So many things came together as a result of that race, it was a brilliant day that brought pleasure to so many people with ramifications that ex-tended way beyond the confines of Cheltenham racecourse and a fantastic race won by one of the great Gold Cup horses.

What makes a great Gold Cup horse? For me they're a classier type of animal all round, with pace and stamina and maybe just a little bit more about them than a National horse. Few horses seem to adapt fully to the demands of both races. Long Run won the Gold Cup in 2011, for example, but when he ran in the 2014 Grand National he fell at Valentine's. Many Clouds won my last National in 2015 but in the Gold Cup a few weeks earlier he couldn't finish higher than sixth. Each race suits some horses better than others. Synchronised seemed to be more of a Grand National horse before we regarded him as a Gold Cup horse because he'd won the Midlands National over four miles one furlong then the Welsh Grand National over three miles five, both of which are extreme distances for a racehorse, but the three-mile Lexus Chase showed that he was a natural Gold Cup runner.

As you'll have gathered by now I love the Cheltenham Festival and the Gold Cup in particular. Yes there's the National and the King George VI Chase and any number of other great races in Britain and Ireland, but Cheltenham was always the first date I'd look for in the racing calendar, the highlight of my racing year and the meeting I looked forward to the most. I had some good Cheltenhams, some great Cheltenhams and some rotten Cheltenhams over the years, but I never had a single dull Cheltenham. It's an event like no other because every horse is geared up to winning the Cheltenham Festival: you go to the sales at the beginning of the year, ask people what are they looking for and they'll all be trying to find a horse that can win at Cheltenham. If a horse wins at the festival a lot of owners and trainers will put them away for the rest of the season, thinking, he's done enough, we'll mind him now until next year.

Cheltenham has the best atmosphere largely because it has

the best horses and the best racing: it's like the finals, where the best in the sport compete in front of 60,000 people every day. There's no atmosphere in racing like it, it's racing as pure theatre and the air crackles with the intensity of it all. The crowd is what lifts any big sporting event to a different level and the Cheltenham crowds are like no other, the most enthusiastic and knowledgeable people who ever gather at a racecourse. Traditionally there's a big Irish contingent at Cheltenham too, which adds extra fizz to the atmosphere. The Irish who come over to the festival contribute massively to making it what it is, bringing a huge fun element to it and helping to lift Cheltenham head and shoulders above any other race meeting. As an Irishman, whenever I'd win a race I could sense the electric charge in the air as the atmosphere lifted even more. It's the same for any winner with Irish connections, like a little piece of the country has transplanted itself across the Irish Sea. It helps that Paddy's Day usually falls during the festival too, and people even make it their annual holiday, coming over year after year, booking the following year's accommodation as they leave. In my view no other racing event – and very few sporting events in general – has that sense of ritual and that draw that's about more than just sport. Even without the wonderful, knowledgeable crowds that flock to the racecourse every year, even if you ran it in front of empty stands, Cheltenham would be the pinnacle of the jumps season because of the sheer quality of horses and races involved. Adding the crowd factor to the equation helps to make it one of the premier sporting events in the British calendar.

My first ride at the Cheltenham Festival was seventeen years and two days before I won on Synchronised and you couldn't devise a greater contrast if you tried. A month earlier I'd ridden

Supreme Master for Claire Johnsey to a good win in a novices' hurdle at Ascot over two miles, but at Cheltenham over the same distance he was out in the betting at 100/1 before the race. He travelled well for most of the way, but where Synchronised got faster as the race went on Supreme Master was going backwards over the last few flights and finished sixteenth. But I was, what, twenty years old, in my first season in England as a conditional and riding at my first Cheltenham so I couldn't really complain. I'm sure I did, though. Straightaway I was captivated by the atmosphere and the pageantry that are unique to Cheltenham and I knew immediately that I wanted more of it. But I also wanted to win.

Recently I went to Eve's school sports day. The teachers there were big on the 'it's about taking part' message, that winning isn't important. Whenever I hear that it strikes me as the biggest load of bollocks I've ever heard, because no sport is just about taking part – it's about winning. Why would you even bother in the first place if you weren't trying to win? On that first day at Cheltenham, 14 March 1995, I would certainly have been happy to be taking part, but I wasn't just there to make up the numbers.

Two days later, I was riding in my first Gold Cup. Toby Balding's Beech Road was another horse with long odds. He'd been a great hurdler in his day and had a lot of success under Richard Guest, including a thrilling finish to win the Champion Hurdle in 1989. He wasn't so good over fences, however, and at thirteen years old in the 1995 Gold Cup he started at 100/1, odds that seemed vindicated as the horse was never truly in contention and came in seventh. He gave me a good ride, though, and I took a small amount of pleasure from the fact we finished ahead of the previous year's winner Jodami. Most of all I was intoxicated by the whole experience of riding in the pinnacle steeplechase of the National Hunt season and my first experience of racing in front of an enormous crowd. I was very conscious of it in the parade ring, more so than during the race itself, as I looked across from my lofty position on the horse at the constantly moving tides of faces and the noisy hubbub of these thousands of racegoers, but it didn't make me nervous or uneasy because I just couldn't wait to get out there and ride a horse in the Gold Cup. Races like that were part of the reason I wanted to be a jockey. Even as a kid I knew all about the Cheltenham Gold Cup: I'd watched it on the television and my dad and Billy knew people who'd travelled over to England to watch it, some of them every year. To be riding in it myself only five years after I'd left Billy's made me proud as I pictured everyone gathered around the television at home, looking out for me in the pack, listening for my name in the commentary.

I had a few rides at Cheltenham the following year, but one clear memory of that particular festival was a row with a trainer whose name I'm not going to mention here because I reckon she doesn't deserve the ink. We had an argument over a horse I was supposed to ride for her and her husband at the festival but I decided instead to ride a few other horses for David Nicholson. His jockey Adrian Maguire had been injured in a fall which freed up some very good rides which David asked me if I'd be interested in taking. One was Jack Tanner in the Sun Alliance Hurdle, a horse called Zabadi in the Triumph Hurdle, and a really good horse called Barton Bank in the Gold Cup. I sensed it was an all-or-nothing offer and these rides were too good to turn down, so I went with David. When I spoke to this husband and wife training team and told them I wasn't going to ride their horse they didn't take it well. They probably did have the roots of a grievance but sometimes these things happen, it's part of racing. David Nicholson was a champion trainer and he'd specifically asked for me once it was clear Adrian was out of contention, so there was never any question in my mind that riding for David was the right thing for me to do. However, no matter how much justification they might have felt they had, and it wasn't much, I thought their reaction was completely out of proportion to the situation. Let's just say that I got a call from the trainer's wife – the trainer himself having already registered his displeasure with Dave Roberts – telling me in no uncertain terms exactly what she thought of me. I thought it was over the top and lacked class, not to mention the fact their horse ran out at the first flight anyway; but what a thing to do, no matter how aggrieved you might feel. The horse still ran and a good jockey still rode it, it really wasn't that important.

At the end of it all, however, I still had a fair few good rides in 1996. It was my first year going for the jockeys' title and I was leading in the championship going into Cheltenham, where I'd never won. Granted I'd had barely a handful of rides at that stage, but being ahead in the championship in my first year as a professional made me aware of a little more pressure on me. Could this upstart hack it on the biggest stage of all? Could he prove he was as good as his place in the jockeys' championship might suggest?

In the Sun Alliance I had a good ride on Jack Tanner; he was in touch most of the way round, but a mistake at the third last saw him drop out of contention. It was a similar story on Zabadi the following day in the Triumph Hurdle. I felt Barton Bank was a good shout for the Gold Cup, though. The previous season he should have won the King George VI Chase at Kempton but when well clear going into the last he somehow managed to unseat Adrian Maguire. Again despite being in touch most of the way round in the Gold Cup, a mistake at the seventh pulled us back from the leaders and Barton Bank came in a long way behind the winner, Conor O'Dwyer on Imperial Call. Seven years earlier as 'wee Anthony' I'd led up Conor at Downpatrick when he rode a winner on a horse of Billy Rock's called Wood Louse. Now here we were, both of us riding in the Cheltenham Gold Cup. Billy must have been as proud as punch.

My final ride that year was on Kibreet in the Grand Annual for Philip Hobbs, and by that stage I think I'd have sold my granny to win a race, any race, at Cheltenham. Kibreet was a good shout. I'd won on him at Ascot the previous November and, while he hadn't covered himself in glory since I knew Philip had been preparing him all year with the Grand Annual in mind. Sure enough we came home by a good four lengths for my first ever win at the Cheltenham Festival. It was a significant win, not just in the hindsight terms of the amazing bond I'd develop with the festival over the next couple of decades, but in making me feel not only that I'd arrived but also that I belonged. Being top of the jockeys' championship in my first professional season probably had a few people in the game watching me with a keen critical eye, and coming away with no winners might have left question marks over my suitability to sit at the top table. I wouldn't have liked that much, but winning on Kibreet helped to demonstrate that I meant business and was worthy of the position my stats had put me in. I also took a tiny bit of additional satisfaction from the fact a certain lady would have opened the papers to read about me winning rather than the misfortune she'd wished upon me.

My 1997 Cheltenham didn't get off to a great start when I had a bit of a falling out with Martin Pipe before racing got under way after I was held up at a corporate reception, making me a few minutes late for an event he was hosting for his Racing Club. After Martin had let me know of his displeasure in no uncertain terms I went out and rode Or Royal for him and David Johnson in the Arkle. Or Royal was a very good horse on whom I'd been beaten at Ascot a few months earlier because he'd hit the front too soon. He wasn't a horse that should be in the lead too early because it basically made him stop, so in the Arkle I knew I had to hold him back as far as I could in the early stages and tuck in behind the leaders. When Richard Dunwoody took a tumble on the highly fancied Mulligan four out I knew my chances had just got better and as we came to the second last it was between Or Royal and Jamie Osborne on Squire Silk. A slight mistake from Or Royal at that fence lost us vital ground but the horse had a great will to win and hauled Squire Silk back to win by half a length.

The winning feeling was tempered slightly by the bust-up with Martin earlier in the day, and when he came to say well done I gobbed off at him which, whatever the rights and wrongs, wasn't the way to address the situation. To Martin's credit he didn't react, indeed, the incident was never referred to again and I turned my attention to the next race, the Champion Hurdle. I'm still a little bit embarrassed about the incident, though.

Make A Stand had improved out of all recognition from the beginning of the season. Since being beaten in a handicap hurdle at Cheltenham's November meeting the horse had improved by, no exaggeration, three stone by the time the Champion Hurdle came around. He'd just got better and better as the year went on and I'd had good wins on him at Ascot and at Kempton. I was injured for the Tote Gold Trophy at Newbury in early February but Chris Maude rode him to what was Make A Stand's fourth consecutive win and in one of the season's more prestigious handicap hurdles, too.

He was still a novice so could have run in the novice hurdle at the start of the day, but Martin being the genius that he is decided to put him straight into the Champion Hurdle instead, and what a great decision that turned out to be. In contrast to Or Royal in the previous race Make A Stand made all the running from the off and I don't think I even saw another horse. He'd had a pretty mediocre career on the Flat, but Martin had had an inkling he'd make a brilliant jumper and he was absolutely right. This fair-to-middling flat horse had been transformed into a Champion Hurdler who jumped like a dream and broke the track record in the process. Sadly he had injury problems after that and was never the same horse, but for those few months at the end of 1996 and start of 1997 Make A Stand was one of the most exciting horses I ever rode. He was an incredibly fast jumper; the main reason why other horses couldn't catch him was because he was so fast through the air, and was practically unbeatable in his prime.

This was only my third season riding in Britain and I'd now won the Champion Hurdle. I'd been champion jockey once and was on course to retain the title, and I knew that if you wanted to be the best jockey you had to win the best races. The Champion Hurdle is certainly one of those, but the pinnacle of them all is, of course, the Gold Cup.

When Noel Chance had asked me to ride Mr Mulligan in the King George VI Chase at Kempton on Boxing Day I jumped at the opportunity because I knew this was a special horse. He was normally under Richard Johnson but Richard was riding for David Johnson at Wetherby that day, and Noel told me that if things went well at Kempton I'd keep the ride on what was a Gold Cup horse. There was the shadow of a doubt over him that day as he'd missed a couple of weeks with a stone bruise in his hoof and he was up against Richard Dunwoody on One Man, who'd won the race the previous year and was strongly fancied to win it again.

The King George is a fast race and Mr Mulligan led from the front until we turned for home with three to jump, when One Man nosed ahead and I sensed that missing fortnight creeping up Mr Mulligan's legs. He'd worked really hard all the way round but just didn't seem to have enough in the tank to haul back One Man. I gave him a kick as we jumped the last in the hope it might produce some magic, but it turned out he was just too tired to respond. He clipped the fence and down we went.

Despite this setback I still believed this was a great Gold Cup horse and told Noel as much as soon as I saw him. I wanted the ride, I said, because a fully-fit Mr Mulligan would be a match for any horse in the race. Unfortunately the fall had given the horse a haematoma in his hindquarter and a pulled ligament in his back, which meant some pretty intensive treatment lay ahead if he was going to be ready. He missed the Irish Hennessy and a fortnight before the Gold Cup we took him to Newbury for a gallop after racing had finished for the day.

We worked Mr Mulligan that day with a novice four-year-old called Sunley Secure, but he worked terribly, really, really bad. I came in aghast and told Noel I was very concerned. I rang Dave Roberts straightaway and said I didn't want to ride this horse at Cheltenham any more because he wouldn't win a sack race let alone the Gold Cup. Martin Pipe had another couple of horses lined up for the Gold Cup, Cyborgo and Challenger Du Luc, who I felt were both great horses on whom I might have a better chance than I would on Mr Mulligan. Noel saw my dilemma and said to me, look, why don't you come and jump some fences on him during the week and see if you can get a feel for him then? I was happy to do that for Noel but I still had grave doubts about the horse. Deep down I knew Mr Mulligan could thrive in the Gold Cup, but given the problems he'd had and the evidence of the terrible gallop at Newbury I wondered whether it might be a step too far in the circumstances. I went to school at Noel's during the week and, wouldn't you know it, he jumped beautifully and gave me a much better feel, almost unrecognisable as the same horse from Newbury. I rang Dave and told him Mr Mulligan was jumping well and I'd stick with him.

It was lucky for me that I did. I still had that Newbury disaster at the back of my mind and wasn't confident going into the race and the bookies seemed to agree with me: Mr Mulligan went to the start at 20/1. However after the first circuit I could feel he was travelling well and I knew he had that most important attribute for a Gold Cup horse: he was a stayer. Fair play to Noel Chance, despite all the obstacles put in front of him he had Mr Mulligan in great shape on the day and had worked miracles to get him ready. It did him great credit to have kept such faith in the horse all along. Mr Mulligan was never a particularly easy ride, he was a little bit straight-backed and wasn't a natural jumper, but he was a doer, a galloper, and when he hit the front I knew it would take a very special horse indeed to get past him. This time it was One Man who didn't have an answer as Mr Mulligan powered through to win the Gold Cup with good old Barton Bank nine lengths back in second.

I was delighted for Noel, delighted for the horse and, of course, delighted for myself. In only my third Cheltenham I'd won both the Champion Hurdle and now the Gold Cup, something only three other jockeys in the history of the festival could claim. The great Norman Williamson had done it two years earlier, Fred Winter pulled it off in 1961 and Aubrey Brabazon had achieved the historic double twice, in 1949 and 1950. I think I'm right in saying it hasn't been done since, either. Along with the Grand National, the Champion Hurdle and the Gold Cup make up the three biggest races in the National Hunt calendar so to win two of them in a week was something very special, and something that would cement my special relationship with the Cheltenham Festival for ever. Whatever happened in the rest of my career nobody could take away the fact that I'd won the Champion Hurdle and the Gold Cup at the same festival. A knock-on effect of that historic double was that it made me feel for the first time that I genuinely deserved to be champion jockey, because those are the races you are judged by beyond statistics. Yes, a win at Cheltenham counts the same numerically as a win at Ayr or Plumpton, but people naturally look to how you perform on the big occasions in the races that stick in the memory, the races with the biggest audiences, the ones that get talked about in the bars and the pubs, so to win both Cheltenham's marquee races was, I knew, a significant career milestone that I hoped would dispel any possible notions that I was a flash in the pan.

Riding for the winning machine known as Martin Pipe helped,

of course, because it almost guaranteed the champion jockey's title, but it couldn't guarantee you were going to win the big races. I was making my mark in the best possible fashion and driving away from Cheltenham in 1997 was the first time I'd felt anything like comfortable in my position as a jockey.

I had another great festival the following year, finishing as the leading jockey with five wins. Only Fred Winter and Jamie Osborne had ever matched that so it was an ideal way to follow up the double of the previous year and again made me feel I was here to stay. Even now, all these years later, people still bring up that meeting. A lot of the Liverpool football team were there that week, and I was – and still am – very friendly with Robbie Fowler and Steve McManaman in particular. I think it was they who'd arranged to bring the rest of the lads down and they backed nearly all my winners, making it a pretty enjoyable meeting for them. Any time I see any of that team now they always mention it. I was on the panel for the quiz show *A League Of Their Own* recently with Jamie Redknapp and he brought it up then. Razor Ruddock is another one that talks about it a lot whenever our paths cross. Sometimes, if I'm feeling generous, I don't even mention Michael Thomas, 1989 and 'it's up for grabs now'.

The only dark cloud over that festival came in the Gold Cup. I was riding Cyborgo for Martin Pipe and just when we were coming out of the back straight for the first time I felt him go lame. There was nothing for it but to take him out of the race so I called out my intention and pulled him away to the right. Coming from behind me was See More Business, one of the fancied horses trained by Paul Nicholls, whom I unwittingly carried out with me along with another of Martin's horses Indian

Tracker. This caused a bit of friction between Martin and Paul who already had a bit of history, but it was a complete accident, just one of those things, and it was just very unfortunate that what happened had such an impact on the race.

It certainly didn't ruin the great memories I have of that year's Cheltenham though. In fact I must have got more excited than usual because when I won the last race of the festival, the Vincent O'Brien County Handicap Hurdle on Blowing Wind, I attempted the first – and last – flying dismount of my career. Whatever possessed me to do it I don't know, maybe one of the lads dared me, but I didn't fancy ever doing it again. I'd leave that kind of thing to Frankie.

While my overriding memory of the 2000 Cheltenham Festival will always be the tragedy that befell Gloria Victis, before the Gold Cup I did have a very memorable win in the Queen Mother Champion Chase. The Champion Chase was always one of my favourite races even though this was the only occasion on which I won it: two miles run at speed over fences. If the Gold Cup, Champion Hurdle and Grand National make up a 'big three', for me the Champion Chase is just behind at number four. Although Edredon Bleu had finished second behind Call Equiname the previous year – by a length and a quarter, I was gutted – he hadn't been in great form leading up to the festival. Yet I knew this was the perfect race for him and the conditions on the day meant he had a really good chance. He was a front-runner, a fast, slick jumper, very economical over the fences, nearly too economical at times because he'd had a couple of falls. He went off quick right from the start and jumped the last slightly ahead of Norman Williamson on Direct Route. Norman managed to nose ahead in the closing stages but in the last seventy-odd yards

Edredon Bleu fought back brilliantly and the two horses were pretty much head-to-head at the line. Edredon Bleu just stole it by the shortest of short heads in one of those finishes where another stride past and Norman might have won or a stride earlier and Norman might have won then, too. But just on the line my horse's head was down at exactly the right time and there's no better feeling than having one of those go your way. I've been on the other side of it and the sense of frustration is agonising. Sometimes you can have an inkling as to whether you've won or not in a situation like that, but when you're as close as we were that day you've no idea where the winning post is because you've got your head down and you're giving it your all. Sometimes you have a fair idea because you can see where the grass line is on the ground, or if you're close enough to the post itself you might catch it out of the corner of your eye, but that day we were in the middle of the track and neither Norman nor I had a clue as we waited for the announcement. To beat Norman in a tight finish like that was very satisfying because he was a brilliant jockey, but it could quite easily have gone the other way. It's a situation that can give you the biggest high or the greatest low all inside the space of a heartbeat; it was a thrilling finish to a brilliant race. The Champion Chase is a fantastic spectacle at the best of times – I always tell people that they should go right down to the fence to watch the Champion Chase because that's as fast as chasers go and it's an amazing experience to be up close – and Edredon Bleu truly graced the race with a magnificent, exciting win. I count winning the Champion Chase that year as definitely one of the highlights of my career.

After a run of good Cheltenhams, my 2002 and 2003 festivals were underwhelming by comparison. That's just how it is – no matter who you are or what you've won before there's no divine right to win at the festival. You're starting level with the best horses and jockeys in the business and you have to learn to take the bad ones on the chin as much as you can.

The death of Valiramix in 2002 cast a dark cloud and did have a big effect on me mentally. I didn't like the criticism that was levelled at me afterwards but it was a valuable lesson about not letting criticism – or indeed praise – get under your skin. I'd realised early on that reacting to criticism caught you in a spiral from which it was difficult to extricate yourself so I learned to ignore it and rise above it. What happened to Valiramix got to me, nobody seemed to appreciate it, a few people took aim at me as a result and nothing will change that. But quite frankly I didn't care. I would never have said it at the time, but especially now I'm retired I don't mind admitting that I really didn't care. I happily concede that for a long period during my career I could be selfish and self-centred: I knew what I wanted to achieve and I wasn't going to give any ground to anyone to achieve it if I could possibly avoid it. The only opinion that really mattered to me was my own. I twigged early on not to get wrapped up in what people wrote about me, no matter whether it was good or bad, because all the while people were writing good stuff, it was inevitable there'd be bad stuff somewhere down the line and it was easier just not to bother with any of it. It can be very nice to read someone writing about how brilliant you are, but the nature of sport is that you're not going to be brilliant every day, as much as you'd like to be. There will be bad days where you'll come away wishing you could go back and do it again, have another crack at it, but that's just not the way it works; when a day does pan out like that people will write things about you that don't make you feel good. You can tell yourself that it's wrong, that it's ill-informed, that you'd felt the same way after Gloria Victis as you had after Valiramix but nobody slagged you off then because the meeting finished and the whole sport was looking the other way, but then you're in danger of letting things eat away at you, and that's not healthy. Ignoring it was definitely the best policy.

Disappointing Cheltenhams would get me down. I'd end up in very bad form afterwards because it was a stage on which I loved to perform and which meant a great deal to me, but it's one of those things and when things do go badly you have to find aspects of it that you can learn from. It's becoming a bit of a cliché in sport, football managers coming out after bad defeats and saying they were concentrating on the positives, but it's what you have to do or you'll go nuts just brooding about how badly things had gone. Cheltenham became a little easier when they extended the festival to four days because it gave you more chances to win there and less chance of coming away feeling terrible because over three days it wasn't so easy to turn around a bad run. 2003 was a particularly rotten year. It was just after I'd had my collarbone x-rayed by Martin's vet but the racing fates extended me no sympathy: I fell in the Arkle and I fell in the Champion Hurdle. I fell in the Champion Chase and I had a particularly sore tumble in the Grand Annual. I had one win, on Liberman in the Champion Bumper.

Bad years like that were hard to take, but they did help me appreciate things more when they went my way. It was important to bear in mind that Cheltenham was the pinnacle: the best jockeys on the best horses in the best races in the land and it wasn't easy to win there. The Jonjo O'Neills, John Francomes and Peter Scudamores had even less success there than I did during their careers, so it was important to remember that there would always be fallow periods. It didn't mean I had to enjoy them though.

My next truly memorable Cheltenham ride came in 2006 on Brave Inca in the Champion Hurdle. He'd finished third the previous year under Barry Cash but then fallen at Aintree. In the winter of 2005–6 I had three good wins on him at Punchestown, in the Morgiana Hurdle in November, then in a two-mile grade one hurdle at the end of December and a similar race a month later. I was very lucky to make the Morgiana at all, let alone win it, because a little over two hours before I was due to ride Brave Inca in south County Dublin I was sitting on the tarmac at Heathrow on an Aer Lingus plane delayed for three hours because of fog. Finally we got the all clear to take off but I was still going to cut it very fine. I will always be grateful to the pilot that day, a guy called Shay Pardy, because he said that when we landed he'd get me off the moment the plane stopped. JP sent his helicopter to Dublin airport to meet me and Shay arranged for a car to be sitting at the bottom of the steps as soon as the door opened to take me to the helicopter. As far as I remember the wheels hit the runway at 1.35, I was on the helicopter within two minutes and something like twelve minutes later we landed at the racecourse. You're meant to weigh out fifteen minutes ahead of the race but the Irish Turf Club kindly cut me some slack in the extreme circumstances and let me weigh out a few minutes late. It was some team effort between Shay Pardy, the car driver and the lads flying the helicopter but it paid off as Brave Inca ended up winning the race and finally, after a day that had been stressful from eight o'clock that morning I could exhale and relax a little bit.

He beat the highly regarded Harchibald in that race and again in his next win at Leopardstown in December which really boded well for the Champion Hurdle. He went into Cheltenham as favourite for the race and, having run well the previous year, I really fancied him even though five of the first seven horses home in 2005 were running again, not least Hardy Eustace who was going for a hat-trick of Champion Hurdles. The race went to the last, we were neck and neck with Hardy Eustace most of the way and had to hold off a late challenge from Macs Joy, but Brave Inca was a really, really tough horse and no one was going to take him coming up the hill.

Brave Inca was a very good horse and a great character, and trainer Colm Murphy had done a brilliant job with him. I won on him again at Fairyhouse later that year but after that I was jocked off in favour of Ruby for the December Festival Hurdle at the end of 2008. I was disappointed, pissed off even, but I wasn't particularly surprised. Barry Cash, who'd ridden him with great success over the couple of years before I first rode him had been jocked off Brave Inca too, and he hadn't done a lot wrong on him. Having done it once I guess it was pretty much inevitable the owners might do it again. One thing I learned in racing was that when it comes to a really good horse like that, one on which I managed to win a Champion Hurdle and a number of other great races, memories can be short. It's not as simple as only being as good as your last race, but it does help keep you on your toes and as a result it wasn't the biggest shock in the world when I was jocked off Brave Inca. Leopards don't change their spots, as the fella might say. I wasn't bitter though, as I'd had a really good time out of him. He was a great character too and I'd trust that horse over the people that owned him any day of the week.

In that same year I won on Black Jack Ketchum, one of my favourite horses, in a grade two novices' hurdle. He was owned by Derek and Gay Smith, although Gay deserves more of the credit as Derek dealt mainly with their flat horses. Black Jack Ketchum was one of the bankers of the meeting because he'd won all five of his races up to that point, went into the race as a short-priced favourite and won like a short-priced favourite. He was a talented horse, but the reason I got such a big thrill out of winning on Black Jack Ketchum was that he was such a brilliant character. He was immensely likeable, the kind of horse that you could bring into your sitting room and he'd sit there watching television with you, a really likeable animal. When you caught his eye it was as if he was looking back at you saying, 'yeah, I know what you're thinking'. I love that I was able to ride a winner at Cheltenham on Black Jack Ketchum, one of the best equine characters I ever met. He's now retired and living in Barbados, probably enjoying his retirement better than I am. Next time I'm over there I might drop in on him and watch a bit of television.

The other horse on which I won in 2006 was the James Fanshawe-trained Reveillez, one of JP's horses, in the Jewson Novices' Handicap Chase. Reveillez hadn't been well laid out for the race. The previous year I'd ridden him at Cheltenham in the Sun Alliance Novices' Hurdle and came in sixth. We prepared him for a handicap at Cheltenham purely on the basis that he wasn't able to win a grade one hurdle so we thought he might not win a grade one over fences either. We went down the handicap chase route instead and, sure enough, he managed to win at the first time of asking. It was testament to James Fanshawe that he'd done such a great job gearing him up for the race. Reveillez was my first Cheltenham Festival winner as JP and Noreen's retained jockey, so that was a big thing for me, not least because having invested heavily in the horse JP had a good few quid on him at 9/2. That day everybody ended up happy.

As I've already mentioned, the death of Wichita Lineman in 2009 was another equine fatality that hit me hard, but I look back on his win in the 2007 Brit Insurance Novices' Hurdle with great affection. Wichita Lineman was a proper tough little horse. Like Black Jack Ketchum he'd won his share as a novice hurdler as well: the Challow Hurdle at Newbury which is a grade one, and also the Classic Novices' Hurdle at Cheltenham's January meeting. In fact, of the four rides I'd had on him before the Brit Insurance he won three and lost the fourth, in November at Cheltenham, by half a length. It was no surprise he went into the Brit Insurance as 11/8 favourite: he was a horse in great form and was a little bit like Synchronised in that he was a good stayer, perfect for coming up the hill at Cheltenham. You could ride him pretty close to the pace because you knew he was going to stay the three miles really well; he was a straightforward ride and he won that race very well indeed. Again like Synchronised and Black Jack Ketchum he had a lovely manner, a very good way about him. As we already know, he came from nowhere to win the William Hill in 2009 which shows just what a tough horse of immense character he was. Wichita Lineman had astonishing courage and I don't think he ever got the credit he undoubtedly deserved. He wasn't the best horse I ever rode, nor the most gifted, but he had the most incredible determination and will to win. Wichita Lineman was a real character of immense promise who alas had a tragic, premature end. We'll never know what he might have gone on to achieve.

Probably the best year of my career was 2010. Don't Push It won the National, of course, but also Synchronised won the Midlands Grand National, I was voted Sports Personality of the Year, received an OBE, won the Galway Plate on Finger Onthe Pulse, and also won the Champion Hurdle on Binocular, who was probably the surprise package of the lot. A week before Cheltenham Binocular wasn't supposed to be running. I'd had a couple of rides on him early in the season in which he disappointed, and despite winning the Contenders Hurdle at Sandown in February I felt something wasn't right with the horse. He was supposed to be improving towards Cheltenham but he'd made no progress at all. Something must have been bothering him but it would take more specialised knowledge than mine to find out what it was. I told his trainer Nicky Henderson what I thought and he had several people look at him but everyone was left scratching their heads. There was no evidence at all of any physical issue, outwardly the horse seemed as right as rain.

JP called me a couple of weeks before Cheltenham and said it was looking almost certain Binocular wasn't going to make the Champion Hurdle and he was going to take him back to Martinstown Stud, his estate in Ireland. While there JP's vets John Halley and Ger Kelly gave the horse a good going over, while the equine back specialist Mary Bromiley also became involved. A few days later JP rang me to say that, believe it or not, Binocular was on his way back.

I went to Nicky Henderson's in the week of the race and rode Binocular over five flights of hurdles and to my astonishment the horse was going like lightning. I was overjoyed: I'd gone from having a good ride in the Champion Hurdle to having no ride in the Champion Hurdle then back to having a good ride in the Champion Hurdle in the space of just over a week. I don't know what John, Ger and Mary did, but whatever it was put the horse in flying form.

In the run-up to the race my only reservation was that travelling back and forth to Ireland so close to the festival the way he had might have unsettled him. But I needn't have worried. He travelled like a dream and when we came around the last bend I just let him go and he shot to the line to win by three and a half lengths. It was an incredible feat on everyone's part to bring the horse back from nowhere to win one of the biggest races of the National Hunt season. Binocular was a fantastic, fast hurdler with a great technique in the same mould as Make A Stand. In hindsight he should really have won more than one Champion Hurdle, he certainly had the ability. He'd been a little unlucky I felt to be beaten by Punjabi, another Nicky Henderson horse, the previous year in a very close finish along with Celestial Halo as I don't think he'd quite got to his peak in time. Another month and he might well have won that one too. He did seem to be hampered by little issues that were difficult to diagnose though, which meant it wasn't easy to keep him right. The fact he won that 2010 race despite such an idiosyncratic preparation demonstrates just the kind of quality horse he was.

The nature of that win underlined just what an amazing year I had in 2010, a year when fate seemed to give me the nod more times than was really necessary. Topping everything off that year was receiving my OBE from the Queen – eventually. Obviously it's a great honour to be recognised in such a way, especially for doing something I love. I'm in awe of the community workers and public servants who receive honours, for me they're the most deserving recipients you could imagine. I ride horses because I love riding horses and was lucky enough to make my living from it for more than twenty years, so it was humbling to receive the honour alongside such deserving recipients.

The only question was, when would I go and pick it up? Every time Buckingham Palace sent through prospective dates they'd be important racing days and I wouldn't be able to go. Well, strictly speaking I could or should have gone, but I was so wrapped up in retaining my champion jockey's title the idea of missing a day's racing for anything other than an injury that physically prevented me from getting on a horse gave me the heebie-jeebies. As a result I ended up inadvertently putting back the trip to Buckingham Palace to collect my OBE for quite a long time. An embarrassingly long time, in hindsight: it's obviously not the right thing to do to keep Her Majesty waiting like that.

It's well known that the Queen is a great fan and patron of racing. She's very knowledgeable and is always well up on the horses. When I stepped forward to receive my OBE she said something along the lines of, 'It's very nice of you to join us at last.' When I heard that I was mortified, but she said it with a twinkle in her eye, and I've been invited to Windsor Castle for a reception during Royal Ascot since so I can't have offended her too grievously. It was a bit of an 'oops' moment, but I think she appreciated the circumstances: the Queen of England and I don't have a great deal in common, it must be said, but the one thing we do share is racing and she's a very understanding lady. I hope.

A few people asked me when I received my OBE (and the MBE I'd been awarded in 2003) whether there was any issue about accepting it, being from a Northern Irish Catholic family. My answer was, not really, no. Times change and you have to move on. Without getting too heavily into politics, what has happened in the north of Ireland in recent years is very positive, in my view, and the Queen herself has played a big part in the warming of relations. The Queen is a very well-informed woman who has a strong sense of empathy; she appreciates that in any conflict there are two sides and is well able to see the bigger picture. When the Queen visited Ireland in May 2011 I thought she was brilliant. She got everything right, from arriving wearing green to speaking in the Irish language at a reception at Dublin Castle to paying her respects at the Republican memorial in Dublin. That visit helped Anglo-Irish relations take a huge step forward. Some people said that it was a pity it didn't happen sooner but maybe it wasn't the right time before then. She undoubtedly gained a lot of trust and a lot of respect among the Irish people during that visit. There's a lot of history in the Irish situation, some of it still very recent, and I don't think you can blame a lot of people for their stance on it whatever side they're on because there are deep wounds that will take a long time to heal. As time goes on, though, hopefully it'll get better. It *must* get better, and give and take on both sides is the only way to move things further forward. As people grow older the youth will see less of the conflict: it's an old cliché but time really is the great healer.

On top of helping defuse political tensions, the Queen is also absolutely brilliant for racing, something I've seen first-hand at Royal Ascot. Her Majesty always has quite a few horses in training which is good for the industry, and as a keen owner and breeder she's continued the royal equine legacy of her mother with great enthusiasm. There will come a time when the Queen isn't around any more and only then will people realise how important she is to the world of racing. Royal Ascot is a very special meeting anyway, but the Queen makes it what it is. Hopefully Charles, or even William or Harry, will take up the family racing mantle when she's gone. Who knows, maybe someone might give Harry a good horse and it might get him interested – I think he might find it entertaining and it might even benefit his social life and his social skills. Not that he needs any training when it comes to his social life, of course, but becoming involved in racing might be good for him and he might enjoy it. I've only met him and William briefly, but they seem to me like very normal people who probably don't get to live very normal lives. I reckon Harry's got the best side of the draw, though, a little less pressure being another step away from the throne. Who knows, we might end up seeing him at Cheltenham as a spectator one day.

For me, I'll have to get used to going back to the Cheltenham Festival as a spectator myself, which will be a little odd, certainly at first. The first time I go back I can see myself trying to stroll into the weighing room out of sheer force of habit. I can see it taking a while to get used to going back as a civilian. It's a festival of which I've been a part as a jockey for more than two decades and had some of the greatest – and not so great – moments of my career there. Looking out from the stands across the course it'll be strange to reflect on the triumphs, disasters, victories and tragedies I've had out there on the course. I've more than twenty years' worth of memories, hopes, dreams, sweat and blood soaked into that turf, and I know as soon as I go back it'll all suddenly seem a very long time ago. Especially when I see other jockeys winning on horses I'd have probably been riding. But there have been plenty of jockeys before me who've had to cope with that kind of feeling and there'll be plenty more after me, so I'm no different from anyone else in that sense. I love racing and I love the best racing so I'll always look forward to Cheltenham and will still enjoy it. It goes without saying that I'd enjoy it more if I was competing and especially if I was winning, but I'll definitely look forward to it as the highlight of my racing year, the same as ever. I'll doubtless see a few old ghosts as I gaze across the track, but I'll also see some great racing. The best, in fact.

ELEVEN

Mountain Tunes, Towcester
7 November 2013

Once the epidural and painkillers had worn off following the battering I'd received from Quantitativeeasing at Cheltenham that put me in intensive care, my biggest concern was missing the start of the 2013–14 season. For the first time ever my customary campaign plan of riding as many winners as possible as early as possible, the strategy that had always served me so well, clearly wasn't going to happen and I was in grumpy form when I went to Sandown with Chanelle and Eve to collect my 2013 jockeys' championship trophy. I was still very sore from the injuries but the physical pain was being matched by the mental torture of being at the races but unable to ride and knowing that I was still realistically a few weeks away from riding.

I was soon given a hefty and welcome dose of reality, however, because that day was the last time I ever saw David Johnson, for whom I'd ridden a great number of winners over the years on the likes of Well Chief, Or Royal and Champleve. David also had a wonderful horse called Cyfor Malta, on whom I rode a good few memorable winners. Cyfor Malta had a rare combination of good looks and natural talent and there was a tangible swagger in the way he held himself. If he'd been a human being I think I'd have hated him, to be quite honest. There was a bit of Eric Cantona about him (and he was actually French, which adds to the comparison), a puffed-up sense that he knew exactly how good he was, ears permanently pricked up, looking at you as if to say, 'OK, you can look at me from there all right, just don't come any closer.'

He was the apple of Martin Pipe's eye from an early stage. His stable was opposite Martin's office and often I'd be in the yard in the morning and see Martin arrive, give him a good pat and then go into the office to start the business of the day. This happened every day, and I doubt I ever saw Martin have as much unadulterated affection for a horse as he did for Cyfor Malta.

I won on him at Cheltenham in the 1998 Cathcart as a five-year-old and again in the John Hughes Trophy by thirteen lengths over the Grand National fences, the first five-year-old ever to win over the Grand National fences. I remember mentioning to Martin before the race the fact that a five-year-old had never won on the course before. He smiled and said there'd never been a Cyfor Malta before. Sure enough he was electric all the way round, absolutely romping home. At the end of the year he won the Murphy's Gold Cup, surging ahead in the race but then deciding to pretty much saunter over the line, all cocky and preening, and only won by a length.

Early in 1999 Cyfor Malta won the Pillar Property Chase against See More Business, Cyborgo and Go Ballistic, but sadly he got injured after that, and we had to watch two of the horses beaten by him that day, and well beaten too, go on to finish first and second in the Gold Cup. He came back from that injury but after two years out I don't think he was ever really the same horse again. I'd left Cheltenham after he'd won the Pillar massively excited about Cyfor Malta, convinced he wasn't just a Gold Cup horse but a Gold Cup winner waiting to happen. Sadly, especially for the owners, it wasn't to be. I was very sorry for David that Cyfor Malta never fulfilled the promise he'd shown at the back end of the nineties because the Johnsons were a wonderful family and I'm proud to have ridden the winners I did for them. Both David and his wife Shirley were very good to me when I was riding for the Pipes, just lovely people for whom I'd always had great time.

That day at Sandown I was in one of the hospitality suites after the champion jockey presentation feeling very sore and very sorry for myself when David sat down next to me and began telling me what he'd been through with his cancer: the chemo, the pain, the sickness, all of it. At the end of it, he asked how I was doing. If anyone else had asked I'd have probably launched into a moan about my terrible luck in not being able to ride, but having just heard David describing his ordeal, all I could say was, 'Oh, me? I'm grand.' It put me in a bit of a daze, sitting there talking to David Johnson at Sandown and thinking about how miserable I'd been feeling when here was someone with good cause to be miserable yet who was being so positive about his situation. I'd spent the day up to that point silently fuming at being at a racecourse and not racing, absorbed in my own world, railing against the terrible injustice of missing the start of the season, and here was David, staying positive, talking about going to America for some new treatment that was going to help him.

He even looked to me like he could be getting better. He didn't look a million dollars or anything but he looked OK and was in pretty good form, yet two months later he was dead. Like the rest of the racing world, I was deeply saddened by the news. He was only 67, and a young 67 at that. He left a great racing legacy, a National winner in Comply Or Die in 1998 and he was six times champion owner over jumps, and the way he'd embraced life and tackled his illness head-on was characteristic of a very tough, dignified and ultimately very nice man.

Walking around Sandown after seeing David, for the last time as it turned out, people were asking me how I was and all I could reply was that I was very lucky. It was a day I'll never forget. I'd sat chatting to him for quite a while after the first race, but after the second my head was so mashed by it all that I said to Chanelle, 'I need to get out of here, I can't watch this.' We left before the main race, the Bet365 Gold Cup, the big end-of-season handicap, but I just couldn't stick around. I just wanted to go home. As well as the conversation with David I was discomfited by being a spectator. I didn't know what to do, who to talk to, where to go or which way to turn from the familiar rhythms and routines of the weighing room. It was a strange and sobering experience all round.

The next day was a Sunday and we had a few people to the house for lunch to mark the beginning of the new season. Around the table were Mick Fitzgerald and his wife Chloe, Richard Hughes and his wife Lizzie, and Carl Llewellyn who isn't married. There was racing on at Wetherby that day, the first day of the season, and although we had the football on after lunch we were constantly flicking back to keep up with the results as they came in from Yorkshire. Jason Maguire rode a winner. Then another. And another. Then he had four winners and I was sitting there with the remote control in my hand, all the noise and the craic from the room fading into the background, obsessing about how we weren't even one full day into the season and I was already four wins behind in the jockeys' championship. I was still the best part of a month away from a return to the saddle too, by which time there could be dozens of jockeys well ahead of me by the time I was back riding. I'd never been in that position before in my life. I found myself shuffling round the house, still sore, obsessively keeping tabs on who was winning what and where. At the end of the first week in May, the week I turned 39 and entered my fortieth year, there were plenty of lads riding well and Jason had ridden another six winners, leaving me ten behind the lead and absolutely powerless to do anything about it all the time I was sitting on my arse at home. It was the worst feeling, that helplessness, that powerlessness to prevent jockeys pulling away from me in the championship. It was like the worst anxiety dream you could devise for me, where I'm trying to ride but can't move as my number of winners sticks stubbornly on zero and every jockey in the land surges ahead leaving me behind. Except this was no dream. I was living it.

I had to set myself a target to return to the saddle, a realistic one but one that would have me back riding as quickly as possible. The twentieth seemed as good a day as any to come back so I'd aim for that, but as the day drew closer I was still feeling my injuries and thinking, fuck, I'm never going to be able to do this. Dave Roberts, knowing I was on my way back but not certain as to how quickly, rang to ask how I was and I said, 'Not great Dave, but I am getting better and still definitely on for the twentieth.'

'Great,' he said, 'I'm glad to hear you're on the mend because Jonjo has a horse running at Ludlow on the sixteenth called Church Field. It'll probably win, so if you feel up to it you could ride that if you like.'

Fuck, I thought, I'm still touch and go to be back for the twentieth and here's Dave talking about the sixteenth.

'Sure,' I suddenly heard a voice that sounded very much like mine saying, 'I'll ride Church Field on the sixteenth, stick me down, no bother.'

I hadn't even sat on a horse since falling off Quantitativeeasing at Cheltenham. I went over to Jonjo's at Jackdaws Castle the day before the race to ride out, just to get the feel of being on a horse again, and when I did it felt absolutely horrendous. Twenty-six days after the fall the pain was still terrible and I was absolutely in bits. Jonjo asked me how I felt, and I was honest with him: horrific. He asked if I needed a bit more time but my stubbornness kicked in and I said, no way, I'm going to ride tomorrow. I'd agreed to the ride, tomorrow was my target return, and there was no way I was going to pull out of it now.

'As long as I can get on that horse,' I said to Jonjo, 'I'll be racing.'

I went up to Ludlow the next day and rode Church Field and I've never, ever felt as bad on a horse in all my life as I did that day. Every movement the horse made had me wincing, but despite carrying this wincing bag of aching bones on his back he managed to win. I'd ridden my first race of the season and got off the mark in the jockeys' championship, but it certainly wasn't pretty. When I got home and watched the race back I saw that when I crossed the line I was practically curled up in the foetal position on the back of the horse.

I spoke to Dave afterwards and told him I'd have to be very, very selective over my rides for the next couple of weeks because if I had a fall during that time there was a fair to middling chance I would never get up. I was as far behind in the championship as I'd ever been in my life, trailing by about twenty, so I didn't want to lose any more rides than was absolutely necessary, but in the short term at least they had to be horses who had an excellent chance of winning before they'd even stepped on the track. Realistically I shouldn't have been anywhere near a horse for another fortnight but I couldn't risk dropping back any further in the championship. Even if I just held my own for a couple of weeks and made sure that I didn't fall any further behind I'd have something to build on by the time I was properly fit again. Plus, for all the agony and risk involved, I simply couldn't face another two weeks watching racing on the TV and seeing horses I should have been riding winning for other jockeys.

That fortnight was one of the most agonising of my career. The pain was constant, but I managed to ride sixteen winners, more than one a day, and at least stay in touch in the championship. People often ask me about my biggest achievements and while the National, the Gold Cup and breaking Sir Gordon Richards' record all spring instantly to mind, to be honest I think those two weeks in the summer of 2013 should be up there too. It really wasn't pleasant at all and in hindsight I've no idea how I got through them. It wasn't just riding the winners that made it a notable achievement either: the fact I avoided falling was massively important, because I'm sure even one regulation, run-of-the-mill, everyday fall during that fortnight would have finished me off and possibly seen me kiss goodbye to the jockeys' championship for that season. The thought of that makes me shudder even today. I took a big gamble doing what I did, but thankfully it paid off.

Once I was back approaching full fitness I managed to put a pretty good run together. My delayed start to the campaign hadn't put breaking records out of my head entirely, but I was obviously a long, long way behind riding my fastest fifty winners. I still needed a goal to aim for, albeit a slightly reduced one in the circumstances, so set myself the target of riding 200 winners. If I could do that, I thought, then there was a very good chance indeed I'd be champion jockey again. Peter Scudamore rode 221 winners in a season once when he was riding for Martin Pipe, but aside from that no other jockey but me had ever won more than 200 winners over jumps in a single season. It was an ideal target, then, because if I could ride 200 winners it was almost certain I'd be champion jockey.

On the way to 200 I knew I'd pass another major milestone in my career: my 4,000th winner. While it was always there looming just over the horizon it wasn't something to which I gave a great deal of thought because, barring a career-threatening injury, it was certain to come at some point. It was a different situation from trying to break Sir Gordon Richards' record when there was the strict deadline of a single season, meaning I couldn't afford to be injured or suspended. The 4,000 landmark was open-ended: as long as I was able to ride I was going to ride my 4,000th winner at some point.

The press began to flag it up when I'd got to within a dozen or so wins of the magic figure. It was only then I turned my thoughts seriously towards it, looking ahead to the rides I had and scoping out when, where and how it might happen. I had long conversations over the phone with Dave about it, because to make it something really special was going to take a little bit of planning. There was something very important that I wanted in place when it happened: I was adamant that I wanted to ride my 4,000th winner on one of JP's horses. JP and Noreen had been very, very good to me over the previous decade so I wanted my landmark winner to be in their colours. I wanted to look back at the photographs and see myself in the green and gold, the same colours I'd been wearing on Don't Push It, Synchronised and in all the other great moments of the second half of my career. To achieve this I had to start picking and choosing my rides carefully the nearer I got to the landmark.

On 6 November I rode my 3,999 winner in a handicap hurdle at Chepstow on a horse of Jonjo's called Minella For Steak, which on paper set things up quite nicely for riding at Towcester the next day. JP and his son John were already planning to be there and Chanelle, Eve and Archie were also going for the day. As it happened my dad and my brother Colm happened to be over from Ireland for the week as well so they'd be there too, as would Jonjo and Jackie. Towcester is barely an hour from London and is a track that doesn't charge for entry, so it was going to be quite a big thing if I could pull it off there. I would never be one to take anything for granted, let alone actually tempt fate, but just as had happened on previous landmark days in my career the signs were good for a memorable occasion, as long as I could do my bit by riding the crucial winner. And I only had two rides.

The first was Church Field, on whom I'd had that terrible first ride of the season at Ludlow, in a handicap hurdle and then Mountain Tunes in a novices' hurdle over two and a half miles. If neither of them came in, I had one ride the following day at Southwell in a bumper on a horse called Forthefunofit.

Southwell is three hours from home and two and a half from London. Forthefunofit was running in the last race of the day: all in all it wasn't a particularly auspicious scenario for people to turn out and watch, so if I could pass the milestone at Towcester it would make a lot of people very happy.

I'd ridden another winner on Church Field after Ludlow, at Market Rasen, but he was a wee bit sluggish that day at Towcester and came in fifth. He'd gone up in the handicap after winning a few races and struggled a little as a result, but to be fair to the horse he ran OK.

The focus shifted to Mountain Tunes. He'd only ever had two races before that day, a couple of point to points in Ireland earlier in the year of which he'd won one, so he was a little bit green and for a lot of the way around Towcester that day he never looked like he was going to win. Even as late as between the second last and last hurdles he was in fourth position and not giving much of an indication he was capable of coming through, but Towcester has a gruelling uphill finish, possibly the stiffest in the country, and if ever fortunes can change dramatically on a race track it's in that final straight at Towcester.

Mountain Tunes started to make ground and was third approaching the last, where he managed to jump into the horse beside him, Panama Petrus under Aidan Coleman, and the horses collided in mid-air. That frightened him a little bit but seemed to do him good because then he really got motoring. Panama Petrus had been thrown off his stride and dropped back, and that just left Jamie Moore on Kris Spin in front of us with Mountain Tunes really picking up steam. Sure enough, with fifty yards to go he powered ahead and managed to do enough to win by half a length.

Considering it was such a landmark race I didn't think I'd given Mountain Tunes a good ride, at least not as good a ride as it might have looked. There were times during the race that he could have been in a better position, or rather I could have made it a little easier for him at least. He was an inexperienced horse and some of the positions I got him in early on were a bit of a shock to the horse, I think, leaving him unsure how to react. In some ways it was about teaching him and in others it should have been about making it as easy as possible for him. But he managed to win, and that was the most important thing.

A whole rush of different emotions coursed through me after we crossed the line. Relief, a great deal of fulfilment and, for possibly the first time ever, a genuine sense of achievement, more so than when winning the National or the Gold Cup, and in a different way to breaking Sir Gordon Richards' record. I've always identified that as my greatest achievement, especially viewed from the distance of a decade, but at Towcester on Mountain Tunes I felt instantly a great sense of achievement, more than ever before. It's hard to explain. Lots of people have ridden winners in the Grand National and the Gold Cup. Lots of people have won the jockeys' championship. One day, now I'm out of the way, someone may well break my record of 289 winners in a season. I'm pretty convinced, though, that no jump jockey will ever ride 4,000 winners again. Thundering past the winning post at Towcester that day, for the first time in my career I really felt that I'd achieved something that no other National Hunt jockey will ever do. No other jump jockey has ever reached even 3,000 and only a handful have passed 2,000, so it's very unlikely that anyone else will reach 4,000. If they do, fair play to them, they'll be absolutely knackered – I just hope I won't be around to see it.

Again I'd been lucky in the way everything came together for me that day. To have my dad and my brother there, Chanelle, Eve – on the day before her sixth birthday – and baby Archie there, Dave Roberts, Jonjo and Jackie, JP and his son John, most of the important people in my racing and personal lives were all there to see it. It was even nice that everyone there had free entry too, and that's before JP decided to mark the occasion by buying everyone at the races a drink, a round for about 5,000 people.

There was a lot of media attention too and I'd done quite a few interviews in the run-up to the day, so I was aware that it was a bit of a story but I certainly didn't expect it to get such widespread coverage. I shouldn't imagine many racing stories have ever made the evening television news, so it was nice from that point of view to see the sport break out of its cultural cocoon.

So great was the interest in fact that I had to give a press conference after the race. Normally you'd speak to a couple of journalists who'd catch you outside the weighing room or wherever, lads you saw all over the country and knew by name, but this time there seemed to be such a lot of media attention that my media manager Claire Burns decided it was easier to get everyone together at once, stick me in front of a banner and behind a microphone to have questions fired at me.

When I passed 3,000 winners a lot of the press started asking me when I was going to retire, but that day at Towcester the questioning interestingly went the other way: did I think I could ride 5,000 winners? At the time I was actually in a bit of a dream world over it all and at one point in that post-4,000 haze I admit that I did actually think I could feasibly get to 5,000. But at the same time there was always the thought at the back of my mind reminding me that if I could win twenty jockeys' championships that would be a good time to stop. When I considered it in a bit more depth I realised that to get to 5,000 winners I'd have to ride 250 every year until I was forty-four years old even if I could maintain that consistent level of performance, and I didn't fancy that so much. Plus if I was still riding at forty-four at the same level of intensity as I always had people would think I wasn't right in the head. I thought I'd done pretty well to get to nearly forty-one years old as a jump jockey. That's a good age. If a jump jockey makes it to their late thirties they're doing pretty well. But forty-four? Nope. Too far.

Having said all that, I do and probably always will believe that I was capable of riding 5,000 winners if I'd kept going. Quite simply I didn't want to. I always had that horror of going on for too long, and if it ever got to the stage where I was still riding and I wasn't champion jockey, well, that would have undone all the good work that I'd done to win twenty straight jockeys' championships. It would have undermined everything and ruined everything and I know I wouldn't have coped with that at all well.

Overall though, it was nice to note how in the space of a thousand winners the tone of questioning had shifted from 'When are you going to stop?' to 'How long will you keep going?'

I'd been very lucky again. I couldn't have planned that 4,000th win any better if I'd tried. If I hadn't won on Mountain Tunes and I'd gone to Southwell the next day it wouldn't have had nearly the same thrill, and I mean no disrespect to Southwell when I say that. As it was it was a big deal on a big day and I think the way things worked out was fantastic for the sport in general.

That evening everyone decamped to a pub in which I have a share called The Outside Chance in Manton, people who hadn't been at the races that day but who I wanted to be part of the day. People like Terry Biddlecombe, God rest him, who was champion jockey three times in the 1960s and won the 1969 Cheltenham Gold Cup on Woodland Venture at odds of 100/8. Terry was married to Henrietta Knight and between them they trained some amazing horses on whom I had some fantastic rides, horses like Best Mate and Edredon Bleu. For some reason Terry always had great time for me and the feeling was definitely mutual. He hadn't been in the best of health for a while. Hen had given up training the previous year in order to care for him and I remember her saying that night, 'You're the only person he'd get out of bed to go and see.' I should doubt he was in many pubs in his later years, but he was in a fair few in his riding days if the stories are true – the way Terry told it he was the ultimate playboy who'd given George Best a run for his money in his time – so I was delighted to see him there that night to be a part of the celebrations. Terry died seven weeks later, and I treasure the memories of seeing him that night, in great form and enjoying the party.

John Francome was there that evening, too. He was champion jockey seven times: John McCririck calls him the greatest jockey of them all and he's probably the most natural rider I've ever seen in my life. He said something to me that night that really astounded me, especially as it came from him.

'Do you realise,' he said, 'that you've ridden a hundred winners for every year of your life? I don't think anyone else will ever be able to do that.'

I'm a numbers man as you know, always have been, and this was a stat that appealed to me very much. When I turned it over in my mind it struck me that even though Sir Gordon Richards won 4,870 races during his career he was riding until he was 55 years old. Break it down another way and I rode 200 winners for every year I was champion jockey, which is a pretty impressive average.

I looked around the pub at some of the faces, seeing groups and knots of people talking and laughing and sharing my land-mark day and realised that nearly everyone in that room had contributed in varying degrees to my achieving that extraordi-nary record. Suddenly I found myself overwhelmed by a wave of gratitude. Everywhere I looked, whichever way I turned, I saw another face, another person who'd helped me along the way during my career in a whole variety of ways.

Then I caught sight of two fellas chatting together on the far side of the bar who'd helped me achieve the milestone I'd reached that day probably more than most. They were the two men who'd certainly had the biggest influence on the second decade of my career: J.P. McManus and Jonjo O'Neill.

The roots of my riding for JP go deep enough to reach as far as Jim Bolger's yard at Coolcullen. Christy Roche was stable jockey when I was apprenticed at Jim's and once he'd finished riding went on to train horses for JP. I heard later that one of the first things Christy ever said to JP about me was, 'That fucking McCoy, he should be handicapped.' JP told me later that Christy was the first person to make him consider employing me and that early but pithy appraisal of my abilities helped to convince him to keep a close eye on my career. Christy was someone I always got on really well with and ended up riding a few good winners for. I won on Like-A-Butterfly for him a couple of times, who was one of the best horses Christy ever trained for JP. She was a very good mare, one of the very few horses to have won a grade one bumper, a grade one hurdle race and a grade one chase. In the space of a month in the spring of 2005 I won the Powers Gold Cup at Fairyhouse on her and the Mildmay Novice Chase at Aintree. For a mare she was very big, strong and bullish, with plenty about her: she wasn't the type to get bullied in a race. Sometimes when you ride a mare over jumps they can be a little bit more timid than the geldings, but Like-A-Butterfly could hold her own and fight her corner, typical of Christy Roche.

It was Jonjo who first approached me directly about riding for JP at the Cheltenham April meeting in 2003. I'd already ridden a good few winners for him along the way, and got to know him better when he moved his operation down from Cumbria to Jackdaws Castle near Cheltenham in 2001. When he first spoke to me about it I was more than happy at Martin Pipe's, where I had access to some amazing horses and fabulous facilities and, as I never tire of reiterating, if you rode for Martin Pipe you were pretty much guaranteed to be champion jockey. I was still happy in my job, indeed I was always happy when riding for the Pipes. I just wasn't ready for a change and didn't feel the time was right. In addition I didn't feel that at that stage either Jonjo or JP had quite enough ammunition to tempt me away from the Pipes anyway, even if I had been looking to get away. So, I said thanks, Jonjo, but no thanks and that was that.

Our paths crossed again at the Cheltenham April meeting a year later. I'd just won the end-of-season grade 2 handicap chase on a horse of Martin's called Seebald, owned by Steve McManaman and Robbie Fowler, and after the race Jonjo collared me and asked again whether I'd be interested in speaking to JP about becoming his jockey. My first instinct was to give the same answer I had the previous year, but then I thought, why not, a chat's a chat with no obligation on either side. Let's hear what the story is.

I still wasn't necessarily thinking of leaving the Pipes. I was happy there and still riding plenty of winners for them, but that nagging feeling that anyone would have been champion jockey with advantages the Pipes gave them was making me ponder whether I wasn't having things a little too easy. Maybe, I thought, I needed to prove to myself that I was champion jockey on my own merits rather than just being a jockey-shaped cog in a well-oiled winning machine. I'd also been keeping half an eye out for Jonjo over the previous year and had noticed him becoming numerically stronger, which was important to me in my desire to be champion jockey. I agreed to have a conversation with JP the following evening at the Lygon Arms in Broadway, where he was staying while he was over at the races, along with his racing manager Frank Berry and of course Jonjo. I hadn't had many dealings with JP at that stage so was intrigued to meet him and instantly I found him very engaging with a gift for encouraging you to engage with him too.

It's as true today as it was that night in the spring of 2004: J.P. McManus doesn't say a great deal, but when he does it's well worth listening to. He told me what he was planning, that they were expanding his racing operation but making it better as well as bigger. It all sounded very convincing and appealing and by the end of the evening I had pretty much given JP my verbal assurance that I would come and ride for him. So much for just going and having a chat, but I trust my instincts and my instincts during that meeting assured me that moving to the McManus operation would be the right thing for me to do. After what I'd heard from JP, Frank and Jonjo in the Lygon Arms that night

I was convinced that I could still be champion jockey not just away from the Pipes but also as part of JP's organisation.

Once I'd said yes, JP was keen to formalise everything straightaway so they could make an announcement to the press as soon as possible. That wasn't a problem for me, but my immediate priority was to tell the Pipes. The last thing I wanted was for them to hear the news second-hand and the least that I owed them after all they'd done for me was to tell them face-to-face.

Telling the Pipes I was leaving them for J.P. McManus was one of the hardest things I've ever had to do. They'd been like a family to me for seven years, I'd spoken to them every day and the relationship we had was much, much more than a working one. JP was keen for me to tell them as soon as possible – as well as wanting to announce the news I suppose he might have been worried I'd mull it over and change my mind – but that suited me: the longer I left it the more anxious I'd get and the bigger deal it would become. I've thought about it a lot since and sometimes I wonder whether, had JP not encouraged me to go straight to the Pipes and tell them, I might actually have struggled to find the bottle to do it, and changed my mind.

I drove over to Somerset to see the Pipes the same evening on what was probably the most nerve-racking journey I've ever undertaken. When I arrived and gave them the news I don't think it came as a complete surprise. The first thing Martin said when I told him I'd been offered another job was to ask whether it was with JP, so he must have sniffed something in the air. Martin had probably noticed JP was acquiring more good horses and generally getting stronger, and I was after all the champion jockey and the obvious target for an ambitious operation, so if he hadn't been exactly expecting my news it wouldn't have been a complete bolt from the blue.

Martin asked if JP had offered me a retainer, which he had, and immediately offered to match it.

'It's not about money, Martin,' I said. 'If I felt a retainer was an issue between us I would have said so, but it isn't and never has been. I feel it's the right time for me to try a new challenge, to prove to myself that I can be champion jockey without riding for you. I need to do this for my own peace of mind and sense of self-worth.'

To my relief he replied that he found this totally understandable and I guess he felt a little happier knowing that I was going purely for racing reasons rather than for money.

Suddenly everything was in motion. I'd spoken briefly to Dave Roberts about the situation, and to Chanelle of course, but like all the major decisions I've made in my life it was my decision alone. I'm lucky to have some good friends whose opinions I value and respect, and there are times when I ring them for advice and to sound them out, but something as big as leaving the Pipes and going to JP had to be my decision. I didn't want anyone clouding my judgement or making me think differently when I'd already reached the right conclusion on my own.

I was a little daunted, I don't mind admitting. With it happening so quickly and so close to the end of the season, it took a while to sink in that I was starting a new campaign, the latest defence of my champion jockey title, without the backing of the Pipes.

The *Racing Post* made it their cover story when the news broke with an image – I still have it at the house – of Jonjo and JP either side of me superimposed over a sunrise with the headline 'A

New Dawn'. Then almost before I knew it the season started and I commenced my quest for enough winners to secure my tenth jockeys' championship. In a sense the swiftness with which the move happened was a blessing: there was less time to ruminate about it and having to focus on racing again straightaway made the whole situation seem less of a massive deal.

On a practical, everyday level very little changed as I'd ridden for Jonjo frequently over the years and indeed he had been a major factor in convincing me to move to JP. Jonjo has an outstanding reputation as a trainer, just as he had an outstanding reputation as a jockey, but he's also a lovely guy into the bargain. I've always said that in order to maintain a long and fruitful working partnership with someone, liking them is a key requirement. I've been lucky throughout my career that the key people I've worked with became friends as well as colleagues or employers and the same is true with Jonjo. I liked him from the very beginning, he was ambitious and I enjoyed his company very much, which made what could have been a difficult transition a lot easier.

He's one of the very best trainers in the business, too, with a fantastic knowledge of horses. He can read them instinctively and sense when a horse is starting to bloom or come to hand, and has a gift for tying that in to the animal's improvement as a racer. Synchronised was a great example: Jonjo transformed him from a handicap chaser winning the Midlands Grand National, probably the slowest race you can get, to winning the Gold Cup at Cheltenham, one of the fastest races in the calendar. It needs a really special knack with horses to pull off something like that and Jonjo is as good a trainer of a staying chaser as I've ever seen as well as being a talent spotter second to none. If I wanted to find a horse capable of winning the Grand National then Jonjo would be the man I'd task to find it. When I look back on some of the horses he's had in the National over the years it's astonishing Don't Push It is his only winner. Clan Royal could easily have won Nationals, Don't Push It was third as well as winning, Butler's Cabin could have won for him the year he fell at Becher's the second time around, even Shutthefrontdoor ran a great race in my last National ride.

Another thing I admire about Jonjo is his open-mindedness, he's always prepared to change and adapt. As I write this they're implementing a new regime at Jackdaws Castle, trying to make things work better because Jonjo feels that in the last couple of years he hasn't made the progress he'd have liked in order to challenge people like Paul Nicholls for the trainers' championship. So he's changed the routines and the way the horses are being trained because he wants to get better. You have to keep adapting in order to move forward, keep examining different angles as routes to improvement, and Jonjo's very good at that. He's very open to change and aware that you can't stand still and expect to make progress.

He's a great people person too. He's aware of the owner's lot; that they have other commitments and racing is their hobby, the way they blow off steam from the other compartments of their life by doing something they enjoy. So when the owners come down to the yard to see their horse or go for a day at the races Jonjo and his wife Jackie work hard to make it as enjoyable as possible for them. He recognises the importance of the trainer's role in making them feel there is a good reason for them having a horse in training, and how rewarding it can be for them even if the horse isn't beating all comers in every single race.

It's all part of what a good, kind person he is, immensely trust-worthy and always having a laugh and a joke to put you at your ease. Being a Corkman you wouldn't know whether he's at the wind-up or telling you the truth half the time, but he's a very genuine person which is very important when you're dealing with people's money and people's hobbies.

I've great time for Jonjo, as a person and as a trainer. He's given me three of the greatest days of my racing life and been a great influence on me. It meant a lot to me that I was riding one of his horses in my last race and I was glad that he was one of the first people I saw when I dismounted for the very last time from Box Office. When I watched the coverage of that last day at Sandown a few days later I saw a moment that was just typical Jonjo O'Neill. As Channel 4 waited for me to come back in they were interviewing people at the winner's enclosure who were saying some lovely, emotional things about the occasion. They put the microphone under Jonjo's nose expecting more of the same, but what they got was, 'Well, after the ride he's just given that horse, I tell you, he's never riding for me again.'

That was typical Jonjo, the iconoclast, always ready with a smart, cheeky thing to say, always making you laugh, always making you feel at ease.

I didn't really know JP at the start and I was a little in awe of him for quite a while. He was my boss, after all, and a very successful, very influential man. During the first three or four years I worked for JP I was always very wary about what I said to him, trying to say the right thing and certainly trying to avoid getting on the wrong side of him.

Racing is JP's hobby. It's his reward for working hard and be-coming successful, an enjoyable distraction from the working world and something he looks forward to. It's a bit like support-ing your football team in a way, when the anticipation of the match at the weekend, when you can roar and shout and let off a bit of steam, helps get you through the working week, and JP is the same with racing. He's fortunate to be in the position he is, being able to indulge his passion for horses in the way he does. If money can't buy you happiness it can certainly buy you time, and JP is able to give over large chunks of his time to the sport he loves which has knock-on benefits for everyone, from the champion jockey to the guy putting on his bets at the Tote window.

In this knowledge I was conscious of what I said to JP and wanted to keep him happy. I was always a little sheepish about ringing him or speaking to him in the early days because he was employing me, I was on the books in a way that I wasn't officially when I was with Martin, even though we'd had the understanding we did. The relationship with JP felt different from that at first, there was more of a respectful distance on my part, but as time passed I relaxed a little, we spoke more, spent more time together, I began to feel much more relaxed in his company and our working relationship became underpinned by a close personal friendship. I wouldn't like to set about ruining his reputation by saying we're a little bit alike, but in some ways maybe there are similarities. There are occasions when I don't think JP is a great talker, that he's a little like me in that some-times he can't be arsed with it, but the more time I spent in his company the more I liked being in his company. Eventually our relationship developed to the stage where I felt I could have my say and tell him what I really thought without it undermining the boss/employee working relationship in any way. We have conversations like two mates would have in the pub, just like I was watching him having with Jonjo in The Outside Chance, and I enjoy his company very much. I'm honestly not just saying that because he's the boss but JP knows me well enough to know that if I didn't like his company and hadn't wanted to ride for him any more, at any point, I would absolutely have told him so. And vice versa, of course.

I really enjoyed riding for both of them very much. Indeed I've been lucky enough to enjoy working for all the people whose paths have crossed with mine over the years, from Billy Rock and Jim Bolger – much and all as I've often said I hated him – to Toby Balding, the Pipes, JP and Jonjo and of course Dave Roberts. Billy gave me the perfect grounding in racing and showed careful responsibility for my future when he told me it was time to take the next step and that it should be with Jim. Jim played as big a part in my career as anyone in moulding me and instilling good habits the way he did. Toby helped me out and showed me the ropes in an almost paternal fashion, showing great kindness to a skinny kid from a small village in Ireland fresh off the boat, while the Pipes were like a surrogate family to me for the best part of eight years. Martin's mother Betty would always hand him a little packet of raisins or wine gums to pass on if she knew he was going to see me that day, something that carried on even after I'd left Martin's and the raisins and wine gums would still turn up.

Even after I'd gone to work for JP and Jonjo I used to stop in and see Betty if I was passing on my way to Newton Abbot or Exeter or somewhere down in that direction. I loved her company, to the extent where even though Betty's house was at the top of Martin's drive I'd visit her and generally not pop in and see Martin. And of course, whenever I left Betty's the little paper bag of raisins or wine gums would always be pressed into my hand as I walked out of the door.

I enjoyed riding for JP and Jonjo as much as I enjoyed riding for the Pipes to the extent that even though I've stopped racing I'm going to remain involved with the horses. I had some of my greatest days in racing thanks to them and it means so much to me that they were all in JP's and Noreen's colours. It's funny how everything changes with time: before riding for JP I'd ridden a lot for David Johnson via the Pipes and when people first saw me in the green and gold they'd say, 'That doesn't look right, it doesn't look as good on you as the Johnsons' blue and green', yet my career almost came to be defined by the green and gold. Eve used to think the colours were mine and mine alone, while Archie used to point at the television and get excited when he saw me in the green and gold before he'd even turned two. Those colours have had a huge influence and impact on my life and many people put the two naturally together. But they're not mine any more. Other jockeys will wear them, deserve to wear them and will wear them with distinction and that's fine with me. As long as they don't break any of my records, of course.

I was always proud to wear the green and gold colours because I like the whole McManus family very much. It's a little bit like our house in that JP thinks he's the boss but it's actually his wife Noreen who's firmly in charge. Actually, maybe that's why I identify with them so closely. JP and Noreen's children John, Suzanne and Kieran all love their racing too and love a day out at the races. They were all there to celebrate the Grand National and the Gold Cup, which helped to make them even more fulfilling days because you can see you're making a lot of people happy. It's a very pleasing ripple effect from winning a big race: you sense your own happiness and sense of achievement passing through others who have an emotional investment in the occasion. That, for me, is what racing is about: achieving goals and success and making good people happy into the bargain. I've had a great deal of good days with the McManuses and I sincerely hope they can continue now I've retired.

Looking round The Outside Chance that night, hours after riding my 4,000th winner, seeing friends, family and colleagues, past and present, all mixed together, the air filled with the hubbub of conversation and pierced by bursts of laughter, I allowed myself a rare feeling of accomplishment. Nobody, I felt, would ever know a feeling like this because nobody, surely, would ride 4,000 winners ever again. For all the jockeys' championships, the National and Gold Cup wins, this achievement was mine and mine alone, nobody could match it and nobody could take it away from me.

I'd toyed mentally with the idea of making it to 5,000 winners, but the euphoria that had fuelled such thoughts earlier in the day had tempered a little and I reverted instead to my notion of retiring once I reached twenty jockeys' titles. That still seemed like a plausible aim and was still a year and a half away, so I didn't really need to think about it too much yet. But yes, twenty titles, that sounded like a good way to finish. Then I reminded myself that I hadn't secured number nineteen yet. A win at Southwell on Forthefunofit the following day would help with that. It would be the four-year-old's first race but I felt he had a good chance. Imagine that, though: a first race. I was 4,000 winners in and I found myself thinking how much I'd like to go back and start all over again. And this time, do it better.

TWELVE

Schooling horses, Jackdaws Castle
7 May 2015

It was good to feel normal again.

Just for a while I was back in the old routine. I'd left the house about 6.20, my breath clouding on the chill morning air as I walked out to the car, and arrived at Jackdaws Castle just under an hour later. I've never been a morning person in my life, but in the late spring when the sky's turquoise, the sun's just on its way up and there's a bit of mist settling in the dips in the landscape, not to mention there being hardly anyone on the roads, it's an uplifting time to be out and about. I went into the office, made myself a cup of tea, sat down, licked my thumb and had a quick leaf through the *Racing Post* until Jonjo arrived, smiling as ever. A crunch of footsteps on gravel, the slamming of doors and we were in the jeep and heading for the gallops.

It had been a strange few weeks. The days leading up to Sandown had me almost in a trance, the day itself flashed by in a blizzard of emotions, and the time since had felt relaxed and happy but curiously directionless. When your body's been used to doing something for twenty-odd years it's hard to suddenly stop doing it altogether, so when Jonjo said he'd have a couple of horses working that morning I volunteered to give one of them a workout.

Being back on a horse drew all the strands that had drifted apart over the previous weeks back together and I truly felt like me again. It had been the longest time in my life other than through injury that I'd not ridden a horse and I'd really missed it. Strip away everything else, the titles, the stats, the wins, the weighing in, weighing out, the saunas, the travelling, the stewards, the punters, the bookies, the parade rings and winner's enclosures, and you're left with the simple pleasure of riding a horse. Being high up on the animal, leaving all your cares and worries at ground level and it being just the two of you, guiding each other, helping each other, working together to give each other as much pleasure as possible. Being on the gallops that morning, feeling the thunder of the hooves beneath me, the roar of the wind in my ears, the heady musk of horse and turf in my nostrils, made things feel normal again.

Schooling horses is an important part of their development. Most people only see racehorses when they're at the races but the real work is done at the stables and on the gallops, honing their jumping skills and giving them good fast run-outs to keep them at the top of their game. With the young horses it's about learning their craft, for the older ones it's just good for their muscles, keeping the horses toned as well as keeping them happy psychologically. These animals are born to race and are at their happiest out on the gallops being put through their paces. Of the more experienced horses at Jonjo's I used to look forward to riding out on Minella Rocco or More Of That in particular. More Of That won the World Hurdle at Cheltenham a couple of years ago with Barry Geraghty riding him but I won on him a couple of times and I'll probably school him over fences a few times before he goes novice chasing.

There are five hurdles and five fences at Jackdaws Castle, and I gave the horse two goes over the fences, just to keep its eye in, good for the muscles, good for the mind, for horse and jockey. Some mornings while I was still riding I'd be schooling up to a dozen horses at a time but I'd be on each one for only five minutes. The stable lads would have them warmed up and when I'd finished the lads would take them away and cool them down. It's a good way to judge the strengths and weaknesses of the younger horses and identify things that maybe need working on. Some will be natural jumpers, some will need work on their jumping. It's also good to get a feel for what kind of form the older horses are in, too.

We went back to the office afterwards for another cup of tea and a bit of a chat. Then Jonjo stood up, shook my hand and said he had to go off and attend to a bit of business somewhere, and then things suddenly weren't normal any more.

This used to be the point in the morning at which I'd leave Jackdaws Castle and head off to wherever I was racing, settling down in the back of the car for a sleep as my driver Steve nosed us onto the motorway and drove me to wherever I'd be trying to rack up a few more winners that afternoon. Now I wasn't racing any more. The horses I was schooling, I'd never ride them in a race. Whatever form I was finding the older horses in was information I'd pass on to other jockeys. There would be no dismounting with butterflies in my stomach as I thought, this could be a Gold Cup horse or a Champion Hurdler, no thrill going over a jump and thinking this, this horse could be the one for the National. There would be no fastest fifty winners, hundred winners, two hundred winners and certainly no three hundred winners. There would be no more colours hanging on the peg, no more weighing room banter and no more winner's enclosure presentations. In the changing rooms at Cheltenham and Aintree there were now places where I *used* to sit.

It was an odd feeling, knowing that I'd leave Jonjo's and go home for the day, pottering about with the television on in the background and keeping half an eye on the racing, but it was a feeling tempered with relief. It might sound strange, given most of this story has been about how competitive I am, but I haven't missed the competitive side of racing at all. I have missed race riding, I've definitely missed that, but I certainly haven't missed being in the car for however many hours every day. It was actually quite nice sitting in the kitchen at home as Eve and Archie ran about the place, looking at the *Racing Post* and seeing early season cards for places like Cartmel and Hexham, both eight-hour round trips at least from home and the kind of journeys I used to make all the time early in the season to break the lads' hearts and hopes of getting anywhere near the jockeys' championship title, and just thinking, I might watch those races if I've nothing else on.

I look at the paper now, see those early season meetings where there's only one a day and they could be anywhere, usually a very long way away, and I think, I am so happy I'm not doing that. It's a whole new sensation for me, looking at the paper and thinking, Jesus, I don't want to go there, because in the past I've always *had* to do it and there was no weighing up the pros and cons. Already, not even a season into retirement, I sometimes wonder how I managed to motivate myself to do that every day of every week of every year. Sometimes it feels like it was a different person going to all those meetings and it'll be even more mystifying when the winter comes. In the winter I'd go to places like Carlisle at a time of year when flying back isn't possible because it's dark at half past three, so by the time you've showered and changed and got to wherever it is the little planes fly out of it's too late. And it's expensive of course. When I was riding my car used to do up to 75,000 miles a year – if I've ridden the equivalent of going twice around the world then I've definitely gone around it a few more times on top of that in cars. In twenty years there can't be anyone who spent more time in a car than I did.

I do miss the riding side of it, the little routines and rhythms of racing that became second nature over the years, but I've been keeping busy, playing golf at a couple of nice tournaments with Lee Westwood, Shane Lowry and Ricky Fowler, all top, top professionals, and if I was still riding obviously I wouldn't have even thought about taking time out to do that. I've been going out more too, becoming much more sociable, and it's nice not having to watch what I eat so closely. I've certainly enjoyed being out at night and not looking at my watch thinking, I need to go home or I'll be tired for racing, or getting halfway through a meal out, stopping and thinking, shit, I wonder what weight I'll be in the morning. These days I'm even eating biscuits all the time and it's great. The only thing worrying me on that front is that my clothes might not fit any more. I put on about ten or twelve pounds in the first month after I retired, and there's no way I'm buying a whole new wardrobe. I haven't got on the scales and thought, jeez, how am I that weight? But I'm going to keep reasonably fit and I wouldn't want to put on many more pounds than I've gained since I retired.

I miss the weighing room with all the banter and the camaraderie. I'll miss Dickie Johnson whom I've known for twenty years around the circuit, and I've only spoken to Dave Roberts a couple of times when I used to speak to him every day. The close friends I've made through racing, lads like Carl, Fitzy and Dominic Elsworth, they're all retired now too of course so we'll still be dragging each other around the golf course, and I've been lucky in that the trainers I've ridden for call for a chat now and again, so I am keeping in touch. And there *are* things I miss. I miss the discipline, the regime and the routine. I miss the structure racing gave my life a little bit.

In general as I write this I'm coping OK and haven't found it difficult suddenly being away from the closeted everyday world in which I was hot-housed for more than two decades. Those words may come back to haunt me, of course, and it may well be different come the winter when the better horses start to come out and there's good racing on a Saturday featuring good horses that I've ridden before. I might not be so chilled about it when I'm watching my old rides winning big races and hearing people talking about how great the jockey is. When those days arrive I wouldn't be human if I didn't suck my teeth and think, that could have been me. I'm sure there will be days when it isn't OK, when I'll really miss racing and wish I could be back out there thundering around Cheltenham or soaring over Becher's Brook. I hope that happens, in fact, because I'm lucky enough to have done a job that I loved for a very long time in which the highs were very high indeed and I *want* to miss it. Chanelle's dad, with his business partner Paul Chaplin, have a horse with Jonjo called Rock N Rhythm that I'd won on three weeks before I retired. A week after Sandown, on the Bank Holiday Monday, Rock N Rhythm won at Kempton and Richard Johnson rode it, which gave me a few pangs. I was jealous that Richard had ridden it and I was jealous that he was riding full stop, but ultimately I was glad he'd ridden it, especially if it helped him towards the jockey's championship. I saw Jezki win at Punchestown during a week in which JP had ten winners of which I'd have ridden probably five, so that was a strange feeling, but at no time have I ever regretted my decision to retire when I did. I'm not a jockey any more, I'll keep reminding myself of that and just move on. I know retiring was definitely the right thing to do and it's vindicated by the fact I can watch a race like the one at Kempton and think, oh man, I could still be doing that rather than, I remember that race last year and I didn't fancy it. It shows that I retired for the right reasons.

The immediate aftermath of Sandown was a busy time so I didn't have time to ruminate much anyway. The following day, the Sunday, we had a hundred people to the house for lunch and it was a fantastic occasion. At the end of the night – or rather, early the next morning – there were still probably about a dozen people left and I was related to most of them other than Dominic Elsworth and his wife Louise, who's Jonjo's daughter, and Denise Byrne, a good friend of ours, and I basically had to come downstairs and ask if there was any chance they could fuck off home.

On the Monday I played a bit of golf with Mick Fitz and Richard Hughes, then went to Ireland on the Tuesday morning where I had arranged to go and see Robbie McNamara in hospital. Robbie had a fall from a horse called Bursledon in a handicap hurdle at Wexford on 10 April 2015, the Friday of Aintree, suffering serious injuries to his chest, abdomen and spine. The following day, when he should have been alongside me at Aintree riding Lord Windermere in the Grand National, Robbie was recovering from emergency surgery in Dublin's Mater Hospital that saved his life but might not have saved his ability to walk again.

Robbie, whom I'd got to know quite well over the previous five or six years, is still only in his mid-twenties. He was friendly with a couple of the Irish lads I know, Alain Cawley, who comes with us to Portugal playing golf every year, and Shane Donohoe, and Robbie started coming along on the golf trips where I got to know him pretty well. The operation he had was a serious one in which two titanium bars were inserted either side of his spine to stabilise him, but when he came round from the surgery he was paralysed from the waist down. As I write, nobody's sure if it's permanent or not but Robbie's a very positive young man who will I hope bounce back from his terrible injuries. He's already making plans to become a trainer, and when I saw him he was talking about getting back playing golf again. That wasn't just empty talk or denial either, he absolutely meant it. And if anyone can, Robbie can.

Once I'd seen Robbie I went to watch the racing at Punchestown and the day after that I travelled west to see Robbie's first cousin John Thomas McNamara, who is paralysed from the neck down after a fall at Cheltenham in 2013.

He'd been riding a horse of Jonjo's called Galaxy Rock in the Kim Muir on the third day of the festival when the horse fell at the first and put JT on the ground head first. He fractured two vertebrae in his neck, had to be airlifted from the course to Frenchay Hospital in Bristol and was put into an induced coma after surgery. He came round to the news that he was permanently paralysed from the neck down. I'd known John Thomas for a good while on the circuit, he was one of the older lads like me, and the thing I remember most vividly about his fall is being in the weighing room that day at Cheltenham, hearing the thump of the air ambulance's rotors as it passed overhead and seeing John Thomas's clothes hanging up on his peg where he'd left them barely an hour earlier. There were rumours flying around that he'd been resuscitated a couple of times on the track, that the only reason he was alive was that there was an anaesthetist at the fence he fell at, that he was dead. The medical care at racing today is better than ever so we knew he was in the best possible hands and apparently there was an anaesthetist at the first fence who acted quickly to possibly save JT's life, but the thing I remember most clearly is just staring at his clothes on the peg and thinking over and over: he might never be back for them. He might never be back.

I saw JT on the Wednesday of Punchestown and I hadn't seen him for a while. I'd been to visit him in the Frenchay not long after the fall, and I saw him when he'd been transferred to Mater Hospital in Dublin and when he was moved to Southport, and I'd visited him and Caroline at their bungalow in Limerick around Christmas time after he'd been finally able to go home. But I have to admit that since I'd been seriously considering retirement in that latter part of my last season I hadn't been to see him at all. I'd found the prospect of going to see him really tough all of a sudden and hadn't been for probably four or five months, the longest I'd gone without seeing him since the fall two years earlier.

But finally I was able to get myself to Limerick and meet him at his yard. As well as Caroline he has two carers looking after him who bring him down to the yard in his specially adapted wheelchair. He has twenty horses in training in the winter; when I saw him he was down to about ten because it was the end of the season, but however many there are JT is there first thing every morning regardless, telling the lads what to do with the horses and watching them being schooled. I spent a good couple of hours with him that day and the time flew by in his company. I found him utterly inspiring but seeing him like that was heartbreaking. Considering the extent of his injuries – he breathes through a ventilator, although he can come off it for three or four hours at a time – it's incredible that he can get out in the yard with the horses at all the way he does. It must be what keeps him going, that and his amazing wife and their three kids, but for someone who's devoted his life to horses, who loves the animals and loved riding them, it must break his heart being able to look at them and watch them but not touch them.

Coming away from John Thomas's house I felt so incredibly lucky that after all the rides I'd had, more than any other jockey, and all the falls I'd had, I was able to retire on my own terms and, literally, walk away. I turned and looked back at JT's house and thought, there's a lad, riding as an amateur because he loved the sport, who went out one day, got a bad fall and his life was changed for ever. So, disjointed and all as I was finding being re-tired and going to Punchestown as a civilian, as my wife calls it, every time there's been a moment where I've felt sad or sorry for myself, I've pulled myself up short by thinking about those two lads, first cousins from the same family, facing the same uncertain futures. Facing them square on, of course, with outstanding courage and determination, but facing them nonetheless and nothing I've had to deal with seems remotely difficult when set against that. I was lucky, I got out in one piece and have very little to worry about. John Thomas and Robbie keep me from moping around or telling myself that I've had it tough, that retiring was a tough decision to make. Well, at least that decision was in my hands because it had been taken entirely out of theirs. I found things a lot easier after that trip to Ireland and seeing the McNamaras. They helped keep everything in perspective and, once again, made me realise just how lucky I am.

That trip also made me reflect on how I'd changed as a person over the years. Having children definitely helped me and my career in ways I hadn't anticipated. Obviously they made me happier, there's no prouder father in the land than me, but you sometimes hear it said that when people in sport get married and have kids they lose their edge and start having different priorities. It was something I was genuinely worried about – look at how I tried to put off marrying Chanelle for as long as I did – and there's no doubt that when you have kids you do have different priorities because they are immediately the most important thing in your life. Contrary to what I'd feared, having the children made me a better person and a better sportsman because they stopped me from getting too up or too down. When I came home from racing, no matter whether I'd had a brilliant day or a rotten day Eve and Archie didn't give a toss. All that mattered was that Daddy was home and they were delighted to see me and that immediately took my racing cares away. Well, most of them.

One of my good friends, Gary Brown, was staying with us recently, saw me playing with Archie and said to Chanelle, 'Oh, it looks like Anthony's found someone who actually likes him at last.' In a lot of ways he's right. Well, obviously Eve likes me too, but for the first time ever I know for sure that there are two people in the world who definitely like me, and like me unconditionally. Eve and Archie have made me much more aware of kids at the races, too. Whenever there were children looking for photographs and autographs I'd make an extra effort to smile and be nice to them because I'd think, if this was my daughter and some sports person didn't give them the time of day, I'd see the look of disappointment on their face and think, who does that prick think he is? So when I signed a racecard for a youngster, or posed for a photograph with them and saw the look on their face afterwards, I'd superimpose that same look on Eve's face or Archie's face and I'd think, I've helped make that wee kid's day, and I've helped make his parents' day as well.

Aside from children, I found it easier to give people more of my time over the years and I do think I became a better person as I got older. I've Chanelle to thank for that to a great extent. It's not a nice thing to admit but it's an unfortunate fact that as a sports person, especially one in an individual rather than team sport, you have to be very selfish. I spent most of my life thinking it was all about me because to be good at something and dominate my sport, being self-centred goes with the territory. It has to be all about you and I certainly thought for pretty much my whole career that it really was all about me. Before Eve and Archie were born I didn't really care about anyone else, I was just wrapped up in riding winners and anything or anyone that got in the way of that was a problem. Chanelle copped most of the fallout from that in the early years of our relationship because I wasn't used to anyone else being important except me. It's a hard thing to admit but I've changed enough since to recognise it and acknowledge it and I've certainly got Chanelle to thank for that. And in Eve and Archie, now there are two people in the world whom I care about more than anything, and as long as they're all right I can carry on. It really is no longer all about me.

I became more comfortable with myself as I got older, happier in my own skin and happier with what I'd achieved. As the years passed I started to enjoy myself more, my career became less about punishment and more about fulfilment. Even when I'd been champion jockey for ten years I didn't really feel any sense of achievement. It was the same when I'd won a dozen titles, even when I'd been champion jockey for fifteen years I felt I'd done nothing to permit myself to feel any kind of professional satisfaction and I was no better than or different from anyone else. It took riding my 4,000th winner to allow me any sense of achievement, because that was the first time I felt I'd done something unique and possibly unsurpassable.

So yes, I'm sure I did change as a person and I'm sure it was for the better. It was also vital for me as a jockey and vital for me as a human being, because anyone who doesn't change doesn't go anywhere. You need a routine that works but you need to be prepared to adapt that routine when the circumstances demand it. It's something that took me a while to learn, but I think I managed to harness my stubbornness and make it work for me rather than punish me. Partly as a result of that, mostly because of my wife and children, I definitely became a happier person as I got older. Where once I didn't feel I had any right to be happy, getting older, getting married and having children allowed me to appreciate what I've done and gave me the permission to enjoy it a little more.

This was demonstrated most obviously during my retirement weeks and in particular during that last day at Sandown. It's an occasion that I think of often and it still feels a bit surreal. I couldn't believe the affection that washed down from the stands; that 18,000 people had turned out. The people at Sandown told me they could have sold thousands more tickets, and when I heard that then I thought at least I've done a bit of good for the sport. Well, either that or people were showing up to make sure I really did pack it in.

Some journalists and commentators were calling it the 'longest farewell tour in history', but it never really felt like a farewell tour and I never intended it to be that way. There were times when I was embarrassed about the attention and times when I wondered whether people were suspicious I was doing it for the publicity, but the last thing I've ever wanted has been publicity. I just loved being a jockey. I wanted to ride winners and I loved riding horses. I didn't want to ride more winners than anyone else in order that I could get publicity for it, not at all, and I'm pretty sure the way things panned out did racing no harm whatsoever. Racing has been so good to me, and when I look back to that day at Sandown I feel like I gave a little bit back to it, that I'd tried to repay it in some way for the enjoyment it gave me and the life I've led and at least a portion of that debt has been cleared.

In the days following my final race I'd often pull out my phone and read a text I received from Sir Alex Ferguson not long after I'd announced my retirement. I'm not trying to drop names or anything, but the text meant a lot to me and I'd re-read every now and again when doubts about retiring would cloud my mind and it soon helped to dispel them. It read:

> Tony, I'm so happy for you on announcing your retirement. It's the right decision at the right time of your life. Many people would differ from my view, but I've been at the top, I know how expectations have filled your life, but you know your body better than anyone else and the continual demands on yourself for excellence wears you down. I felt it in my last few years at United but I kept saying to myself, 'just one more'. The energy you need to do it is indescribable. It is heart wrenching as I was built as a winner and I couldn't think about losing. One more time. I had to go out as a winner. You have made a great decision Tony. Many people will be advising you on what to do in your retirement, but you do what you want to do. It has been a pleasure watching you.
>
> Alex Ferguson

One of the questions I've been asked most often since I retired is what I'll do to replace the buzz I got from riding winners, the feeling that drove me on and motivated me for two decades. You hear other sports people talking about their difficulty in finding something to replace the intensity of the pursuit of sporting excellence and, as someone who was very driven all through my riding career, there was a worry that I'd find life difficult once I'd stopped riding. It did concern me a little when I looked ahead to life as an ex-jockey, and I know it's very early for me to be saying this, but as far as I'm concerned the buzz has gone. It's not there any more. There is no replacing the buzz because there's nothing to replace. That chapter has closed and it's time to look forward.

Whether you're a footballer, a golfer, whatever your sport might be, once your time is gone, that's it, finished, done. You can try to find something to replace that buzz by all means, but, believe me, it ain't coming back. Sport is a short career: I'm a veteran and I'm only just into my forties. Every sports person is going to have to do something different eventually and, who knows, you might find something that gives you a feeling that replicates the drive and desire you had in your first career, it might even be a buzz, but it's not going to be *that* buzz. So, right now, I'm not seeing my post-riding career as a quest to find something to replace that feeling because as far as I'm concerned the feeling I got from racing is gone.

I wonder whether for some retired sports people when they talk about missing the buzz they actually mean they're missing the adulation, being in the public eye. Is it that they miss the buzz of walking down the street and people knowing who they are? The autograph requests, the people slinging an arm around their shoulder for a selfie? Do they miss people talking about them? As Oscar Wilde said, the only thing worse than being talked about is not being talked about: is that the problem? That's certainly not the case for me. I can see why some people might find the adulation rewarding, even intoxicating, but giving in to it can never end well because ultimately, it's fleeting. Next year, possibly even by the time you read this, someone else will be champion jockey. The media will be saying, 'Oh, isn't he great, and you know what? He might be the best we've ever seen.' That's the way it goes: people forget about you very quickly. In golf people are raving about Jordan Spieth being the best golfer anyone's ever seen, meanwhile Tiger Woods slinks dejectedly out of a side door and no one notices. In football they talk about

Messi versus Ronaldo as the double-header for the greatest footballer ever because a fifteen-year-old kid wouldn't know who George Best was, or Pelé or Diego Maradona. It's all subjective, all about opinions, everyone's got one and as time passes there'll be more opinions about more players and jockeys.

I'm not interested in any of that and I'm certainly not interested in going looking for the fucking buzz. Something will come along that I'll enjoy very much, I'm sure, something that I'll look forward to doing and that I'll find very fulfilling (don't forget that I'm well versed in bulling cows, thanks to Billy Rock . . .) but there won't be a buzz because I don't need one. Rest assured, there's no big dark void where racing used to be eating away at the core of my being and leaving my retirement stretching out in front of me like a yawning chasm of ennui. I'll be fine. There's no buzz, and I'll be fine.

As for what I'll do, I've no firm plans as yet. I know people have speculated about my becoming a trainer, but I can tell you now that will never happen. For one thing, if someone held a gun to my head and told me I had to be a trainer it would be of flat horses, and I look at Aidan O'Brien, who's had eleven Irish Derby winners, five English and won every classic going and he's barely five years older than I am, so what's the point in my starting now? I'm never going to beat that. Also, as I said earlier, there's not the same sense of discipline about the younger jockeys that there used to be in my time at Jim Bolger's, you couldn't pull that off in the modern world, so training is not going to be an option for me.

I have been doing plenty of bits and pieces to keep myself busy. I did a talk for *The Times* newspaper at a conference where the first speaker was David Cameron, the second was Nicola

Sturgeon, and then there was me. I didn't have much to follow up with after those two, as you can probably imagine. I wrote a novel a couple of years ago, which was something I enjoyed very much. It was a bit racy – I roped in my wife and her friends for those parts – but I have that in mind as the first of a trilogy, so you never know, there could be more to come. In fact, the next festival I'll be attending in Cheltenham will be the literary festival, believe it or not.

As for racing, sometimes I think I've left it in a good state and sometimes I'm not so sure about it. I know some of the big yards are having problems employing stable staff at the moment and it worries me that fewer people are coming into the sport to work. Another big worry is that there seems to be far fewer jockeys riding now than there were when I started riding. In my first season there was something in the region of 150 licensed National Hunt jockeys but that figure is now down to around ninety. It's a bit of a worry. I don't know if the life of a professional jockey is financially less appealing to people or whether there are other reasons. Whatever the cause I worry about the overall standard of jockeyship because competition makes people better, and if there are half the number of jockeys the level of competition drops accordingly. I don't believe the standard of riding is generally as good as it was ten years ago. I said this in an interview a few months before I retired and it came across as if I was saying there were no jockeys as good as those who were around a decade ago, which isn't remotely what I meant. I meant there isn't the *depth* there used to be. There are still great jockeys and some of the leading jockeys today are every bit as good, if not better than the great names of the past, but without them racing against each other that will always remain an opinion rather than incontrovertible fact. There are people who wouldn't put me in their list of top ten jump jockeys: that's just the way people are and that's fine with me. When I retired people were selecting my top ten rides: they were all different and all of them were different to the ten I'd pick.

But in my opinion the standard of the top jockeys will always be consistently good. Take the leading jockeys of today, lads like Richard Johnson, Ruby Walsh, Barry Geraghty, then go back to Richard Dunwoody, Adrian Maguire, Norman Williamson, Peter Scudamore, John Francome, Jonjo O'Neill, Fred Winter, you can go right back to Fred Archer in the nineteenth century; people will put up an argument that *he* was the best, no, he was the best, rubbish, it was *him*, he was definitely the best. That's how people are and it's that kind of debate that makes sport so fascinating, but all those names are worthy of being mentioned in the same breath as each other.

Overall I think racing is doing pretty well. Indeed, given the shortage of jockeys I wouldn't mind having another go myself, going back to the beginning and starting out again. I'd do a few things differently, and surely to God things would turn out better next time round, but even if I can't go right to the back of the queue and begin all over again I'll still ride horses. I love riding, I have done ever since my dad first put me on a horse and I can't imagine life without it even if I'm not actually racing any more. I'll keep schooling horses and riding out at Jonjo's and might even ride a few more round the country for JP. It won't be the same as racing, but I love riding and I like schooling, I get a real kick from it. It'll keep me fit, too; I like being fit and am definitely not going to turn into a fat fella. I'm pretty sure I look a little less gaunt than when I was sweating out the pounds every day to make the weight – I think I might even have cheeks, now – but I've been doing a good bit of bike riding lately and there are a few friends who want me to have a go at the amateur stages of the Tour de France, so I might have a crack at that.

Whatever I do, though, I fully intend to embrace the future rather than wallow in the past. I reckon I've got that out of the way in these pages. I received some very nice letters on my retirement from some great people from the racing world. I'll treasure all of them, but one that stands out in my mind came from John Magnier. At the end of a letter that expressed some wonderful sentiments and good wishes, he finished with the words, 'keep looking forward'.

And he's right. You don't go anywhere if you don't look forward.

Notable Career Feats

Winners Ridden

National Hunt winners in Great Britain

Season	Winners
1994–95	74
1995–96	175
1996–97	190
1997–98	253
1998–99	186
1999–00	245
2000–01	191
2001–02	289*
2002–03	258
2003–04	209
2004–05	200
2005–06	178
2006–07	184
2007–08	140
2008–09	186
2009–10	195
2010–11	218
2011–12	199
2012–13	185
2013–14	218
2014–15	231

*A British Horse Racing record for the most winners ridden in a season by a jockey (flat or jumps)

National Hunt winners in Ireland

Season	Winners
1993–94	3
1994–95	4
1995–96	7
1996–97	2
1997–98	8
1998–99	4
1999–00	7
2000–01	0
2001–02	1
2002–03	0
2003–04	0
2004–05	13
2005–06	22
2006–07	7
2007–08	8
2008–09	5
2009–10	6
2010–11	6
2011–12	12
2012–13	8
2013–14	11
2014–15	10

Winning milestones

1,000th winner – **Majadou**, Cheltenham, 11 December 1999
2,000th winner – **Magical Bailiwick**, Wincanton, 17 January 2004

3,000th winner – **Restless D'Artaix**, Plumpton, 9 February 2009

4,000th winner – **Mountain Tunes**, Towcester, 7 November 2013

Big Race Wins

Grand Nationals

Grand National – **Don't Push It** (2010)
Irish Grand National – **Butler's Cabin** (2007)
Midlands Grand National – **Synchronised** (2010)
Scottish Grand National – **Belmont King** (1997)
Welsh Grand National – **Synchronised** (2010)

Cheltenham Festival

Albert Bartlett Novices' Hurdle – **Black Jack Ketchum** (2006), **Wichita Lineman** (2007), **At Fishers Cross** (2013)
Arkle Challenge Trophy – **Or Royal** (1997), **Champleve** (1998), **Well Chief** (2004)
Byrne Group Plate – **Majadou** (1999)
Cathcart Challenge Cup – **Cyfor Malta** (1998), **Royal Auclair** (2002)
Champion Bumper – **Liberman** (2003)
Champion Hurdle – **Make A Stand** (1997), **Brave Inca** (2006), **Binocular** (2010)
Cheltenham Gold Cup – **Mr Mulligan** (1997), **Synchronised** (2012)
County Hurdle – **Blowing Wind** (1998), **Alderwood** (2012)
Festival Trophy Handicap Chase – **Wichita Lineman** (2009)

JLT Novices' Chase – **Noble Prince** (2011), **Taquin Du Seuil** (2014)

Jewson Novices' Handicap Chase – **Reveillez** (2006)

Johnny Henderson Grand Annual Chase – **Kibreet** (1996), **Edredon Bleu** (1998), **Alderwood** (2013)

Pertemps Final – **Unsinkable Boxer** (1998)

Queen Mother Champion Chase – **Edredon Bleu** (2000)

RSA Chase – **Albertas Run** (2008)

Ryanair Chase – **Albertas Run** (2010, 2011), **Uxizandre** (2015)

Supreme Novices' Hurdle – **Hors La Loi III** (1999)

Other notable races

Aintree Hurdle – **Pridwell** (1998), **Jezki** (2015)

Ascot Chase – **Tresor de Mai** (2002), **Tiutchev** (2003)

Bet365 Gold Cup – **Bounce Back** (2002), **Hennessy** (2009)

Betfred Bowl – **Tiutchev** (2004), **Exotic Dancer** (2007)

Celebration Chase – **Edredon Bleu** (2001), **Seebald** (2003), **French Opera** (2011)

Champion Four Year Old Hurdle – **Shaunies Lady** (1996)

Christmas Hurdle – **Straw Bear** (2006), **Binocular** (2010, 2011), **Darlan** (2012), **My Tent Or Yours** (2013)

December Festival Hurdle – **Brave Inca** (2005)

Fighting Fifth Hurdle – **Straw Bear** (2006), **My Tent Or Yours** (2013)

Galway Hurdle – **Toast the Spreece** (1997), **Thomas Edison** (2014)

Galway Plate – **Finger Onthe Pulse** (2010), **Carlingford Lough** (2013)

Hatton's Grace Hurdle – **Brave Inca** (2006), **Jezki** (2013)

Hennessy Gold Cup (Ireland) – **Carlingford Lough** (2015)

International Hurdle – **Valiramix** (2001), **Binocular** (2008)

Irish Champion Hurdle – **Brave Inca** (2006)

King George VI Chase – **Best Mate** (2002)

Lexus Chase – **Exotic Dancer** (2008), **Synchronised** (2011)

Liverpool Hurdle – **Galant Moss** (1999), **Deano's Beeno** (2003)

Long Walk Hurdle – **Deano's Beeno** (2002), **Big Buck's** (2010, 2011)

Melling Chase – **Viking Flagship** (1996), **Albertas Run** (2010), **Don Cossack** (2015)

Morgiana Hurdle – **Brave Inca** (2005)

Paddy Power Gold Cup – **Cyfor Malta** (1998), **Lady Cricket** (2000), **Shooting Light** (2001), **Exotic Dancer** (2007)

Powers Gold Cup – **Like-a-Butterfly** (2005), **Justified** (2006), **Gilgamboa** (2015)

Punchestown Champion Hurdle – **Brave Inca** (2005), **Jezki** (2014)

Tingle Creek Chase – **Master Minded** (2008)

Tolworth Hurdle – **Iznogoud** (2001), **Royal Boy** (2014)

Victor Chandler Chase – **Nordance Prince** (2000), **Master Minded** (2011)

World Series Hurdle – **Derrymoyle** (1998), **Refinement** (2007)

INDEX

Index

Index

Index

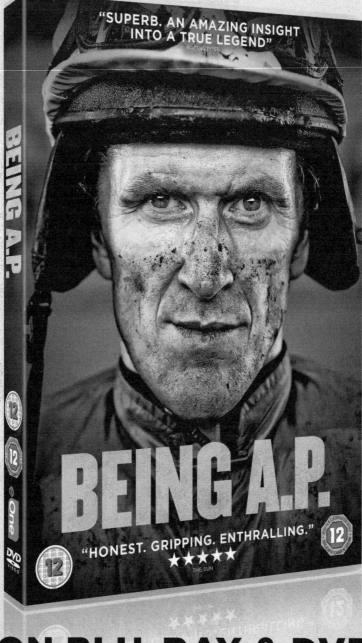

"FANTASTIC... A COMPELLING PORTRAIT OF AN EXTRAORDINARY SPORTSMAN"

THE MAIL ON SUNDAY

"SUPERB. AN AMAZING INSIGHT INTO A TRUE LEGEND"
RACING POST

BEING A.P.

"HONEST. GRIPPING. ENTHRALLING."
★★★★★
THE SUN

12

ON BLU-RAY & DVD

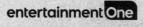